DISTRIBUTED COMPUTING
Associated Combinatorial Problems

ADVANCED TOPICS IN COMPUTER SCIENCE SERIES

Consulting Editors

Professor V. J. RAYWARD SMITH
School of Information Systems
University of East Anglia
Norwich, UK

Professor F. WARREN BURTON
School of Computing Science
Simon Fraser University
Burnaby, Canada

This is a brand new series of texts aimed at postgraduates and advanced students of Computer Science in polytechnics and universities. The titles will also be invaluable reading for researchers in this field.

ADVANCED TOPICS IN COMPUTER SCIENCE SERIES

DISTRIBUTED COMPUTING
Associated Combinatorial Problems

BRIAN BOFFEY MSc, PhD

Department of Statistics and Computational Mathematics
University of Liverpool

OXFORD

BLACKWELL SCIENTIFIC PUBLICATIONS

LONDON EDINBURGH BOSTON

MELBOURNE PARIS BERLIN VIENNA

© Brian Boffey 1992

Blackwell Scientific Publications
Editorial offices:
Osney Mead, Oxford OX2 0EL
25 John Street, London WC1N 2BL
23 Ainslie Place, Edinburgh EH3 6AJ
3 Cambridge Center, Cambridge,
   Massachusetts 02142, USA
54 University Street, Carlton
   Victoria 3053, Australia

Other Editorial Offices:
Librairie Arnette SA
2, rue Casimir-Delavigne
75006 Paris
France

Blackwell Wissenschaft-Verlag
Meinekestrasse 4
D-1000 Berlin 15
Germany

Blackwell MZV
Feldgasse 13
A-1238 Wien
Austria

First published 1992

Printed and bound in Great Britain by
Hartnolls, Bodmin, Cornwall

DISTRIBUTORS

Marston Book Services Ltd
PO Box 87
Oxford OX2 0DT
(*Orders:* Tel: 0865 791155
         Fax: 0865 791927
         Telex: 837515)

USA
Blackwell Scientific Publications, Inc.
3 Cambridge Center
Cambridge, MA 02142
(*Orders:* Tel: 800 759-6102)

Canada
Oxford University Press
70 Wynford Drive
Don Mills
Ontario M3C 1J9
(*Orders:* Tel: 416 441-2941)

Australia
Blackwell Scientific Publications
(Australia) Pty Ltd
54 University Street
Carlton, Victoria 3053
(*Orders:* Tel 03 347-0300)

British Library
Cataloguing in Publication Data
Boffey, Brian
   Distributed computing: associated
   combinatorial problems.
   I. Title
   004.36

   ISBN 0–632–02828–9

Library of Congress
Cataloging in Publication Data
Boffey, Brian.
     Distributed computing : associated
     combinatorial problems / Brian Boffey.
         p.   cm.
     Includes bibliographical references
     and index.
     ISBN 0–632–02828–9
     1. Electronic data processing—
     Distributed processing.
     2. Computer networks.   I. Title.
     QA76.9.D5B647   1992
     004'.36—dc20   91–35682
                                              CIP

Contents

Preface

The present text differs from almost all others on computer networks and distributed computing because of the emphasis on associated combinatorial problems. As such it should be of use to at least two groups of readers. First, computer scientists who are familiar with computer networks and wish to learn more about network design and other combinatorial problems. The second group comprises operations researchers, mathematicians and others who are interested in obtaining a wider knowledge of techniques for solving combinatorial problems. For the latter, the book provides an introduction to combinatorial optimisation within the setting of an interesting applications area; an introductory chapter is also included to give sufficient background for the applications to be appreciated.

There are many problems of a combinatorial nature related to computer networks and not all could be covered adequately in the space available, even if this were desirable. The final choice of topics was naturally influenced by the author's knowledge and interests. There are three main themes: routing of packets through a network (chapters 2 and 3); network design (chapters 4 and 5); location of software (chapter 6). Topics such as error detecting/correcting codes and cryptography are adequately treated elsewhere and are not included. It had been hoped to include more on software location and distributed databases, but this was decided against for reasons of space and because the area seems to be in a less coherent and developed state compared to 'hardware oriented' problems.

In order to make the material presented accessible to as wide an audience as possible the necessary mathematical background is developed gradually as the book proceeds. Thus, formal mathematical prerequisites are modest:- a familiarity with set theoretic notation, the concept of matrix and matrix multiplication, sets of linear equations, differentiation (including partial differentiation) and an elementary knowledge of probability and linear programming. Broadly speaking the necessary background can be obtained from a first course in operations research techniques.

Much of the first three chapters could be included in a final year undergraduate course. However, the material of chapters 4 to 6 is more suitable for postgraduate study. To aid understanding, a large number of numerical example problems are solved in detail. Also, for use by instructors, exercises of varying difficulty are included at the ends of chapters. The ends of proofs of theorem and solutions of examples are marked by an open square '$\square$'.

This author has frequently been frustrated by references in the literature to internal reports and conference papers which are difficult or well nigh impossible to obtain. Consequently a policy has been adopted that only readily available material (books and papers in recognised journals) be included in the reference section.

I would like to express my gratitude to David Downham, Larry LeBlanc, Chris Potts, Les Proll, Vic Rayward-Smith, Alan Veevers and Derek Yates whose comments on the manuscript have led to many improvements. Thanks are due to Mike Hennell who kindly provided access to desktop publishing facilities, and to Blackwell Scientific Publications for their patience during the long gestation period of this book. Finally, I would like to acknowledge the many researchers, too numerous to mention by name, whose work has led to this book being possible.

Chapter 1

Introduction

Rudimentary computer networks were introduced with the connection of remote terminals to central computers to support remote job entry and time sharing; often a (smaller) front-end computer was used to off-load communications control from the central processor.

Around 1970, ARPA (The Advanced Research Projects Agency of the US Department of Defense) introduced ARPANET (now known as DARPANET, but the original name will be retained here), which has been developing since. Other early developments include:

(i) *public data networks* in which sites belonging to independent organisations are connected via a subnet operated by a common carrier; TYMNET is a notable early example.

(ii) *network families* introduced by computer manufacturers to interconnect hardware produced by them but tailored to the actual hardware owned by particular customers; examples are IBM's SNA and Digital's DECnet.

Over the past two decades there has been much progress. Computer networks have found wide application and have developed in many different ways. They are used in banking and other areas of finance, airline reservation, for holding library databases, for defence applications, for inventory-distribution systems, to support electronic mail, and in many other ways. They may be dedicated or general purpose; they range from a single computer with connected data terminals to very large networks connected in a complex way; they include local area networks (LANs) connecting microcomputers (perhaps within a single building) and wide area networks (WANs) which operate over more than one continent; they may be privately owned or with independent sites communicating via a publicly owned subnet. Computers may be connected together in a ring, tree, or more complex way, and the transmission medium may be coaxial cable, twisted wire pairs, fibre optics, radio or communications satellite. It is thus seen that the diversity of computer networks is enormous. Broadly speaking, the primary concern here is with large, wide area, packet switching networks with a complex topology.

Section 1.1 gives a very general discussion on computer networks used for distributed computing. In order to avoid unnecessary detail, a 'generalised' model network is introduced in section 1.2. Some details of the various components will be given, though of necessity many technical details are glossed over and for further information the interested reader is referred to one of the standard texts (for example: Bertsekas and Gallager, 1987; Schwartz, 1987; Stallings, 1988; Tanenbaum, 1989).

1.1 COMPUTER COMMUNICATION

Why should anyone be interested in connecting computers together anyway? Answers to this are: to facilitate the passing of information (eg. electronic mail) and for sharing of resources.

Resource sharing

Examples of resource sharing are:
  (1) retrieving information from (part of) a database which is held at a remote site. Of course, in principle at least, each site could have a copy of the database but this is likely to be more expensive, perhaps prohibitively so. Storage space of the sites holding the database is being shared.
  (2) transferring a program to a remote site for execution because of large processing or storage requirements or a need for other facilities not available locally. In this case the storage, processing power or other resource of the receiving site is being shared.
  (3) transferring a program to another site because the local site is heavily loaded. Such load-sharing may be used to remedy a temporary local shortage on the part of the local site.
  (4) splitting a job into modules which are run concurrently at different sites so as to obtain the final results more quickly. This may be essential in time-critical situations as may arise in military applications. The general computing resources of the sites are being pooled over the interval of time during which the program executes.

Another advantage of distributed computation is that it enables computing facilities to be enhanced by relatively small increments as the need arises; that is, extendability is improved. It is thus seen that there are advantages to be gained from distributed computing which can out-weigh the communication overheads incurred. Whatever the application, when a message is to be transmitted it is generally important that this be effected quickly and accurately.

Reliable communication

A message is of no use if it doesn't arrive at its destination, and is of little or no value if it arrives in a corrupted state. That is, the communi-cation must be *reliable*. For speech, *small* losses of information can be tolerated but for others, such as information on bank transactions, the re-liability must be effectively 100%. (*Guaranteed* 100% accuracy is not achievable but the chances of error can be reduced to an exceedingly small quantity.)

Generally, higher reliability may be achieved by building in a certain amount of *redundancy*. This is exemplified by natural languages where a few missing letters or a missing word very often do not lead to any loss of understanding. Indeed, in English, many messages can be understood even if all vowels are purged. It should be clear however, that any superimposed character errors are more likely to lead to loss of under-standing than would be the case for the unpurged version of the message. Redundancy can be built into computer messages using simple *parity* checks or the more sophisticated *cyclic redundancy code* checks. The latter are designed, among other things, to trap *bursts* of bits in error such as might occur through electrical noise (crackle) on a tele-phone line.

Clearly, a short message is more likely to be transmitted unscathed than is a long one. For a message containing several million bits the chance of one or more errors occurring might be greater than that of none occurring, and a few tries may be necessary before the message is trans-mitted correctly even though the total number of bits in error is quite small. This difficulty may be resolved by splitting a message into *pack-ets* of information typically containing of the order of 1000 bits each. This saving more than offsets the attendant increase in overheads.

What should be done when an error is detected? In real life a person not 'catching' all that has been said might request repetition of the appro-priate part of the message. In a similar way if it is detected that a packet contains an error then a request may be made for that packet to be retransmitted (cf. section 1.2). Although great care is taken to trap transmission errors it is theoretically possible for a message to be incorrectly transmitted but accepted because all the checks applied are satisfied. Thus, we can never be *certain* that a message gets through correctly, but the chances of errors remaining can be made *very small* indeed.

The above discussion relates to a single link whereas several links may be required to form a path from the origin of a message to its destination; with this in mind further *end-to-end* checks may be applied at the destination.

Computer networks are designed to accommodate expected average traffic conditions. However, traffic is often *'bursty'* in nature - for example when a large file is to be transferred many packets will follow one another in quick succession along a particular path. In order to prevent such conditions causing confusion, the entry of new packets into the network may be restricted by *flow control* procedures.

Open Systems Interconnection (OSI)

It is a very complex task to arrange for the effective interconnection of different types of computer having different operating systems and supporting different software. Moreover, it is important that the addition of a new computer site into a network should not necessitate extensive software modifications throughout the network. With such points in mind a *layered* approach is adopted to computer network design. The *O*pen *S*ystems *I*nterconnection (or OSI) reference model will now be described briefly.

The OSI reference model has seven layers, which, for convenience we split into the four upper levels and the three lower levels; the levels are:

    7. Application Layer

    6. Presentation Layer

    5. Session Layer   *Upper levels*

    4. Transport Layer

    3. Network Layer

    2. Data Link Control Layer   *Lower levels*

    1. Physical Layer

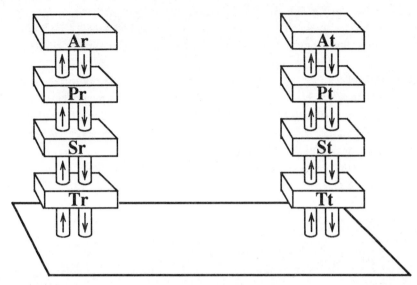

Figure 1.1 The upper levels of the OSI layered model; *r* is the origin node and *t* the destination node.

Layers 4-7, referred to here as the upper levels, are all concerned with communication from one *external site r* (the origin) to another external site *t* (the destination); that is, with end-to-end matters. In fact, each layer can only communicate directly with the layer below and (except for layer 7) the layer above (cf. figure 1.1). However, for each level it is as if the 'conversation' were between the *same* levels at the origin and the destination via a *virtual link* with the appropriate attributes. In particular, Transport Layer *Tr converses with Tt*, using a virtual link provided by the lower levels of *r* and *t* and of other intermediate nodes (cf. figure 1.2). This concept of a virtual link may be likened to the communication at sea between two ship's captains in which the captain of the first ship sends a message, in English, to his radio operator who transmits the message in Morse code which is received on the second ship and then, after conversion to English, relayed to its captain. To the captains of the two ships it is as though there is a virtual link along which messages are transmitted in English; in principle at least, there is no need for the captains to understand Morse code or even know that it is used!

The *applications layer* is the domain of the user and so is dependent on what the user wishes to achieve. Certain, frequently used services (data encryption for security, data compression, code conversion, ...) are provided by the *presentation layer*. The *session layer* is concerned with setting up and managing *sessions* (the connection of one user to another), and will check *access rights*. The lowest level of the end-to-end layers is the *transport layer* which splits messages up into suitably sized *packets* to which a few bits are added (at the front) to form a *header* H_t. It is at this level that several low rate sessions may be multiplexed together or a high rate session split into two or more. (The corresponding splitting or aggregating will be performed in the transport layer of the destination site.) Flow control and error recovery may also be performed by the transport layer.

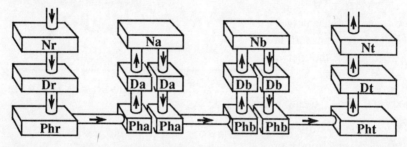

Figure 1.2 The lower levels in the OSI hierarchy assuming that there are two intermediate nodes *a* and *b* between the origin *r* and the destination *t*. Note that only the route from *r* to *t* is given; there will be a corresponding route in the opposite direction.

Turning now to the lower levels, the lowest of these, the *physical layer* is the only layer in which actual communication between nodes takes place. This layer includes the communication channel (wire, fibre optics or whatever) and associated interfaces (modems etc). It provides a '*virtual bit pipe*' for the data link control layer. 'Bits enter at one end and leave at the other' as far as the physical layer is concerned, and the bit patterns have no structure or intrinsic meaning.

Data Link Control (DLC) Layer

DLC operates on units called *frames* each of which consists of a *frame header* H_d, followed by a packet passed down from the network layer followed a *frame trailer* T_d. H_d indicates the start of the frame, what kind of packet it is carrying, etc.; T_d includes a *cyclic redundancy code* (or CRC) which is used for error detection, and an indication of the end of the frame. The frame header and trailer are added by DLC and for the HDLC protocol (cf. Bertsekas and Gallager, 1987) they comprise in total 48 bits, a not inconsiderable overhead. The order in which the sending DLC receives frames is maintained by the receiving DLC even though it may accept them out of order from the associated physical layer.

Thus DLC is responsible for error detection and provides for the network layer a **reliable** virtual pipe for transmission of packets.

Network Layer

The final layer to be described, and the one of most interest in this text, is the network layer. Whereas the perspective of the upper levels is end-to-end and that of the physical layer and DLC is of individual links, the perspective of the network layer is network wide. This layer takes packets from the transport layer at the origin and is responsible for routing them through the network, probably taking account of congestion in links in some way.

The journey of a message

To complete this discussion of OSI, we will look at the journey taken by a message sent from a user at r to a user at t assuming that a session has already been set up. The message is passed down to the presentation layer (Pr in figure 1.1) to the session layer Sr to the transport layer Tr. At this level the message is split into packets and the header H_t added. Each packet is passed down to network layer Nr and another header H_n prepended. Then it is passed to DLC Dr, a header H_d prepended and a trailer T_d appended to form a frame which is passed down to physical layer Phr. The frame with the form shown in figure 1.3 is now transmitted to the physical layer Pha of the next node, a, along its route. It then goes up to Da (cf. figure 1.2), has the frame header and trailer stripped off, and, assuming it is accepted as being without error, is passed up to Na where the header H_n is stripped off and replaced by another one, after which it is passed down to Da corresponding to the next link of its journey, and so on as indicated by figure 1.2.

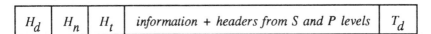

| H_d | H_n | H_t | information + headers from S and P levels | T_d |

Figure 1.3 The form of a frame showing added headers and trailer.

Although the terms frame and packet have both been used we shall from now on use the term 'packet' to mean either as, for our purposes, the difference is not particularly important except in so far as there is a certain amount of overhead represented by the extra bits added to the 'raw data'.

X.25

There are many public networks (corresponding to the communications subnets in our model of figure 1.4), owned by governments and private companies, which provide a communications service to those organizations that wish to subscribe.   Then, whatever the set of protocols used *internally* in such a network, it is clearly desirable that there be standard interfaces between the network and subscriber equipment.   The standard (strictly, a recommendation) X.25 was developed by CCITT (Comité Consultatif International Télégraphique et Téléphonique).   For the purposes of the present text it is only necessary to know that it corresponds to the lowest three layers of the OSI model (figure 1.2) and is virtual circuit oriented.   For a detailed description the reader may refer to Barnett and Maynard-Smith (1988).

1.2 POINT-TO-POINT NETWORKS

For large WANs (wide area networks) it is clearly unrealistic to have every site connected to every other site by a dedicated point-to-point line. Moreover, on grounds of cost, it is desirable to use the available links as effectively as possible. One solution, akin to that of road transportation, is to have a *switching network*, in which there are point-to-point links from each node (junction, roundabout, ...) to only a few other, relatively near, nodes.   Here, switching from link to link is performed by vehicle drivers; on the other hand, in computer networks the packets of information are passive and a processor is required at each node to forward packets on their way correctly. Thus, in a WAN, (computer) sites communicate with each other via a network of links and (switching) *nodes* to form what is termed a *communications subnet* (figure 1.4).

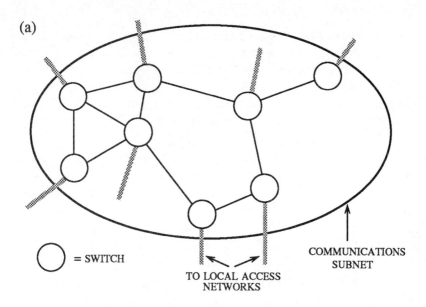

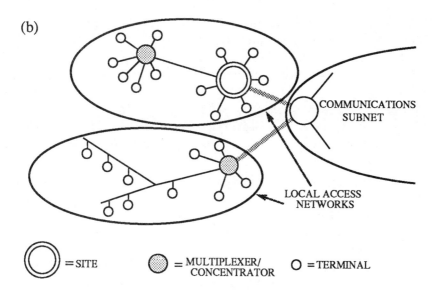

Figure 1.4 Generic models for (a) a communications subnet, and (b) a local access network.

A generic model

There is considerable diversity associated with computer networks and it is to avoid becoming enmeshed in unnecessary details that we shall tend to work with generalised models which capture the common form and relevant features of many actual networks. Further information on more practical aspects are contained in, for example, Tanenbaum (1989), Bertsekas and Gallager (1987) and Stallings (1988).

The generalised model around which we base our investigations is shown in figure 1.4 (cf. Boffey, 1989). *Users* are connected to *sites* via *local access networks*, and sites are connected to other sites via a *communications subnet*. Typically a site is an independent computer system (sometimes called a 'host computer'). *Terminal equipment* (or simply *terminals*) which may be single VDUs or something more elaborate, are connected through a tree network, via *multiplexers* and/or *concentrators* to sites, or perhaps directly to the communications subnet.

Multiplexers and concentrators share a similar purpose, but have the following difference. For traffic *from* terminals, a multiplexer has up to m incoming lines, each with capacity c say, and an outgoing line of capacity $C=mc$; that is, incoming traffic is merged in some way and passed on directly by sharing a higher capacity line. On the other hand, a concentrator (which is microprocessor controlled) makes use of the fact that, for most of the time, information is arriving from only a fraction of the terminals and so more than $m=C/c$ lines from terminals are permitted. In periods of relatively heavy traffic this may lead to the outgoing line temporarily being unable to cope and so data is queued for onward transmission at the earliest opportunity. For traffic going *to* terminals a composite stream of traffic is split into individual streams as appropriate.

Perhaps the distinction between multiplexing and concentration is made clearer by the following road traffic analogies. Consider the merging of single lane roads into a single wider road with the same speed limit and lanes equal in number to the number of merged roads. After being merged the vehicles keep in lane, each lane corresponding to an incoming road (cf. figure 1.5a). This corresponds to *frequency division multiplexing* (FDM) in which traffic from several low capacity lines is sent along a higher capacity line with traffic from each incoming line being forwarded at different frequencies. A similar situation is that in which the incoming m single lane roads have a speed limit of c and are merged into a single lane road with a speed limit of $C = mc$ (cf. figure 1.5b). This corresponds to *time division multiplexing* (TDM) in which traffic from several incoming lines is sent along a higher speed line with time slots available to each in rotation. A third situation is that in which several single lane roads merge to a wider road with the same speed limit but whose width is less than the combined widths of the incoming roads. In periods of low intensity traffic the system operates smoothly but when the intensity is higher, queues may build up from time to time at the junction. This corresponds to concentration (cf. figure 1.5c).

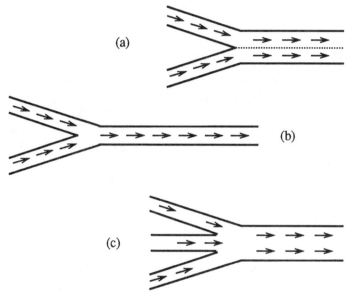

Figure 1.5 Road traffic analogies for (a) FDM, (b) TDM, and (c) concentration.

Although multiplexing and concentration have been described with reference to the local access networks it should be added that they may be used on links of the subnet; the principles are similar.

Retransmission procedures

In order to pass correctly through the subnet, packets should pass correctly along each link on their journey. Section 1.1 mentioned error detection when describing the DLC layer, but did not touch on all the difficulties associated with communication over unreliable links. (Here 'unreliable' merely means that accuracy is less than 100% though, hope-fully, it is very near.)

Consider transmission over a particular link, ij say. Firstly there is the problem of recognition of the start and end of each frame; if these are not determined correctly then a whole frame can be 'lost'. A correct-ly delimited frame is accepted (with the right number of bits) if certain checks are satisfied by the DLC of the receiver node j. A (positive) acknowledgement of some form must then be sent to node i to indicate acceptance (or a negative one if errors are detected). This may take the form of a special control packet or be incorporated into an 'ordinary' frame going from j to i (called *piggybacking*). In either case there is a chance that it will be lost or corrupted.

This poses another problem for i: how long should it wait for an ac-knowledgement (positive or negative)? A packet could be accepted by j yet i could wait forever if the acknowledgement has gone astray. To get round this a *time-out* procedure is adopted whereby a packet is retransmit-ted from i if no acknowledgement has been received within some specified time T. This in turn raises the possibility of j correctly receiv-ing a frame more than once, and this must be distinguished from the case (admittedly not common) in which two successive frames are intended to carry the same data.

A means of doing this is for frames to carry *sequence numbers* in their headers so that if two packets with the same sequence number ar-rive 'close together in time' it is known that the second results from a retransmission and so is discarded. In the absence of line failure or fail-ure of node j, i will eventually succeed in both transmitting a frame and knowing that it has been received correctly. Clearly this may take some while with the result that following frames are held up. A common procedure in practice, however, is to adopt *go back n ARQ* (Automatic *R*epeat re*Q*uest); with this, i is permitted to transmit frames $s+1$, $s+2,..., s+n-1$ before an acknowledgement for frame s is received. If this is not received within a time T or a negative acknowledgement is received, then i retransmits $s, s+1$ etc. Note that it is possible for implicit acknowledgement to be received and acted upon since, when i receives an acknowledgement that frame $s+1$ has been received correctly, it may be inferred that frame s has also been correctly received.

This discussion gives the flavour of difficulties that can arise and how they can be tackled; for a more precise and extensive treatment see Bertsekas and Gallager (1987). What is of relevance to the present work however is that chance events occur which result in 'random' delays (cf. section 3.1), and that the total flow in a network is considerably in excess of the flow of 'actual data' if retransmissions and all types of control packets are accounted for.

Routing

Local access networks usually form a tree structure (that is, contain no closed loops) and so routing of packets is straightforward. This is not the case for the communications subnet. Information is transmitted in small packets from an origin site r via nodes of the subnet to a destination site t. The pair (r, t) will be termed an *origin-destination* (or simply *OD*) pair. Also control packets are generated at subnet nodes and sent to other subnet nodes.

The way in which packets are forwarded through the subnet is determined by a *routing algorithm*. There are many such, and chapters 2 and 3 are devoted to just this topic. One possibility is to treat packets independently whether they belong to the same OD pair or not; this is the so-called *datagram* model. The header contains the identity of the destination t, and based on the knowledge of the current state of the network, the network layer at node a determines which link from a is the most promising along which to transmit the packet. It is clear that different packets belonging to the same message may follow different paths and get out of order when they meet up again, that is, not in the order they started their journey. This means that packets need to be reordered at the destination site (or the node at which they leave the subnet) and for this to be effected each packet must contain a sequence number indicating its position in the message.

An alternative is to a assign a route, called a *virtual circuit*, to a session. A virtual circuit will (usually) not have exclusive use of a link but will share it with other virtual circuits. When a virtual circuit is set up the route it follows is determined by prevailing traffic conditions. A major advantage of virtual circuits is that, barring node or link failure, ordering is strictly maintained. A packet need only contain information as to which virtual circuit it belongs, nodes having routing tables which match incoming circuits with outgoing ones. A slight disadvantage with virtual circuits is that a certain amount of overhead is incurred in setting them up. For a discussion on the relative merits of datagram and virtual circuit routing the reader is referred to Gerla (1985).

In order to keep nodes informed as to the current state of the traffic conditions in the network it is necessary for them to send out information from time to time, giving rise to further control overheads. The routing tables may be determined *centrally* at a *Network Routing Centre* or in a *distributed* fashion.

Congestion

Congestion effects are experienced in computer networks in much the same way as in road networks. [In road networks it is nodes (junctions) that tend to cause congestion. This may also hold for computer networks when high capacity fibre optics links are being employed, but otherwise it is common for limited link capacity to be the cause of congestion.] As the load offered to a computer or road network increases so, at first, the *throughput* (the total rate at which traffic is reaching its destination) will increase. As the offered load increases further the throughput continues but at an ever decreasing rate until a point is reached after which an increment in offered load results in a decrease in throughput. Some authors regard the term 'congestion' as referring to this latter phenomenon only, but in this text the term will be used more widely to refer to situations in which an increase in offered load leads to either a smaller increase in throughput or an actual decrease. The general form of the relation between offered load and throughput for a system exhibiting congestion is illustrated in figure 1.6.

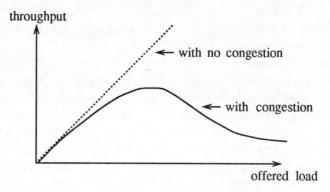

Figure 1.6 Generalised *throughput v offered load* curve for a system exhibiting congestion.

Example 1.1   Figure 1.7 represents part of a computer network; links irrelevant to the discussion are omitted. All packets are of equal length and each link has a capacity of 40 pps ('pps' denoting 'packets per second'). There is a steady stream of packets arising through transfer of three large files from a to g, from b to e and from c to g, in each case at a rate of 30 pps. Traffic corresponding to other OD pairs is to be ignored. What is the maximal throughput?

Solution   Without more information it is impossible to answer this question. However, it can be stated that the maximum throughput cannot exceed 80 pps since this is the most that links d-e and f-g can accommodate together.

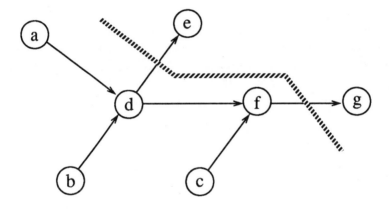

Figure 1.7 Part of a computer network (see text). At most 80 pps can cross the broken line.

First, assume that a packet is always accepted if there is a free buffer in which to store it. At f the link to g cannot cope with traffic at the rate required of it, and so all available buffers at f will fill up (the files being transferred were assumed to be large). Thus even packets transmitted without error must be discarded leading to numerous retransmissions on c-f and d-f. On average, 50% of the accepted packets will belong to each of these links and so the transmission rate on d-f is reduced to a maximum of 20 pps which in turn results in d's buffers filling. In a similar way 50% of packets accepted at d will belong to each of the incoming links reducing the traffic intensity on each to 20 pps. The total throughput is thus only 60 pps but it is *fair* in so far as each OD pair has 2/3 of its requirements met.

Suppose now that buffers at node *d* are allocated for storing packets queuing for link *d-e* or link *d-f* but not both. There is then no hold-up of (*b, e*) traffic and a throughput of 70 pps is achieved. Although it could be argued that this is less fair since (*b, e*) is favoured with a greater rate than the other OD pairs, it is surely better since no OD pair suffers a deterioration in flow rate and one gains. The question of what constitutes a fair policy and how to achieve it is far from trivial; nothing more will be said on this aspect. □

Another difficulty that can arise is that of *deadlock* of which there are various types. Figure 1.8 shows an example in which traffic corresponding to four separate OD pairs needs to use the links *a-b* and *b-c*, *b-c* and *c-d*, *c-d* and *d-a*, and *d-a* and *a-b* respectively, but the appropriate buffers at the four nodes are full. This is an 'indirect' deadlock which is not prevented by allocation of buffers to queues as in example 1.1; however such deadlocks are prevented simply by a different allocation (cf. Gerla and Kleinrock, 1980).

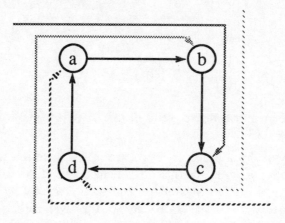

Figure 1.8 Example of an indirect deadlock. The broken lines indicate the desired paths of four streams of packets.

Congestion is not as important an issue as it used to be since the decrease in storage costs now permits sufficient buffer space to be provided for the difficulties described to be unlikely, particularly if the entry of packets into the subnet is controlled (see below).

Flow control

Gerla and Kleinrock (1980) give the following reasons for employing flow control (including congestion control) procedures:

(1) prevention of throughput and response time degradation and loss of efficiency due to network and user overload;

(2) deadlock avoidance;

(3) fair allocation of receivers among competing users;

(4) speed matching between the network and the attached users.

We have touched briefly on the first three of these and now turn to the last. A receiver site which is slow compared to the sender site can cause congestion and so there is a need for *end-to-end* flow control. (Many authors reserve the term 'flow control' for just this.) This may be achieved by some form of acknowledgement of packets from the destination to the origin.

A prominent system of flow control is based on the use of *windows*. The origin will only allow at most *w*, say, despatched but unacknowledged packets for the particular destination concerned. When the destination receives a packet it sends an acknowledgement, or *permit*, for the origin to transmit another packet. The window size *w* may be fixed or variable.

With the use of virtual circuits, flow control is readily effected on a link-by-link basis with each link on the virtual circuit having its own window. When a particular link, *k-m* say, is 'overloaded' packets out of *k* are slowed up with the result that packets build up at *k* until the window for *j-k* starts to limit the flow on *j-k*; this in turn causes packets to build up at *j*, and so on back along the virtual circuit. This is called *backpressure* and is an effective means of keeping packets from swamping a congested region of the network.

1.3 THE DESIGN OF COMPUTER NETWORKS

So far a brief outline has been given of the typical characteristics of computer networks. In practice there is considerable variability and before going on to discuss the problems of design some details of a few real networks are given. First to be given are the historically important, but dissimilar, ARPANET and TYMNET, and then the manufacturers' systems DECnet and SNA. Also mentioned is the public data network PSS.

ARPANET

The Advanced Research Projects Agency Network ARPANET was introduced by the (Defense) Advanced Research Projects Agency of the US Department of Defense at the end of the 1960s and has evolved since. In 1983 it was split into two networks: MILNET, a military network, and ARPANET devoted to research. These networks both became parts of the ARPA Internet. In 1986 ARPANET had about 150 sites connected to a subnet of switching nodes (Quartermain and Hoskins, 1986).

Switching nodes are mostly connected by dedicated 56 kbps links. ('kbps' is an abbreviation for 'kilobits per second'.) The service provided to the sites is virtual circuit and it thus appears to an origin site that there is a fixed route to the destination site. However, between the *entry node* (where packets first enter the subnet) and the *exit node* (where packets leave the subnet) a datagram service is provided. This necessitates packets being resequenced at the exit node.

Information units are messages of up to 8095 bits long which are split into 1 to 8 packets within the subnet. The maximum frame size within the subnet is 1008 bits. Routing of datagrams is determined in a dynamic distributed fashion and is the subject of section 3.5. ARPANET has its own ARQ mechanism for congestion control (Bertsekas and Gallager, 1987).

TYMNET

Initially, TYMNET was designed to provide access to TYMSHARE's timesharing service. From 1976 however, it has been very successfully providing a public data communications service to its customers.

TYMNET is a highly connected network using voice grade 9.6 kbps lines. It is virtual circuit based and packets, which must contain data in multiples of 2 characters, are limited to 66 characters, that is 528 bits of data. A frame generally carries information belonging to several virtual circuits - which might be termed *packet multiplexing*. This can result in characters on a particular virtual circuit becoming spread out or bunched together.

There is a hierarchy of 4 supervisor nodes. The currently active supervisor node performs shortest path calculations for determining virtual circuits.

Go back *n* ARQ is used to control congestion at the data link level. Flow is effected by means of backpressure with window size measured in bytes whose number varies with the virtual circuit. There is no end-to-end flow control.

PSS

In many countries the governmental PTT (Post, Telegraph & Telephone administration) provides a public data network service. In Britain, British Telecom, formerly nationally owned but privatised in 1985, provides PSS (Packet SwitchStream) for use internal to the UK, and IPSS (International Packet SwitchStream) for international connections.

PSS is a hierarchically organised network with interfaces which meet the CCITT X.25 recommendation. Equipment capable of sending and receiving X.25 packets may connect directly to the PSS network via lines operating at 2.4 kbps, 9.6 kbps or 48 kbps. Simple character based terminals may be connected via 300 bps, 1.2 kbps or higher capacity lines to a port of a PAD (Packet Assembler and Disassembler). A PAD creates packets from characters input by its terminals and forwards these packets to a PSS switching node; in the reverse direction a PAD accepts packets from a PSS node and converts them into characters which are output to its terminals.

The PSS network began commercial operation in 1981. In 1987 there were some 4000 customers and port capacity was doubling each year. In 1984 the IPSS gateway provided connections to 56 public packet switched networks in more than 40 countries (Lane, 1987).

Packets are normally limited to $128 \times 8 = 1024$ bits of user data though longer packets can be requested up to a maximum of $1024 \times 8 = 8192$ bits.

DECNET

DECNET is a set of protocols and programs produced by Digital Equipment Corporation for use with its computer systems. The associated network architecture is termed DNA (Digital Network Architecture). Here we shall follow Tanenbaum (1989) in using the term 'DECNET' to mean 'DECNET' and/or 'DNA'.

There are 'many DECNETS' with the physical characteristics of any particular one depending on the equipment purchased by the owner. Packets can contain from 1 to 16383 bytes, that is 8 to 131064 bits, of data.

Routing is similar to that of ARPANET, with datagrams being used, but with user-defined cost functions.

Sliding windows are used for flow control with up to 255 outstanding packets being permitted. Also special *choke* packets are employed.

The layers in the DNA architecture are:

8 User

7 Network Management (NICE)

6 Network Application (Data Access Protocol)

5 Session Control

4 End-to-end communications (Network Services Protocol)

3 Routing (adaptive)

2 Data link (DDCMP, X.25 or ETHERNET)

1 Physical link

SNA

Systems Network Architecture (SNA) was designed to permit customers of IBM equipment to construct private networks. It is more complex than DECNET and has undergone considerable evolution.

SNA provides a virtual circuit service but, unlike TYMNET, it is the source node that constructs the required route. Sessions have a service class (eg. file transfer, interactive, etc). When a session is set up a *virtual route* (comprising a list of nodes on the route to be followed) is selected at the source node for the session. For any OD pair there may be up to 3 service classes and up to 8 virtual routes: a maximum of 24 possibilities in all. The virtual routes corresponding to each OD pair are prepared manually beforehand so that in a sense the routing is static. The particular route finally chosen for a session will depend on the service class and the current load on each of the candidate virtual routes. Also there may be multiple lines between a pair of nodes and these are divided into *transmission groups* with a transmission group usually being homogeneous (eg. using 9.6 kbps lines only). Because of this, as part of establishing a session the virtual route chosen must be mapped onto an *explicit route* which is a sequence of transmission groups. Which line to use within a transmission group is a DLC decision. When there are multiple lines within a transmission group it is possible for packets to be received out of sequence, and so resequencing takes place at each node *en route*.

The layers in the SNA architecture are:

7 Application

6 Network Addressable Unit (NAU) Services

5 Data Flow Control

4 Transmission Control

3 Path Control (routing)

2 Data Link Control (SDLC)

1 Physical

There are very many other networks in existence and for a survey of some of these the reader is referred to Quartermain and Hoskins (1986).

Essential features

From the above brief descriptions of a few networks it is clear that there is considerable diversity in practice; this is lessening with the moves to conformance with the OSI reference model and X.25 recommendation. In our discussions of combinatorial problems associated with computer networks all possible variations cannot be covered, nor is it necessary. What then are the essential features?

Conditions that will typically hold, at least approximately, are that:

(1) the overall network conforms with the generic model of section 1.2; that is, local access networks in the form of trees are connected via a more highly interconnected communications subnet.

(2) there is at most one link between any pair of nodes.

(3) flow is continuous, it being ignored that in reality traffic consists of discrete units, namely bits (and at a higher level packets).

(4) flow is conserved; that is, the proportion of 'lost' packets is assumed to be small enough to be ignored.

(5) the (average) traffic demand for each OD pair is known; overheads (resulting from headers and trailers) are assumed to be included using an appropriate 'expansion factor'.

(6) control traffic (acknowledgements, routing information, flow control information, ...) may be ignored, if necessary being incorporated into the traffic demand in some appropriate way.

(7) the operation of the physical, DLC and four highest layers may be ignored as far as the combinatorial problems of interest to us are concerned.

(8) the communication equipment, including switching nodes, is normally in a working state.

When appropriate, these conditions are assumed to hold unless otherwise
stated or where it is clear from context that one or more do not hold.

Problems to be considered in this text will relate to routing of
packets (chapters 2 and 3), to the design of networks (chapters 4 and 5)
and to the location of software (chapter 6).

Design and problem decomposition

Suppose a network is to be set up to support a large database system, and
that it must connect a given set of customers with given requirements
via a set of switching nodes with specified locations and characteristics.
Even with this amount of initial information and the extensive list of
assumptions made above, a problem of truly enormous computational
difficulty remains. It is necessary to decide:

(1) which switching node each customer should be connected to and
via which route;

(2) locations of any concentrators to be used and their connections;

(3) between which switching nodes links should be placed and what
their capacity should be;

(4) how the database should be split up and where each fragment
should be located.

This is clearly a complex problem, and for other than very small
data sets is not susceptible to solution by exact methods. Fortunately,
it decomposes in a natural way. Firstly the design of the local access
networks and the communications subnet may reasonably be treated
separately. Secondly, the design of the hardware aspects of the network
may be performed separately and before the location of the software components. While it appears that this latter separation might possibly lead
to appreciable suboptimisation, the combined problem seems scarcely to
have been tackled. Even after these, and perhaps further, decompositions
formidable combinatorial problems may remain and it is necessary to
'resort' to approximate methods.

This text will look at some of the combinatorial subproblems that
arise in connection with computer networks and distributed computing.
Attention is restricted to routing algorithms and design problems.
Other combinatorial problems related to error detection, encryption etc.
are not dealt with here but are covered elsewhere.

Chapter 2

Low Intensity Flow

Over a typical minute's operation hundreds, perhaps thousands, of packets will be transmitted over individual links of a computer network. It is, therefore, reasonable to adopt a global view in which the flow is regarded as being of a continuous nature rather than of discrete units. Also, to a first approximation, loss of packets may be ignored. For these reasons it is appropriate to spend some while developing the theory of *conserved* flows.

Consider traffic from node r_1 to s_1 and from r_2 to s_2 ($r_1 \neq r_2$ or $s_1 \neq s_2$), and suppose the routes for these two OD (Origin-Destination) pairs both include a link from i to j and that all packets contain the same number of bits. If average traffic intensities (ie. flow rates) are very low, with no sudden bursts, then packets on the two routes will seldom be competing for the use of the link at the same time. That is, interference is minimal and packets are not held up. Thus the link traversal time resulting from packet-processing at i and transmission over the link ij is nearly the same for every packet; the total delay per unit time for all packets along ij is very nearly proportional to the number of packets transmitted on that link per unit time. (More generally, it is nearly proportional to the total number of bits transmitted when packet lengths vary.) Because of this the term 'linear' flow will be used for the approximation in which the cost of sending a unit of flow along any link is directly proportional to the total flow (rate) in the link. Linear flow leads to simple methods for analysing a network and, though it is often not a realistic approximation in practice, it provides a useful starting point for studying 'non-linear' flow.

No system, however, is without its limitations. For some real world systems, flow may be linear up to a certain level above which the system cannot operate. An example of this is provided by a mountain chair lift; if a single-seat chair leaves every 6 seconds say, then the total travel time is proportional to the total flow (rate) for flows of up to 10 passengers per minute. However, as soon as a rate of 10 passengers per minute is reached the system is 'saturated'; the system does continue to operate but only at the capacity level of 10 passengers per minute. Flows in systems in which links have capacities are termed 'capacitated' flows. For other systems the cost of sending one unit of flow may be an increasing function of the total flow in the link. A section of roadway provides an example; the more traffic there is the slower it tends to go. Flows exhibiting this form of behaviour will be termed 'congested' flows; congested flows are of relevance in the design and analysis of computer networks.

Section 2.1 introduces some graph theoretic terminology that is used throughout this book. This will need to be understood in order to provide a sound foundation for appreciating later developments that are more specifically related to computer networks. Next, conserved linear flows are studied and related to routing.

Routing of packets of information is described in general terms in section 2.3 including hierarchically organised networks. In the following two sections several routing algorithms are described and in the final section the problem of finding alternative routes is addressed.

2.1 NETWORK FLOW

In order to treat network flow mathematically it is necessary first to introduce some graph (network) theoretic terms; these will broadly be in agreement with those of Boffey (1982), relevant differences being in the usage of the terms 'node' and 'link'.

Terminology

A (*directed*) *graph* is a pair (X, A) where X is a non-empty set of *nodes* and A is a set of directed pairs (i, j) of nodes, each pair being called an *arc*. Arcs will usually be written as *i-j*, or simply *ij*. A *path* is a sequence of arcs $i_1 i_2$, $i_2 i_3$, ..., $i_{p-1} i_p$ and will be written $i_1\text{-}i_2\text{-}i_3\text{-} \cdots \text{-}i_p$ or simply $i_1 i_2 i_3 \cdots i_p$. A path is a *circuit* if the first and last nodes i_1 and i_p coincide (thus forming a closed loop), and is *simple* if no nodes coincide, except possibly the first and the last.

Figure 2.1 shows an example of a directed graph with node and arc sets $X = \{a, b, c, d, e, f, g\}$ and $A = \{ab, ba, bc, bd, cd, da, dc, eg, fe, gf\}$. Examples of paths are: *ab*, *abd*, *cdc*, *cdabd* and *egfegfe*. Of these *cdc* and *egfegfe* are circuits, the first being simple; the other paths are simple except for *cdabd*. It will be noticed that the graph consists of two separate parts (called *components*) and so the graph is not *connected*. In this book we shall be concerned with connected graphs and, unless stated to the contrary, it will be assumed that it is possible to go from any node to any other while respecting the directions of the arcs.

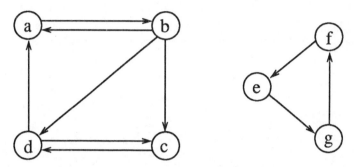

Figure 2.1 A directed graph on seven nodes *a, b, ..., g*. Having more than one component, the graph is not connected.

A directed graph in which arcs occur in pairs, that is *xy* is in the graph if and only if *yx* is, is said to be *symmetric*. It is often convenient to represent symmetric graphs as undirected graphs and vice versa, where an *undirected graph* is a pair (X, E) with X a non-empty node set and E a set of undirected pairs of nodes called *edges*. An edge between i and j will be written *i-j* or simply *ij*, it being understood that *ij* and *ji* represent the same edge. A *chain* is a sequence of edges $i_1 i_2, i_2 i_3, ..., i_{p-1} i_p$ and will be written as $i_1 - i_2 - i_3 - ... - i_p$ or simply $i_1 i_2 i_3 ... i_p$. It is a *cycle* if the first and last nodes i_1 and i_p coincide, and is *simple* if no nodes coincide, except possibly the first and last.

Figure 2.2 shows an example of an undirected graph whose node set is $X = \{a, b, ..., e\}$ and edge set is $E = \{ab, ad, bc, be, cd, ce, de\}$. Examples of chains are: *bc, ede, adecd, bcebceb*. Of these *ede* and *bcebceb* are cycles; *bc* and *ede* are simple.

Frequently we shall merely refer to 'graphs', it being understood from the context whether a directed or undirected graph is implied. Also the term *link* will be used to mean either an arc or an edge, and the term *route* to mean either a path or a chain. The concepts that have been introduced are collected together in table 2.1.

Table 2.1 Some commonly used graph theoretic terminology.

directed	undirected	not specific
node	node	node
arc	edge	link
path	chain	route
circuit	cycle	cycle
simple	simple	simple
connected	connected	connected

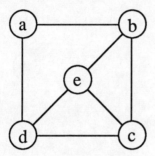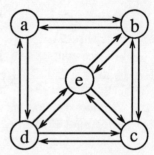

Figure 2.2 On the left is an undirected graph on five nodes and on the right is the corresponding symmetric directed graph.

The problems dealt with in this book involve flows, distances, times, costs, etc., with links having associated capacities, lengths, travel times, costs, etc. Graphs in which links have associated *weights* are often called *networks*, but we shall use the term 'graph' and 'network' more or less interchangeably. For networks with flow in them, *origins* (*destinations*) are nodes at which flow originates (terminates).

The communications subnet of a WAN may be represented by an undirected network (in the graph theoretic sense) when full duplex communication is being used. The node set consists of the switching nodes of the subnet and the edge set comprises the communication links between nodes. However, it is often convenient for computational purposes to use the corresponding symmetric directed network in which, for each pair of directly linked nodes i and j there is an arc ij **and** an (oppositely directed) arc ji (cf. figure 2.2). If simplex communication is being used then a directed graph is of course the appropriate model.

Conserved flows

Suppose that a directed network $N = (X, A)$ is given with $r, t \in N$. Also, for simplicity assume for the moment that the only traffic in the network is from origin r to destination t, all other OD (*Origin-Destination*) pairs being 'inactive'. A *conserved* (*single commodity*) *network flow* relative to OD pair (r,t) is a set of real numbers $\{ x_{ij} \mid \text{all } ij \in A \}$ such that

$$\Sigma_i \, x_{ij} - \Sigma_k \, x_{jk} = \begin{cases} -val & \text{if } j = r & (2.1a) \\ 0 & \text{if } j \neq r, t & (2.1b) \\ val & \text{if } j = t & (2.1c) \end{cases}$$

$$x_{ij} \geq 0. \tag{2.2}$$

x_{ij} is the *arc flow* (per unit time) in arc ij and clearly cannot be negative (hence the constraint 2.2), and the collection of arc flows $\{x_{ij}\}$ forms the network flow which will often be denoted by the vector x, the components of x being the arc flows x_{ij} in some suitable fixed order. The flow is called 'single commodity' because it relates to a single OD pair. Equations (2.1a, b, c) are the *conservation* constraints which state that what flows into a node must flow out. The rate at which flow leaves r is the same as the rate at which flow reaches t and is called the *value* of the flow; it is equal to $\Sigma_k \, x_{rk}$.

Example 2.1 In the computer network subnet shown in figure 2.3, 11 kbps of flow enter the network at node 2 and 11 kbps leave at node 4. [Note that 'bps' stands for 'bits per second' and 'kbps' for 'kilobits per second'.] What paths does the flow take and what is the flow along each of these paths if the arc flows are as indicated?

Solution It is readily checked that the given arc flows are realised by sending

    5 kbps along 2-3-4

    3 kbps along 2-3-7-5-4

    1 kbps along 2-1-6-7-3-4

    1 kbps along 2-1-6-7-5-4

    1 kbps along 2-1-6-5-4.

the flow in arc ij being the sum of the flows on each of the paths (if any) that pass along ij.   □

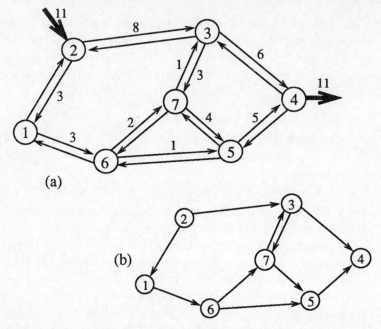

Figure 2.3 A subnet with seven nodes. Arc flows, where non-zero, are shown alongside the corresponding arcs in (a), and the assignment graph associated with the network flow is shown in (b).

For a flow x in a graph G on node set V, the *assignment graph* (*associated with flow x*), is the graph, $G(x)$, on node set V which contains precisely those arcs ij for which the flow is non-zero. Thus, for the network flow of figure 2.3(a) the assignment graph is given by figure 2.3(b), where

> node set $V = \{1, 2, 3, 4, 5, 6, 7\}$
> arc set $A = \{$1-6, 2-1, 2-3, 3-4, 3-7, 5-4, 6-5, 6-7, 7-3, 7-5$\}$.

Path flows and arc flows

The above example demonstrates a different way of viewing a network, namely in terms of 'path flows'. Let π be any path from r to t and x_π a non-negative number. x_π will be called a *path flow* along π from r to t. Note that conservation of flow is taken account of automatically. Unique arc flows x_{ij} corresponding to a set $\{x_\pi\}$ of path flows from r to *t* are given by

$$x_{ij} = \sum_\pi \delta_{ij}^\pi x_\pi \quad \text{where} \quad \delta_{ij}^\pi = \begin{cases} 1 \text{ if } ij \text{ is on } \pi \\ 0 \text{ otherwise.} \end{cases}$$

It should be noted that the set of path flows $\{x_\pi\}$ gives rise to a unique set of arc flows $\{x_{ij}\}$ but the converse is not in general true.

Theorem 2.1 For any conserved flow $x = \{x_{ij}\}$, of value *val* >0, from node r to node t in a network G, there corresponds a (not necessarily unique) set of path flows (including flows round circuits) which yields the given set of arc flows x.

Proof First a flow $y = \{y_{ij}\}$ is introduced which initially is set equal to $x = \{x_{ij}\}$. The proof proceeds, in stages, by reducing the arc flows y_{ij} and replacing them by equivalent path flows x_π and circuit flows x_γ until the assignment graph $G(y)$ consists of nodes only. Clearly at this point the sets $\{x_\pi\}$ and $\{x_\gamma\}$ together describe the same overall network as the set $\{x_{ij}\}$.

Since *val* >0 there must be a path π in $G(y)$ from r to t. Moreover, π may be chosen to be simple (no repeated nodes). Let

$$\varepsilon = \min [val, \min \{ y_{ij} \mid ij \text{ on } \pi\}],$$

and reduce *val* and the flows y_{ij} for ij on π by ε. The flow x_π of value ε together with the *reduced* flow y must equal the original flow x. This procedure is repeated until *val* is reduced to zero, at which point the set of path flows generated, $\{x_\pi\}$, corresponds to a conserved flow from r to t, of value equal to the *initial* value of *val*.

The assignment graph may still contain some arcs, but a similar argument to the above shows that the remaining flow y may be represented by flows x_γ round circuits γ, so that finally the sets $\{x_\pi\}$ and $\{x_\gamma\}$ are such that

$$x_{ij} = \sum_\pi \delta_{ij}^\pi x_\pi + \sum_\gamma \delta_{ij}^\gamma x_\gamma$$

where δ_{ij}^γ is defined analogously to δ_{ij}^π. The following example should clarify the procedure of the above proof. $\square$

Example 2.2 For the set of arc flows $\{x_{ij}\}$ shown in the network of figure 2.4a, find a corresponding set of path and circuit flows.

Solution The assignment graph is shown in figure 2.4b, and in this we generate (say) path r-a-e-$t = \pi_1$. Then

$$\varepsilon = \min [\, val, y_{ra}, y_{ae}, y_{et} \,] = \min [\, 8, 8, 5, 3 \,] = 3$$

and set $x_{\pi_1} = 3$ and

$$y_{ra} \leftarrow 8 - 3 = 5, \quad y_{ae} \leftarrow 5 - 3 = 2, \quad y_{et} \leftarrow 3 - 3 = 0, \quad val \leftarrow 8 - 3 = 5.$$

The modified assignment graph is shown in figure 2.4c. In a similar way setting

$$\pi_2 = r\text{-}a\text{-}e\text{-}f\text{-}t \qquad x_{\pi_2} = 2$$
$$\pi_3 = r\text{-}a\text{-}f\text{-}t \qquad x_{\pi_3} = 2$$
$$\pi_4 = r\text{-}a\text{-}f\text{-}i\text{-}t \qquad x_{\pi_4} = 1$$

and making the appropriate modifications leads to the assignment graph of figure 2.4d. Finally, setting

$$\gamma_1 = g\text{-}c\text{-}b\text{-}f\text{-}g \qquad x_{\gamma_1} = 3$$
$$\gamma_2 = g\text{-}c\text{-}d\text{-}h\text{-}g \qquad x_{\gamma_2} = 2$$

leads to the assignment graph having no arcs. The set

$$\{\, x_{\pi_1}, x_{\pi_2}, x_{\pi_3}, x_{\pi_4} \,\} \cup \{\, x_{\gamma_1}, x_{\gamma_2} \,\}$$

is a set of path and circuit flows which, together yield the arc flows given in figure 2.4a. $\square$

Minimal cost flows

In flow situations there is typically a cost of c_{ij} per unit flow per unit time associated with each link ij (which may represent distance travelled, time taken, cost of using a line, or some other measure). If the flow in ij is x_{ij} per unit time this leads to a cost of $c_{ij}x_{ij}$ per unit time if the flow is assumed to be linear. Aggregating all arc flow costs gives the per unit time network flow cost

$$c(x) = \sum_i \sum_j c_{ij} x_{ij}. \tag{2.3}$$

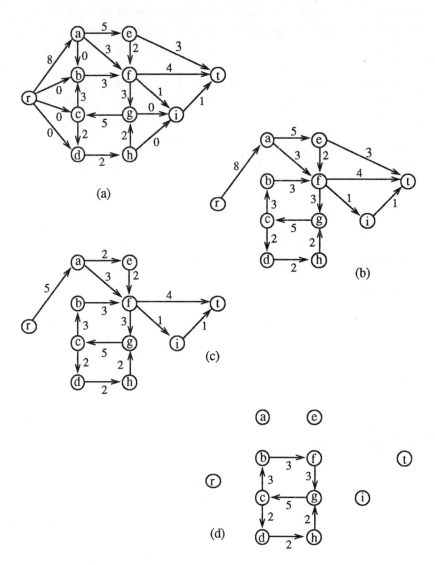

Figure 2.4 A conserved flow pattern **y** is shown in (a) and the corresponding assignment graph in (b). Diagram (c) shows the new assignment graph after 3 units of flow along π_1 have been removed. The assignment graph after flow along π_4 has been removed is shown in (d). Finally this flow is decomposed into flows round circuits *g-c-b-f-g* and *g-c-d-h-g*.

If now, the routing of flow can be controlled (as it can for flow of packets through a computer network) then it is pertinent to ask which routing (that is, flow pattern x) leads to least cost for a specified value of flow.

In order to answer this it is more convenient to look at the path flow formulation. Assuming that the flow $x = \{x_{ij}\}$ is represented in terms of path and circuit flows the cost $c(x)$ may be expressed as

$$c(x) = \sum_i \sum_j c_{ij} x_{ij} = \sum_i \sum_j c_{ij} (\sum_\pi \delta_{ij}^\pi x_\pi + \sum_\gamma \delta_{ij}^\gamma x_\gamma)$$
$$= \sum_\pi (\sum_i \sum_j c_{ij} \delta_{ij}^\pi) x_\pi + \sum_\gamma (\sum_i \sum_j c_{ij} \delta_{ij}^\gamma) x_\gamma$$
$$= \sum_\pi c(\pi) x_\pi + \sum_\gamma c(\gamma) x_\gamma$$

where $c(\pi)$ is the cost of sending one unit of flow along π and $c(\gamma)$ is the cost of sending one unit of flow once round circuit γ. The cost minimization problem posed above may now be formulated as

$$\text{minimize } c(x) = \sum_{i=1}^m c(\pi_i) x_{\pi_i} + \sum_{i=1}^m c(\gamma_i) x_{\gamma_i} \qquad (2.4)$$
$$\text{subject to}$$
$$\sum_{i=1}^m x_{\pi_i} = val$$

where $\{\pi_i\}$ is the set of paths from the origin to the destination. Clearly, since all cost coefficients are positive, the flows round circuits γ_i must be zero in every optimal solution and consequently the second summation in (2.4) may be ignored. With respect to computer networks this means that effort should be made to prevent packets cycling as may happen with some adaptive routing strategies (cf. section 3.5).

Problem (2.4) is a simple example of a 'continuous knapsack problem', and its solution is trivial. Suppose, without loss of generality, that the paths are so numbered that $c(\pi_1) \le c(\pi_2) \le ... \le c(\pi_m)$. Then setting $x_{\pi_1} = val$ gives an optimal solution. [If any other path were used then flow could be switched from it to π_1 without increasing the cost.]

Example 2.3 Suppose the cost per unit flow (in either direction) for each link of the network of figure 2.3 is 4 except links 3-7, 7-5 and 5-4 for which it is 1. What is the cost of the flow given in figure 2.3a?

Find a minimal cost flow and its cost.

Solution The cost of the given flow is readily calculated to be 105 s ('s' standing for 'seconds'). The shortest path is 2-3-7-5-4 of 'length' 7 s and so it is optimal to assign all 11 kbps of flow to it for a total cost of $11 \times 7 = 77$s. □

2.2 CONSERVED FLOW AND TREES

The scope is now widened to include flow to several destinations, though still from a single source r. Indeed, every node other than r may be considered to be a destination but with the possibility that flows to some destinations are zero.

Example 2.4 The network of figure 2.5 represents a possible computer network between the six British cities London (L), Birmingham (B), Cardiff (C), Manchester (M), Norwich (N) and Sheffield (S). Links marked 'f' are 128 kbps lines and those marked 's' are 64 kbps lines. It is decided to assign a 'length' of 1 to f-links and a 'length' of 2 to s-links to reflect the difference in times to transmit a given number of bits. For traffic from London only, find optimal routes for traffic to each of the other cities assuming the linear flow approximation is appropriate.

Solution By inspection it is readily seen that: L-B, L-C, L-B-M, L-N and L-N-S are the shortest routes to B, C, M, N and S respectively. Moreover they are unique shortest routes. Since flow is assumed to be linear there is no interference between flows for different OD pairs and it is therefore optimal to assign

    traffic from L to B to route L-B,
    traffic from L to C to L-C,
    traffic from L to M to L-B-M,
    traffic from L to N to L-N,
    traffic from L to S to L-N-S. □

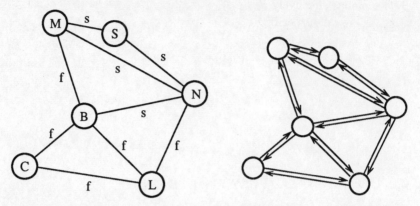

Figure 2.5 Network for example 2.4 in which f-links are twice as fast as s-links. The corresponding symmetric directed graph is shown to the right.

Minimal cost flows and out-trees

Consider the 'subnetwork' obtained from the network of figure 2.5 by removing those links to which no flow has been assigned (in either direction). This new network, shown in figure 2.6, has a special structure; it is connected and possesses no cycles (that is, there are no closed loops).

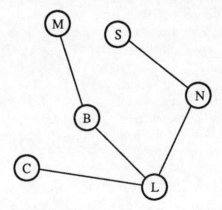

Figure 2.6 The tree rooted at L, on node set {L, B, C, M, N, S} and whose links correspond to links having non-zero assigned flow.

Graphs with this property are called *trees*. Sometimes however, a directed graph without cycles is also loosely referred to as a 'tree' (that is, directions are effectively ignored). On the other hand if all the arcs are directed toward a specified node, g say, (called the *root*) then the graph may be termed an *in-tree* (*rooted* at g), and if all arcs are directed away from the root g then the graph may be termed an *out-tree* (*rooted* at g). These definitions should be clarified by the examples given in figure 2.7.

Figure 2.7 From left to right: examples of a tree, an in-tree and an out-tree.

Theorem 2.2 There is a least cost feasible flow from r for which the associated assignment graph is an out-tree rooted at r.

Proof Such an out-tree may be constructed by starting with the trivial tree T consisting of node r only and repeating the following step until T has 'grown' to contain all the nodes.

STEP Select any node x not yet in T. Suppose π_x is a shortest (ie. least cost) path from x to r, and u is the last node in T which is on π_x. All arcs and nodes on π_x from u to x are added to T. All flow from r to the other added nodes y is directed along the unique paths in T to which these nodes y belong. $\qquad\square$

This may be clearer from the example in figure 2.8 in which T has grown to the tree on the five nodes $\{r, a, b, c, u\}$ indicated by the heavy arcs. Suppose that π_x is the path r-a-u-v-x. Then nodes v and x, and the arcs uv and vx are added to form the updated tree T. Since r-a-u is a shortest path to u and u-v-x is a shortest path from u to x (it is a sub-path of a shortest path) it follows that r-a-u-v-x is a shortest path from r to x also. [Note that if r-a-u-v-x and r-c-u-v-x are both shortest paths from r to x, the length of r-a-u and r-c-u must be equal. However the addition of c-u would have created a cycle.]

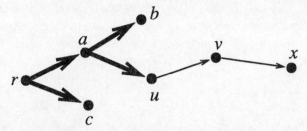

Figure 2.8 Illustration of the growth of the out-tree T (cf. theorem 2.2).

It will now be shown that it is not necessary to distinguish between flows to different destinations as far as cost minimisation is concerned. Let x_{ij}^t be the flow from origin r to destination t that passes along arc ij. Then $x_{ij} = \sum_t x_{ij}^t$ and there will be a set of conservation equations corresponding to each destination t, which, if summed, lead to the *aggregate* conservation constraint equations

$$\sum_i x_{ij} - \sum_k x_{jk} = D_{rj} \quad \text{all } j \neq r.$$

Theorem 2.3 If $x = \{x_{ij}\}$ is a minimal cost network flow in a network N, with node set X and arc set A, which satisfies the aggregate conservation constraints, then there is a set of path flows $\{x_\pi\}$ such that the individual (r, t) conservation constraints are satisfied.

Proof Let $N^* = (X \cup \{T\}, E^*)$ be the network formed from N together with an extra node T and links from each destination t of N to T. In N^*, T is the sole destination with traffic requirement $\sum_j D_{rj}$. The flow x is extended to a flow x^* on N^* by assigning flow D_{rt} to each link $t\text{-}T$ for each destination t of N. $\qquad\qquad\square$

The aggregated problem becomes

minimise $\sum_i \sum_j c_{ij} x_{ij}$

subject to

$$\sum_i x_{ij} - \sum_k x_{jk} = D_{rj} \quad \text{for all } j \neq r.$$

$$x_{ij} \geq 0 \quad \text{for all } i \text{ and } j.$$

Similarly, if there are several origins but only a single destination then the minimal cost flow problem can be treated in the same way, the flow being regarded as that of a single commodity.

Multiple-origin multiple-destination flows

When we turn to the case of many origins and many destinations the situation fundamentally changes. To see why this should be so, consider the problem of figure 2.9, in which it is required to send one unit of flow per unit time from p to v, and one unit of flow per unit time from u to q. Regarded as a single commodity flow the only requirements are that one unit of flow per unit time should enter the network at each of p and u, and one unit of flow per unit time should leave each of q and v. One 'solution' is: $x_{pq} = x_{uv} = 1$ and all other $x_{ij} = 0$. This is not however feasible for the original problem since there is no flow from p to v as required.

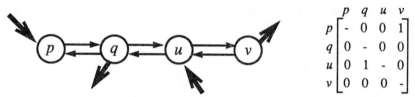

Figure 2.9 A multi-commodity flow. The traffic demand matrix is shown on the right.

It is easily seen that there is no interference between flows from different origins and so the cost minimisation problem when there are multiple origins and destinations can be expressed in the disaggregate form:

minimise $\sum_i \sum_j c_{ij} (\sum_r \sum_t x_{ij}^{rt})$ (2.5)
subject to

$$\sum_i x_{ij}^{rt} - \sum_k x_{jk}^{rt} = \begin{cases} -D_{rt}^{rt} & \text{if } j=r \\ 0 & \text{if } j \neq r, t \\ D_{rt}^{rt} & \text{if } j=t \end{cases} \qquad (2.6)$$

$x_{ij}^{rt} \geq 0$ for all i, j, r and t.   (2.7)

where x_{ij}^{rt} is the flow from origin r to destination t that passes along link ij. For some purposes the corresponding aggregate form minimise $\sum_i \sum_j c_{ij} \sum_r x_{ij}^r$ (2.8)

subject to

$$\sum_i x_{ij}^r - \sum_k x_{jk}^r = \begin{cases} -D_r & j = r \\ D_{rj} & \text{for all } j \neq r \end{cases}$$ (2.9)

$x_{ij}^r \geq 0 \quad \text{for all } i, \text{ and } r.$ (2.10)

is more useful, where x_{ij}^r is the flow in arc ij from source r and D_r is the total flow from r to all other nodes. [Equally, the flows could be aggregrated by origin rather than by destination.]

All that is required to solve the cost minimisation problem is to find separately the shortest paths from each origin r to every other node and to assign the flows accordingly.

Example 2.5   For the network of example 2.4 (reproduced below together with the internode traffic matrix) what routes should be used for flow for each OD pair if the linear approximation is adopted?   With

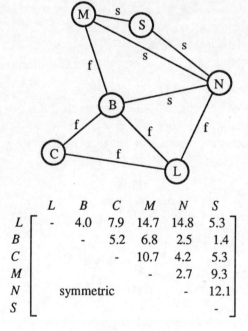

	L	B	C	M	N	S
L	-	4.0	7.9	14.7	14.8	5.3
B		-	5.2	6.8	2.5	1.4
C			-	10.7	4.2	5.3
M				-	2.7	9.3
N		symmetric			-	12.1
S						-

Figure 2.10 Network and associated traffic matrix.

this routing determine the percentage utilisation for each of the links. Does the linear approximation appear to have been justified if packets are all 1000 bits long?

Solution As in example 2.4 s-links will be assigned a length of 2 and f-links a length of 1. Then, by inspection, shortest routes for each OD pair are as given in the following matrix.

	L	B	C	M	N	S
L	-	L-B	L-C	L-B-M	L-N	L-N-S
B		-	B-C	B-M	B-N	B-M-S
C			-	C-B-M	C-L-N	C-L-N-S
M				-	M-N	M-S
N					-	N-S
S						-

Note that the alternative route *C-B-M-S* could have been used for traffic from *C* to *S* instead of *C-L-N-S*. The shortest route for OD pair (I, J) is just the reverse of the shortest route for OD pair (J, I). Recalling that the demand matrix is symmetric and, for each link (in each direction), adding the flows for the routes that pass through that link (in each direction) gives the total flow in each direction in every link. The results are given in tabular form below. [Note that the links carry the stated flow in both directions.]

Table 2.2 Link flows (in kbps) and link utilisations.

Link	Flow	Utilisation
L-B	18.7	15%
L-C	17.4	14%
L-N	29.6	23%
B-C	15.9	12%
B-M	33.6	26%
B-N	2.5	4%
M-S	10.7	17%
M-N	2.7	4%
N-S	22.7	35%

The percentage utilisation is obtained by dividing each link flow by 64 kbps or 128 kbps depending on the particular line speed, and multiplying the result by 100. It is seen that link *N-S* and to a lesser extent *B-M* and *B-C*, cannot reasonably be described as lightly loaded, and so the linear approximation must be slightly dubious (cf. section 3.1).

Finally the average delay d_{av} will be calculated from the formula

$$d_{av} = \frac{\textit{Total time taken for all OD pairs per unit time}}{\textit{Total traffic for all OD pairs}}$$

Total time = 2[(4.0)(1) + (7.9)(1) + (14.7)(2) + (14.8)(1) + (5.3)(3) +

(5.2)(1) + (6.8)(1) +(2.5)(2) + (1.4)(3) + (10.7)(2) +

(4.2)(2) + (5.3)(4) + (2.7)(2) + (9.3)(2) + (12.1)(2)]

= 384.8 (in units of the time to transmit packet on a fast line).

Total traffic = 2[4.0 + 7.9 + 14.7 + 14.8 + 5.3 + 5.2 + 6.8 + 2.5

+ 1.4 +10.7 + 4.2 + 5.3 + 2.7 + 9.3 + 12.1]

= 213.6 kbps,

from which d_{av} is found to be 0.014 (in units of the time to transmit one packet on a fast line). Since a 128 kbps link has had a length of 1 associated with it and each packet contains 1000 bits, it follows that d_{av} = 384.8/128 = 0.1875 s.

An alternative way of calculating total time taken is via the total link flows (cf. table 2.2).

Total time = 2[(18.7)(1) + (17.4)(1) + (29.6)(1) + (15.9)(1) +

(33.6)(1) + (2.5)(2) + (10.7)(2) + (2.7)(2) + (22.7)(2)]

= 384.8 (in units of the time to transmit packet on a fast line).   □

2.3 SHORTEST PATH ROUTING

In a computer network there will be a certain amount of traffic directly between the nodes of the subnet; these will include various types of control packets relating to routing, flow control etc. The majority of subnet traffic, however, originates outside the subnet and finishes outside.

For example, a message sent from a VDU terminal to a remote computer will:

(1) be sent through a local access network to a unique subnet node t;

(2) travel through the subnet using one or more paths to a unique node t;

(3) be sent from t via a local access network to its ultimate destination.

For the purposes of this chapter, which is concerned with routing in the subnet, r will be regarded as the origin and t the destination with the remaining parts of the journey, if any, being understood.

Datagram routing

For linear (ie. steady and low intensity) flow over reliable links the routing problem is straightforward, packets being sent along shortest (least cost) paths. The actual routing of a packet as it passes through a network can be effected readily if each packet contains full details of the route it is to take. This is, however, wasteful of communication capacity since it is only necessary at any node i to know, for each possible destination node t, which outgoing link should be used. Then, if the packet is sent on the correct outgoing link from i, to j say, it will be correctly routed thereafter at j and subsequent nodes. To see this, consider the example of a packet that is to be sent from node 1 to node 3 in the network of figure 2.11.

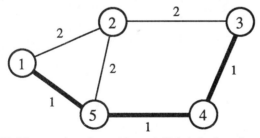

Figure 2.11 The number alongside each link is its length.

Since 1-5-4-3 is the unique shortest path it follows that 5-4-3 and 4-3 must be the unique shortest paths from node 5 to node 3, and from node 4 to node 3 respectively. Consequently, after node 1 has sent the packet along link 1-5, node 5 will take over and automatically route the packet along 5-4, and finally node 4 will send the packet along 4-3 to its destination. This gives rise, at each node i, to a *routing table* $T(i)$ containing a link from i corresponding to each possible destination. Thus, $T(i)$ takes the general form

$T(i)$

Destination	Next node
1	j_1
2	j_2
.	.
i-1	j_{i-1}
i	-
i+1	j_{i+1}
.	.
n	j_n

Example 2.6 For the five node network of figure 2.11, links are full duplex with capacities 32 kbps for 1-2, 2-3 and 2-5, and 64 kbps for the remaining links. Assuming that the linear flow approximation is made, determine routes for each OD pair, and hence determine a routing table for each node.

Solution If fast lines are assigned a length of 1 and slow lines a length of 2, the shortest routes for every OD pair are, by inspection, as given by the following matrix

$$
\begin{array}{c}
\\
1\\
2\\
3\\
4\\
5
\end{array}
\begin{array}{ccccc}
1 & 2 & 3 & 4 & 5 \\
\left[\begin{array}{ccccc}
- & \text{1-2} & \text{1-5-4-3} & \text{1-5-4} & \text{1-5} \\
\text{2-1} & - & \text{2-3} & \left|\begin{array}{c}\text{2-3-4}\\\text{2-5-4}\end{array}\right| & \text{2-5} \\
\text{3-4-5-1} & \text{3-2} & - & \text{3-4} & \text{3-4-5} \\
\text{4-5-1} & \left|\begin{array}{c}\text{4-3-2}\\\text{4-5-2}\end{array}\right| & \text{4-3} & - & \text{4-5} \\
\text{5-1} & \text{5-2} & \text{5-4-3} & \text{5-4} & -
\end{array}\right]
\end{array}
$$

Note that for OD pair $(2,4)$ there are two alternative shortest routes, namely 2-3-4 and 2-5-4; similarly for $(4,2)$ both 4-3-2 and 4-5-2 are shortest routes.

Assuming that for OD pairs $(2,4)$ and $(4,2)$ the alternative paths

2-3-4 and 4-3-2 are chosen respectively then, with t denoting the destination and j_t the next node, the routing tables are

T(1)

t	j_t
1	-
2	2
3	5
4	5
5	5

T(2)

t	j_t
1	1
2	-
3	3
4	3
5	5

T(3)

t	j_t
1	4
2	2
3	-
4	4
5	4

T(4)

t	j_t
1	5
2	3
3	3
4	-
5	5

T(5)

t	j_t
1	1
2	2
3	4
4	4
5	-

For a packet being sent from origin 1 to destination 3, the first link is found from T(1) by inspecting the link entry for $t = 3$, the second link from T(5) by inspecting the link entry for $t = 3$, and finally the last link from T(4) by inspecting the link entry for $t = 3$. The required route is in fact chosen as may be seen from the italicised entries in the above tables. □

Of course conditions are typically varying and link failures occur occasionally. Consequently the above *static* routing scheme is likely to be suboptimal. A simple modification which is satisfactory for relatively slowly varying conditions is to use routing tables as described above but to update them periodically by means of a shortest path calculation based on the extant link lengths.

Virtual circuits

In practice, one origin node is likely to be 'conversing' with only a subset of the possible destination nodes. This means that a larger than necessary routing table might be scanned whenever a packet is received. An alternative scheme using *virtual circuits* will now be described. For simplicity, we temporarily assume that for any OD pair there is at most one conversation taking place at any one time and that links are reliable. Each conversation will have an assigned route which is allocated a distinct number 0, 1, 2, ... Since the same range of numbers is being used by different nodes it seems that there is scope for much confusion. However, there is *no need for a packet to carry the same route number throughout its journey* provided that the correct number is inserted at each node. That is, a correspondence between route numbers carried on incoming packets and route numbers on outgoing packets must be set up. How this works will be illustrated by an example.

Example 2.7 For the network of figure 2.11, suppose that currently there are conversations corresponding to OD pairs

$$(1,2) \quad (1,3) \quad (2,3) \quad (5,4) \quad (1,5) \quad (1,4).$$

Devise a suitable routing table for each node.

Solution Appropriate routing tables for each node are shown in figure 2.12. For their interpretation consider the entries in $T(1)$. On the first line, 'H 0' relates to a message entering the subnet at node 1 on virtual circuit 0, and '2 0' indicates that it is forwarded to node 2 on circuit 0. The second line, 'H 1' relates to a message entering the subnet at node 1 on circuit 1, and '5 0' indicates that it is forwarded to node 5 on circuit 0. Note that there is no confusion between these two circuits labelled '0' since they are received at different nodes. Consider also a message between node 1 and node 4. This enters the subnet at node 1 on circuit 3 and is forwarded to node 5 on circuit 2 as circuits 0 and 1 are already allocated. At node 5 it is received on circuit 2 and is also forwarded on circuit 2 to node 4. At node 4 it is received on circuit 2 but forwarded on circuit 1 since only circuit 1 has been allocated for messages leaving the subnet at node 5. □

Centralised and distributed routing

Routing table calculations may be made *centrally* at a special node called the *Network Routing Centre* (or NRC), or in a distributed way with each node constructing its own tables. Other variations are possible, for example, 'delta routing' (Rudin, 1976). In centralised routing with datagrams, an individual node reports to the NRC on the status of each of its outgoing links; this can be a cost reflecting current delay on the link, type of link etc, and may be set to infinity if the link is down. The

NRC then calculates the routing table for every node and distributes the appropriate table, T(i), to each node i. This clearly generates a large amount of traffic in the region of the NRC as may be seen by the following simple order of magnitude calculation. For a network with n nodes each routing table T(i) will require at least $O(n)$ bits [ignoring the possibility that more bits are needed to represent each of the n possible destinations as n increases]. The NRC must send n-1 such tables over paths which may reasonably be assumed to average $O(\sqrt{n})$ links, and this traffic must be borne by (typically) $O(n)$ links. Hence $O(n.n\sqrt{n})/O(n)$ bits, that is $O(n^{1.5})$ bits are, on average, carried by each link. Since the links in the vicinity of the NRC will be loaded well above average it is seen that the approach is not attractive for large networks if frequent updates are required in order to account for varying conditions.

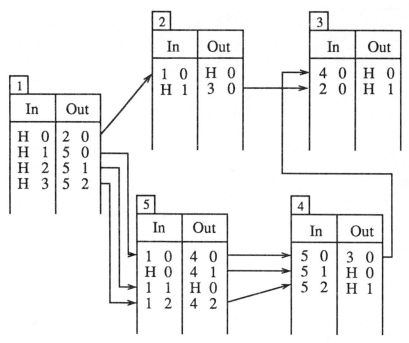

Figure 2.12 Square boxes indicate which node a table relates to. 'H' indicates the corresponding node is a point of entry or exit from the subnet.

The simple distributed alternative for datagrams is for each node to send the status of each of its outgoing links to every other node so that the routing tables may be calculated locally. Although much better than for centralised routing the amount of control traffic carrying routing information is still uncomfortably large, and the nodes are also involved in more computation. The traffic can be reduced if a node only informs other nodes on lengths of its outgoing links when these have changed significantly; more precisely a node will broadcast the new link length of any of its outgoing links whose length has changed by more than a prescribed amount. This is the strategy of the 'new' ARPANET routing scheme (McQuillan et al. 1980).

An alternative distributed scheme, which results in an order of magnitude less routing traffic being generated while still being responsive to changing conditions, is for each node to transmit link status information to its neighbouring nodes only. The effect of a link cost change is thus felt locally very quickly, but takes some time to percolate to more remote parts of the network. (This strategy is described in some detail in section 3.5.)

With virtual circuits, a route is set up for a particular session and normally remains in force for the duration of the session (provided link or node failures do not occur along its route).

The route may be determined centrally, with the most recent data on link costs received at the NRC being used in the calculations. Then the appropriate routing table updates are transmitted to the relevant nodes. An alternative, used in TYMNET II (cf. Tymes, 1981), is for the NRC to construct the route, but for the tables to be set up locally when a special packet, called a *needle*, carrying the route information 'threads' its way along the designated route; the information to be transmitted then follows behind. Finally there is the possibility of a node being responsible for setting up virtual circuits for traffic originating at that node. This could be effected readily if each node i had a datagram-type routing table $T(i)$ stored there.

Centralised routing is simple in concept, but may be seen to have two pronounced disadvantages:

(1) there is the possibility of excessive traffic being generated in the region of the NRC this being exacerbated should a link from the NRC fail;

(2) the network is vulnerable to failure of the NRC itself.

The latter disadvantage may be lessened, at a cost, by having another node on standby to act as NRC.

Hierarchical routing

It has been noted earlier that as the size of a network increases so the routing overhead can grow as a proportion of 'useful work done'. A strategy that is suitable for a 15 node network may be inconvenient for a 100 node network and impractical for a 1000 node network. It may therefore be worthwhile relaxing the requirement that the routes chosen be optimal (with respect to link costs *at the time of calculation*) in order to cut down the routing overhead.

It is fortunate that for large networks the general direction in which to send a packet tends to be clear. Consider the analogy of a journey from Amsterdam to Madrid by rail. It may be decided to split the routing problem into two parts: first decide on the best way of travelling to Spain, then consider the more local problem of getting to Madrid from the chosen entry point. There are two possible entry points from France to Spain by rail, one at either end of the Pyrenees mountains. Suppose that the West entry point is chosen and used not just for travel to Madrid but also for travel from Amsterdam to any Spanish destination. Then, for some destinations the optimal route will have been chosen and for others it will not. However, the selected route will seldom be much in error (as a proportion of the total distance) and so this strategy is a reasonable one to adopt.

Kamoun-Kleinrock hierarchical routing

A node address now comprises a pair (c, n) where c is the *cluster* number and n is the node number within the cluster.

Example 2.8 For the given clustering of nodes shown in figure 2.13 suggest the routing table for node $(3, 2)$.

Solution In order to route packets correctly from node $(3, 2)$ it must be known which is the best next node for each of the possible 'destinations', that is, nodes $(3, 1)$, $(3, 3)$, $(3, 4)$, and clusters $(1, -)$, $(2, -)$ and $(4, -)$. Consequently its routing table could be as shown in figure 2.14. For larger networks the reduction in size of routing tables is likely to be more impressive. The optimal number of clusters is indicated by the following result. □

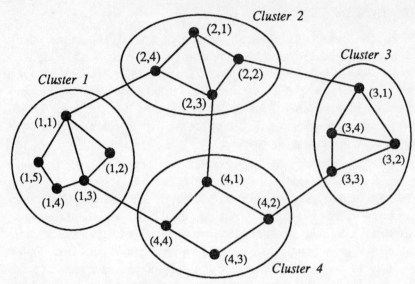

Figure 2.13   An example of a network with a natural clustering of nodes.

Destination	Next node
$(3, 1)$	$(3, 1)$
$(3, 2)$	-
$(3, 3)$	$(3, 3)$
$(3, 4)$	$(3, 4)$
$(1, -)$	$(3, 3)$
$(2, -)$	$(3, 1)$
$(3, -)$	-
$(4, -)$	$(3, 3)$

Figure 2.14 A possible routing table for node $(3, 2)$ of example 2.8.

Theorem 2.4 If the number of nodes, n, is the square of a positive integer then the optimum number of clusters is $\sqrt{n}$, with each cluster containing $\sqrt{n}$ nodes. [If n is not the square of an integer the result is still 'approximately' true.]

Proof Suppose there are c clusters and that cluster i contains $n(i)$ nodes. If k is a node in cluster i then its routing table will contain $n(i)+c$ entries. The optimal number of clusters is found by solving minimise$_c$ $(l = \max_i (n(i) + c))$

subject to

$$\Sigma_{i=1}^{c} \; n(i) = n$$
$$n(i), \; c > 0.$$

For the moment we ignore the obvious requirement that $n(i)$ and c be integers. For each i, $l \geq n(i) + c$, so that summing these inequalities over i gives $lc \geq (\Sigma_{i=1}^{c} n(i)) + c^2$ for fixed c. Since $n(i) = n/c$ gives $l = n/c + c$ and hence $lc \leq (\Sigma_{i=1}^{c} n(i)) + c^2$ it follows that the solution of the above optimisation problem occurs when $n(i) = n/c$ all i.

Letting c vary leads to $\sqrt{n}$ as the optimal value of c implying that each cluster contains $\sqrt{n}$ nodes.

If n happens to be the square of an integer then $\sqrt{n}$ is the optimal value for c and cluster size. It is intuitively clear that, more generally, $c = \lceil \sqrt{n} \rceil$, and $n(i)$ equal to either $\lceil \sqrt{n} \rceil$ or $\lceil \sqrt{n} \rceil$ - 1 will be at least near optimal where '$\lceil \; \rceil$' denotes rounding up to the nearest integer. In fact, Kleinrock and Kamoun (1977) showed that this is indeed optimal. $\qquad\square$

It is interesting to enquire as to how much can be lost by way of increased path lengths. The answer is that in the worst case the path can be as much as three times as long as the optimal path, though in practice the loss will generally be very much less than this.

Theorem 2.5 (Baratz and Jaffe 1986) Suppose, for a given network and clustering, that

(1) routing tables reflect the best (ie. shortest) paths;
(2) no links experience a weight change whilst a message is being sent from any node A to any other node B;
(3) for any two nodes A and B in the same cluster, the shortest route between A and B remains within that cluster;
(4) the weight associated with each link is the same in both directions.

Then, $\omega/\omega_{opt} \leq 3$ where ω_{opt} is the length of a minimal path from A to B and ω is the length of the path actually taken using Kamoun-Kleinrock hierarchical routing.

Proof If A and B are in the same cluster then $\omega = \omega_{opt}$ and there is nothing further to prove.

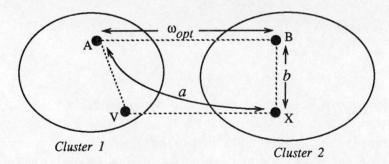

Figure 2.15 The broken lines *AB*, *AV*, *VX* and *XB* are respectively the shortest routes between *A* and *B*, *A* and *V*, *V* and *X*, and *X* and *B* (see theorem 2.5).

Suppose *A* and *B* are in different clusters (cf. figure 2.15) and that *X* is the node in the cluster of B which is closest to *A*. Let *a* be the distance from *A* to *X* and *b* the distance from *X* to *B*, then

(1) $a \le \omega_{opt}$ since *X* is a nearest node to *A* in cluster 2;

(2) length *XA* + length *AB* $\ge$ length *XB* by assumption (3). Also, by assumption (2), length *XA* = *a*. Consequently $a + \omega_{opt} \ge b$.

Combining (1) and (2) gives

$$\omega = a + b \le (\omega_{opt}) + (a + \omega_{opt}) \le 3\omega_{opt}.$$

In fact the worst case can be realised as shown in figure 2.16. $\square$

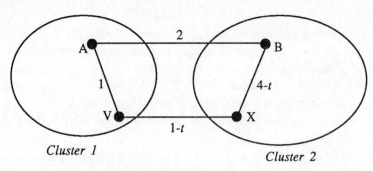

Figure 2.16 A four node two cluster example showing that $\omega = 3\omega_{opt}$ can be realised in Kamoun-Kleinrock hierarchical routing. This may be seen by letting t→0. Each of *AB*, *AV*, *VX* and *XB* are single links whose lengths are shown alongside.

For very large networks, clusters of nodes could themselves be grouped into larger clusters forming a 3-level hierarchy as follows:

level 0 cluster - single node
level 1 cluster - cluster of nodes
level 2 cluster - cluster of level 1 clusters.

The following analogue of theorem 2.4 holds.

Theorem 2.6 For a 3-level hierarchy containing n nodes, the optimal number of clusters (with regard to minimising total storage used by routing tables) is for

each level 1 cluster to contain $n^{1/3}$ nodes
each level 2 cluster to contain $n^{1/3}$ level 1 clusters.

[This is exact if n is the cube of a positive integer; otherwise it only holds approximately.]

Proof See Kleinrock and Kamoun (1977). □

An alternative hierarchical routing scheme

Baratz and Jaffe (1986) suggest an alternative form of hierarchical routing. Instead of only one entry point in a remote cluster for all packets from a given origin node r, they calculate the entry point which is best for the *particular destination within a cluster*. This does, not surprisingly, require more computation and so is only appropriate for virtual circuits where all packets corresponding to a particular session will, under normal circumstances, follow the same route.

This alternative scheme while permitting optimal routing does not represent a return to the non-hierarchical schemes of section 2.3. Each node now keeps entries for only each node in its cluster and each possible entry point (called a *border* node) in remote clusters.

Consider setting up a virtual circuit from node r to node t. Either the optimal path stays within the same cluster as r or it passes through at least one border node. In the latter case, the last border node belonging to a path is called the *critical border node* for that path and is clearly in the same cluster as the destination node. A virtual circuit is determined by the following protocol:

(1) r sends a REQUEST message to t - directly if r and t are in the same cluster; otherwise to each border node in the cluster containing t from whence the message copies are forwarded with the first to reach t being accepted.

(2) t returns to r, along the reverse of the path taken by the accepted REQUEST message copy, a message containing the lengths of the shortest paths from t to each border node in the cluster containing t.

(3) The critical border node for the optimal path from r to t is determined by finding that border node B in t's cluster which minimises $d(r, B) + d(t, B)$ with ties being resolved arbitrarily.

(4) The optimal path is established by using the (clustered) routing tables with r as origin and B as destination then from B using 'local routing' to get to t.

2.4 LABEL-CORRECTING AND LABEL-SETTING

In this section it is assumed, for simplicity, that routing calculations are performed centrally at the NRC. (The routing algorithms introduced may, however, be used in certain forms of distributed routing also.) Since the linear flow approximation is often not well justified, a node may periodically send to the NRC the current arc length estimates for arcs outgoing to its neighbours. (The estimates may be based on queue lengths, time to acknowledgement or a combination of these.) From time to time NRC calculates the new routing tables and transmits the appropriate one back to each subnet node.

It is clear that the many-origin many-destination routing problem may be solved by sequentially finding, for each origin node r, the shortest paths from r to every other node. Thus

REPEATED SINGLE-ORIGIN (RSO) PROCEDURE
For each origin r perform the following step.
STEP Find the shortest path from r to every other node.

Special purpose algorithms exist for simultaneously finding paths from all origins to all destinations (eg. Floyd, 1962; Spira, 1973). However, it has been found, for sparse networks of the type arising in road transportation networks, that it is *much* better to use the RSO procedure. Since computer networks are similarly sparse (though relationships between arc lengths are likely to be different), the RSO procedure is also worth considering in this situation.

Before discussing individual algorithms some terminology will be collected together; terms used here but not explained will be defined in subsequent pages.

a_{ij} the length of arc ij

$d(i,j)$ the shortest distance from node i to node j

r, s particular origin nodes

$d(j)$ an abbreviation for $d(r,j)$

$dist(j)$ an estimate of $d(j)$

$p(j)$ the predecessor of node j on a shortest path from r to j

$T(x)$ a subtree (of the shortest path in-tree) rooted at node x

$\pi(r,a)$ a shortest path from r to node a.

For routing problems in computer networks the arc lengths will be non-negative and under these conditions all the algorithms introduced in this section will work correctly and provide the right solutions. Label-correcting algorithms (see below) are also valid when some arcs have negative lengths though, not surprisingly, they do not work correctly if circuits whose total length is negative are present.

Label-correcting

The basic idea behind single-origin shortest path algorithms is to start with 'estimates' $dist(j)$ for the distances $d(j) = d(r,j)$ from origin r to every node j. These estimates, called *labels,* are continually refined until, providing the algorithm satisfies some modest requirements, they converge to the desired shortest distances (ie. $dist(j) \rightarrow d(j)$ for all j). The following outline algorithm, which is based on this idea, requires the initial estimates to be upper bounds (ie. $dist(j) \geq d(j)$ initially).

Prototype label-correcting algorithm

{ To find the shortest distance from r to every other node.

 Input: a network (X, A) and a set of arc lengths $\{a_{ij}\}$. }

  Set $dist(r) = 0$.

  for all $j \neq r$ **do** set $dist(j)$ to some upper bound on $d(j)$.

  while further changes may be possible **do**

  begin

   Select an arc uv.

   if $dist(u) + a_{uv} < dist(v)$

   then set $dist(v) \leftarrow dist(u) + a_{uv}$ (estimate improvement).

  end

{ Output: $dist(j) = d(j)$ for all j. }

The validity of this algorithm is established from the following results.

Theorem 2.7 Given a set of estimates, $\{dist(j)\}$, satisfying

 (1) $dist(r) = 0$;

 (2) $dist(j) \geq d(j)$ for all j;

then $dist(j) = d(j)$ for all j, if and only if $dist(j) \leq dist(i) + a_{ij}$ for every arc ij.

Proof (A) *Given $dist(j) = d(j)$ for all j.*

Let uv be an arc for which $dist(v) > dist(u) + a_{uv}$. Then

$$\begin{aligned} d(v) &\leq d(u) + a_{uv} && \text{(definition of shortest distance)} \\ &= dist(u) + a_{uv} && \text{(given)} \\ &< dist(v) && \text{(by assumption).} \end{aligned}$$

But this is a contradiction and so the arc uv cannot exist; hence $dist(j) \leq dist(i) + a_{ij}$ for all arcs ij.

(B) *Given $dist(j) \leq dist(i) + a_{ij}$ for all arcs ij.*

Suppose that for some node u, $dist(u) > d(u)$ and that $\pi(r, u)$ is a shortest path from r to u. On $\pi(r, u)$ there will be a first arc pq for which $dist(p)=d(p)$ but $dist(q) \neq d(q)$ (in fact $dist(q)>d(q)$). Then

$$\begin{aligned} dist(q) &\leq dist(p) + a_{pq} && \text{(by assumption)} \\ &= d(p) + a_{pq} \\ &= d(q) && \text{(by shortest path property)} \\ &< dist(q). \end{aligned}$$

But this is a contradiction and so $dist(u)$ must equal $d(u)$. $\qquad\qquad\qquad$ $\square$

Corollary Upon termination, the prototype shortest path algorithm gives the correct shortest distances.

A particular implementation (algorithm (LC-Q) below) of the prototype algorithm will now be presented. A set *CAND*, of 'candidate' nodes, is maintained as a *queue*; that is, an *ordered set* to which elements are added at the 'rear' and removed from the 'front'. All arcs emanating from a given candidate node are considered together. The variables $p(x)$ will be explained later.

Algorithm (LC-Q)
{Label-correcting algorithm, using a queue, for finding a shortest path
from node r to all other nodes.
Input : a network (X, A) and a set of arc lengths $\{a_{ij}\}$. }

$\quad$ Set $CAND = \{r\}$, $dist(r) = 0$; $p(r) = r$, $u = r$.
$\quad$ **for** all $j \neq r$ **do** set $dist(j) = \infty$.
$\quad$ **while** $CAND \neq \varnothing$ **do**
$\quad$ **begin**
$\qquad$ Remove the node u from the front of the queue.
$\qquad$ (ie. $CAND \leftarrow CAND - \{u\}$.)
$\qquad$ **for** each arc uv **do**
$\qquad$ **begin**
$\qquad\quad$ **if** $dist(u) + a_{uv} < dist(v)$
$\qquad\quad$ **then** set $dist(v) \leftarrow dist(u) + a_{uv}$ (estimate improvement),
$\qquad\qquad$ set $p(v) \leftarrow u$, and add v to the rear of the queue if not already in (ie., $CAND \leftarrow CAND \cup \{u\}$).
$\qquad$ **end**
$\quad$ **end**
{Output: if there is no path in the network from r to j then $dist(j)$ has its initial value of ∞ , otherwise $dist(j) = d(j)$ for all .}

Initially, for every $j \neq r$, $dist(j) = \infty$. As soon as $dist(j)$ becomes finite, via $dist(j) \leftarrow dist(i) + a_{ij}$ say, it is set to the length of the shortest path from r to j so far found, this path being called the *incumbent path for node j*. The preceding node on the path is $i = p(j)$ except that $p(r) = r$.

At any time during the application of the algorithm the incumbent path to j may be found (in reverse order) by following the pointers $p(j)$, $p(p(j))$, $p(p(p(j)))$, ... back to r.

Theorem 2.8 Let $C = \{ i \mid dist(i) < \infty \}$ and $A = \{ ji \mid i = p(j), j \neq r\}$ then (C, A) is an in-tree at r. ☐

The in-tree (C, A) will be called the current *shortest distance tree* or merely the *SD-tree*.

Example 2.9 Use algorithm (LC-Q) to find shortest distances from r to every other node of the network of figure 2.17.

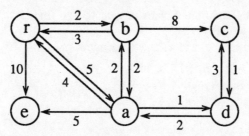

Figure 2.17 It is required to find the shortest distances from r to every other node (cf. examples 2.9 and 2.10).

Solution The course of the solution is shown by the table overleaf in which the circled elements indicate nodes selected from *CAND* for 'scanning'. The small figures to the right indicate the growing SD-tree defined by the pointers $p(x)$. Note that *CAND* is ordered and nodes are always taken from the 'left'.

There are several things that may be learnt even from this small example.

(1) The order in which arcs from a given node are considered can affect the efficiency. For example, if at the first step arc rb is considered before arc ra then b will be ahead of a in the queue. When b is taken from the queue and upon considering arc ba, a has the correct value of $dist(a)$. Hence a will only join the queue once. The reader may verify that successive states of the queue are

$\{r\}, \{b, a, e\}, \{a, e, c\}, \{e, c, d\}, \{c, d\}, \{d\}, \{c\}$

CAND		r	a	b	c	d	e	
{r}	dist(j)	⓪	∞	∞	∞	∞	∞	
	p(j)	r	.	.	.	.	.	
{a,b,e}	dist(j)	0	⑤	2	∞	∞	10	
	p(j)	r	r	r	.	.	r	
{b,e,d}	dist(j)	0	5	②	∞	6	10	
	p(j)	r	r	r	.	a	r	
{e,d,a,c}	dist(j)	0	4	2	10	6	⑩	
	p(j)	r	b	r	b	a	r	
{d,a,c}	dist(j)	0	4	2	10	⑥	10	
	p(j)	r	b	r	b	a	r	
{a,c}	dist(j)	0	④	2	9	6	10	
	p(j)	r	b	r	d	a	r	
{c,d,e}	dist(j)	0	4	2	⑨	5	9	
	p(j)	r	b	r	d	a	a	
{d,e}	dist(j)	0	4	2	9	⑤	9	
	p(j)	r	b	r	d	a	a	
{e,c}	dist(j)	0	4	2	8	5	⑨	
	p(j)	r	b	r	d	a	a	
{c}	dist(j)	0	4	2	⑧	5	9	
	p(j)	r	b	r	d	a	a	

and three iterations are saved. Thus, better performance has been achieved with shorter arcs being considered first; this strategy is generally beneficial. While the necessary processing may not be worthwhile for a one-off calculation, it may in some situations be worth keeping the network with, for each node, the outgoing arcs being kept in order of increasing length.

(2) Another idea (attributed to d'Esopo) that improves the performance on average is to maintain the set of candidate nodes as a *deque* (cf. Boffey and Yates, 1989). Nodes are always taken from the front of the deque. However, a node is placed at the rear if entering *CAND* for the first time; otherwise it is placed at the front.

(3) When finding the distance between relatively close nodes it is clearly wasteful of effort to find the shortest distance to every node of the network. Savings may be made by entering a node x in *CAND* after an update only if $dist(x) \leq dist(t)$.

Label-setting

As noted above, the order in which nodes are selected from *CAND* for scanning influences the effectiveness of a shortest route algorithm. There is always at least one order for which each node needs be scanned only once. An order that achieves this is obtained by at each iteration choosing a node u in *CAND* for which $dist(u) \leq dist(i)$ for all other i in *CAND*. Before proving this the algorithm is presented and an example given.

Algorithm (L-S)

{Dijkstra's algorithm for finding a shortest path from node r to all other nodes.

Input: a network (X, A) and a set of arc lengths $\{a_{ij}\}$. }

   Set $CAND = \{r\}$, $dist(r) = 0$, $p(r) = r$.

   for all $j \neq r$ **do** set $dist(j) = \infty$.

   while $CAND \neq \emptyset$ **do**

   begin

   Remove the node u from *CAND* for which $dist(i)$ is minimal.

   Set $CAND \leftarrow CAND - \{u\}$.

   for each arc uv **do**

   begin

   if $dist(u) + a_{uv} < dist(v)$

   then set $dist(v) \leftarrow dist(u) + a_{uv}$ (estimate improvement),

   set $p(v) \leftarrow u$, and add v to the set *CAND* if not already in (ie. $CAND \leftarrow CAND \cup \{u\}$).

   end

   end

{Output: if there is no path in the network from r to j then $dist(j)$ has its initial value of ∞, otherwise $dist(j) = d(j)$ for all j.}

Nodes in *CAND* are said to be *temporarily labelled*, and those in

   $PERM = \{ x \mid x$ has been selected for removal from *CAND* $\}$

are said to be *permanently labelled* since the values of $dist(u)$ cannot change once u has been selected.

Example 2.10 For the network of figure 2.17 use algorithm (L-S) to find the shortest distance from r to all other nodes.
Solution The solution is given below in tabular form.

CAND		r	a	b	c	d	e
{r}	$dist(j)$	⓪	∞	∞	∞	∞	∞
	$p(j)$	r	.	.	.	.	.
{a,b,e}	$dist(j)$	0	5	②	∞	∞	10
	$p(j)$	r	r	r	.	.	r
{a,e,c}	$dist(j)$	0	④	2	10	∞	10
	$p(j)$	r	b	r	b	a	r
{e,c,d}	$dist(j)$	0	4	2	10	⑤	9
	$p(j)$	r	b	r	b	a	a
{e,c}	$dist(j)$	0	4	2	⑧	5	9
	$p(j)$	r	b	r	d	a	a
{e}	$dist(j)$	0	4	2	8	5	⑨
	$p(j)$	r	b	r	d	a	a
	$dist(j)$	0	4	2	8	5	9
	$p(j)$	r	b	r	d	a	a

The validity of Dijkstra's algorithm rests on the following results.

Theorem 2.9 For each $j \in CAND$, every node other than j on the incumbent path to j is permanently labelled.
Proof When node j first has its label $dist(j)$ changed the above condition holds. It remains true thereafter.

Theorem 2.10 If all link lengths are strictly positive $(a_{ij} > 0)$ then $dist(u) = d(u)$ when node u is selected in algorithm(L-S).
Proof The result is assumed to be true for $|PERM| \leq m$; this is clearly valid for $m = 1$. Suppose now that u is about to be selected as the $(m+1)$st candidate for $PERM$, and let

   π be a shortest path from r to u,
   z be the last node on π which is in $PERM$ and
   y be the successor of z on π.

Then

$$dist(y) = \min_{x \in \text{PERM}} (dist(x) + a_{xy}) \quad \text{(step 2 of algorithm (L-S)}$$
$$\leq dist(z) + a_{zy} \qquad (z \in PERM \text{ by theorem 2.9)}$$
$$= d(z) + a_{zy} \qquad \text{(by induction hypothesis)}$$
$$= d(y) \qquad (\pi \text{ is a shortest path)}$$

The desired result follows by observing that y must coincide with u since otherwise

$$dist(y) = d(y) < \text{length of } \pi \qquad \text{(arcs lengths are positive)}$$
$$= d(u)$$
$$\leq dist(u)$$

and y would have been selected for removal from *CAND*. $\qquad \square$

While Dijkstra's algorithm requires fewer iterations than algorithm (LC-Q) in general, there is a penalty to be paid. This is the necessity of extracting the minimum element of the set $\{dist(j) \mid j \in CAND\}$. For large networks, *CAND* can become large and the effect of maintaining a priority queue can outweigh the benefits of label-setting. Much research has been invested in devising suitable data structures for label-correcting and label-setting algorithms (Gallo and Pallottino, 1986)

An approach which has been particularly successful is the label-correcting / label-setting hybrid of Glover et al (1985 a, b). Strictly, the approach is that of label-correcting, but a node x is heuristically added to the front or rear of a deque depending on the value of $dist(x)$ in such a way that nodes are taken from the front in approximate label-setting order. In this way the computational benefits of label-setting are largely realised without the necessity to maintain a priority queue such as a *heap* for example (cf. Boffey and Yates, 1989).

Making use of earlier calculations

It has long been realised that when computing the shortest paths from a source s to every other node, much work has already been done towards finding the shortest paths from other source nodes. For example, suppose that the shortest distance tree corresponding to source node s is as in figure 2.18. This tree has been split into two subtrees: the subtree $T(r)$ rooted at node r and the subtree $T(s)$ rooted at s which contains the remaining nodes. Then, the shortest path from r to any other node x in $T(r)$ is obtained immediately - it is just that part of the path from s to x that lies in $T(r)$. The other component subtree $T(s)$ also contains valu-

able information. Suppose the correct shortest distance tree corresponding to source s is as in figure 2.18b then this may be obtained by
attaching the subtree $T(z)$ to $T(r)$ by arc uz and replacing arc sr by arc
rs.   In other cases the changes will of course be different but it remains
true that the shortest distance tree at a node r can be built up from the
shortest distance tree at node s by starting with the subtree $T(r)$ and
successively attaching subtrees. Advantage of these facts has been used in
the *integrated single-source* methods of Florian et al. (1981) and Gallo
and Pallottino (1982); however the methods developed are not too
straightforward to code.   A trivial modification to algorithm (LC-Q)
which captures a considerable proportion of the benefits is to change the
setup (prior to **while** loop in algorithm L-S) to

Obtain $d(r, s)$.
Set $dist(r) = 0$; $dist(j) = d(r, s) + d(s, j)$ all $j \neq r$.
Set $CAND = \{r\}$. Set $p(r) = r$.

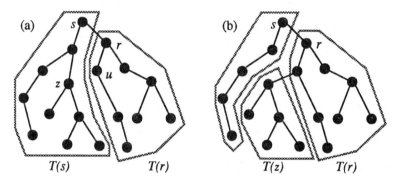

Figure 2.18 Illustration of how $T(s)$ can be grown by attaching subtrees.

Starting with this better estimate, $dist(j)$, of $d(j)$ corresponds to insisting that the incumbent path from r to j must go via s. This apparently
raises a difficulty in that although $d(s, j)$ has already been calculated for
every node j, $d(r, s)$ has not. However, if r and s are close together then
a shortest path from r to s may be found by a relatively inexpensive
local search and this overhead is likely to be offset by gains elsewhere.
Incorporating the method of Glover et al. (1985a, b) should make this
competitive with the earlier mentioned integrated single-source methods.

Another way of using previously gathered information is exploited
in the 'new ARPA routing algorithm' (cf. McQuillan et al. 1980). This
is a distributed scheme in which each node maintains its own SD-tree.

However, instead of performing complete shortest route calculations at each update an incremental update is performed whenever a message is received that a particular link length has changed by a 'significant amount'. Such *asynchronous* updating has the benefit that it tends to improve stability (cf. section 3.4). The method will not be described in full, but the following observations should give the flavour of it:

(1) If a link not in the previous SD-tree increases in length then **no** change to the SD-tree is required;

(2) If a link *uv* in the SD-tree at node *r* increases in length then only the nodes in the subtree at *v* need be considered for reassignment (cf. figure 2.19);

(3) If a link decreases in length then the procedure is more complex (McQuillan et al 1980), though only a subset of the nodes of the SD-tree need be considered for reassignment.

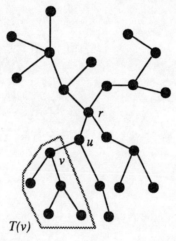

Figure 2.19 If the length of *uv* increases then the only nodes affected are those in *T(v)*.

2.5 VIRTUAL CIRCUIT DETERMINATION

It has been seen that, in order to find the shortest distance from *r* to *t*, it is necessary to find the shortest distances from *r* to (at least) all those nodes *j* which are nearer to *r* than *t* is. However, in practice, there is often extra information available which may be useful. For example, consider the question of finding the (shortest) distance by road from Chicago to Seattle. Any motorist with even a slight knowledge of the USA would not consider making the journey via Baltimore even though the distance from Chicago to Baltimore is less than the distance from Chicago to Seattle. This is reasonable because of the extra knowledge that all road distances are positive and that to go from Chicago to Baltimore would be 'to go in the wrong direction' (more precisely the airline distance from Baltimore to Seattle is greater than the airline distance from Chicago to Seattle). How can extra knowledge be used in general? An (at least partial) answer is based on the notion of a 'consistent' function.

Definition 2.1 A real-valued function h on the node set X of a network (X, A) is *consistent* if $h(i) \le a_{ij} + h(j)$ for all arcs ij.

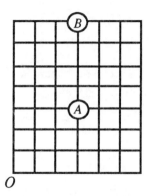

Figure 2.20 A lattice network in which there is a node at every intersection, and the length of each edge is 1. It is required to find the shortest distance from the specified node A to the specified node B.

Example 2.11 The lattice above represents a network in which there is a node at the intersection of each horizontal and each vertical line, and the length of each edge is 1. Relative to the point O each node i may be represented by a pair of coordinates (i_x, i_y); for example, A is the point $(3, 3)$ and B is the point $(3, 7)$. The function h defined by

$$h(i) = \sqrt{\{(B_x - i_x)^2 + (B_y - i_y)^2\}}$$

gives the 'airline' distance from i to B. Show that h is a consistent function.

Solution Denoting by a_{ij} the length of edge ij, and making use of the property that the sum of the lengths of two sides of a triangle is greater than or equal to the length of the third side, gives

$h(i)$ = airline distance from i to B

$\leq$ (airline distance from i to j) + (airline distance from j to B)

$= 1 + h(j) = a_{ij} + h(j)$

as required for consistency.   ☐

We are now in a position to state a refined label-setting algorithm for finding the shortest distance (and path) from origin r to destination t. This algorithm is due to Nemhauser (1972) and is a special case of the A* algorithm of Hart et al. (1968).

Algorithm (N)
{Nemhauser's algorithm to find a shortest path from r to t given a consistent function h.
Input: a network (X, A) and a set of arc lengths $\{a_{ij}\}$. }

   Set $PERM = \emptyset$, $CAND = \{r\}$, $dist(r) = 0$, $p(r) = r$.

   for all $x \neq r$ **do** set $dist(x) = \infty$.

   while $CAND \neq \emptyset$ **do**

   begin

     Select a node u with minimal value of $f(x) = dist(u) + h(u)$.

     $PERM \leftarrow PERM \cup \{u\}$, $CAND \leftarrow CAND - \{u\}$.

     for all arcs uv from u **do**

     begin

       if $dist(u) + a_{uv} < dist(v)$

       then $dist(v) \leftarrow dist(u) + a_{uv}$, $p(v) \leftarrow u$, $CAND \leftarrow CAND \cup \{v\}$.

     end

   end
{Output: $dist(i) = d(i)$ for all i in $PERM$, and the shortest path from r to i is given via p.}

It should be noted that algorithm (N) differs from Dijkstra's method (algorithm (D)) only in the use of $h(u)$ in the selection of the next node u to be added to $PERM$; equivalently, algorithm (D) is a special case of algorithm (N) with $h(x) = 0$ all x. That the algorithm is valid follows from the proof of theorems 2.9 and 2.10 with $f(u) = dist(u) + h(u)$ replacing $dist(u)$.

Example 2.12 It is required to find a shortest path from A to B in the grid network of figure 2.20 above. If the function h^c is defined for all j by

$h(j) = h^c(j) = c \times (\text{airline distance from } j \text{ to } B),$

use algorithm (N) to find the desired path for the following values of c: 0, 0.3, 0.6, 1.0. In each case give the total number of nodes scanned.

Solution First note that h^c is consistant for c in the range $0 \le c \le 1$ as may be seen by a simple modification to the proof of example 2.11.

Figure 2.21a shows the values of the airline distance to B. We shall consider now the case of $c = 0.6$ in some detail. First, node A is scanned and the four adjacent nodes labelled. The distance to each is 1 and, upon adding $0.6 \times airline\ distance\ to\ B$, the values of $f(x)$, rounded to 1 decimal place, for these four nodes are given by (cf. figure 2.21b)

$1 + 0.6 \times 3.0 = 2.8$
$1 + 0.6 \times 4.1 = 3.5$ (twice)
$1 + 0.6 \times 5.0 = 4.0.$

The node with minimal value of $f(x)$ ($= 2.8$) is scanned next and the three adjacent unlabelled nodes are labelled to get the tree of figure 2.21c. Next the node with label 3.2 is scanned to get the tree of figure 2.21d. At this point two nodes tie with labels of 3.5; after scanning both of these, in either order, the situation of figure 2.21e is attained. Notice that these last two scans represent wasted effort since neither node is on the required shortest path to B. The node with label 3.6 is scanned and B becomes temporarily labelled (figure 2.21f). After scanning two nodes with label 3.9, B is selected for scanning and the algorithm terminates. In all, 8 nodes have been scanned (not including B for though it is selected for scanning the scan is not carried out). The final shortest path tree is shown in figure 2.22c.

The final SD-trees corresponding to $c = 0$ (in which case the method degenerates to Dijkstra's), $c = 0.3$ and 1.0 are shown in figures 2.22a, b, d. The computational effort as measured by the number of nodes scanned, is summarised in table 2.3 for the four values of c. As the distance between A and B increases so the saving is proportionately greater.

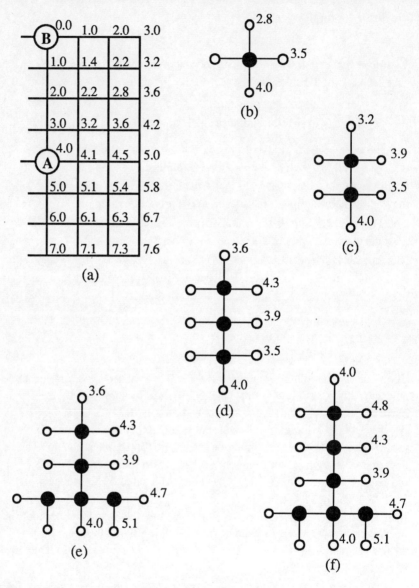

Figure 2.21 The airline distance from each node to B is given in (a) for nodes of the right hand half of the lattice network of figure 2.20; the corresponding figures for the left hand side may be obtained by symmetry. For (b) - (f) see text.

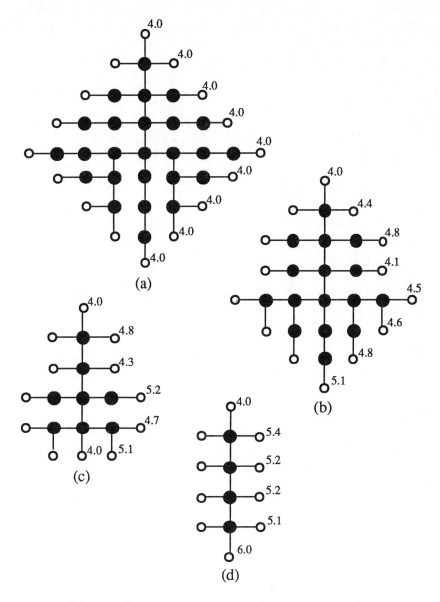

Figure 2.22 The final trees generated by Nemhauser's algorithm when finding the shortest path from node *A* to node *B* in example 2.12. The diagrams (a), (b), (c) and (d) correspond to *c* = 0.0, 0.3, 0.6 and 1.0 respectively. The labels for the left hand sides of the trees may be obtained by symmetry. Note that the tree of (a) is not unique.

Table 2.3 Number of nodes scanned in terms of c.

$c = 0.0$	$c = 0.3$	$c = 0.6$	$c = 1.0$
25	16	8	4

Corresponding figures for the case when B is 5 grid points above A (in a grid network with one extra row of nodes all round for a fair comparison) are

41 nodes scanned if $c = 0$
5 nodes scanned if $c \geq 0.9$.   □

A convenient way of forming consistent functions is provided by theorem 2.11.

Theorem 2.11 A network (X, A) is given with origin node r, destination node t and arc lengths $\{a_{ij}\}_{ij \in A}$. Let $\{b_{ij}\}_{ij \in A}$ be any set of numbers satisfying

$$0 \leq b_{ij} \leq a_{ij} \quad \text{all } ij \in A.$$

Then $h(x) = d^b(x, t)$ all $x \in X$, is a consistent function, where $d^b(x, t)$ denotes the shortest distance from node x to node t using the numbers b_{ij} as arc lengths.

Proof For any arc ij

$$
\begin{aligned}
h(i) = d^b(i, t) \ &\leq d^b(i, j) + d^b(j, t) \quad \text{(definition of shortest path)} \\
&\leq b_{ij} + d^b(j, t) \\
&\leq a_{ij} + d^b(j, t) \\
&= a_{ij} + h(j)
\end{aligned}
$$

and the desired result is established.   □

Example 2.13
(1) Hop function. When the number of 'hops' (that is, number of links traversed) is used as a measure of distance then, for all links ij

$$a_{ij} = \begin{cases} 1 & \text{if } ij \text{ is working} \\ \infty & \text{if } ij \text{ is failed.} \end{cases}$$

For every link ij, b_{ij} is set to 1 giving $h(x) = d^b(x, t)$ to be the number of hops from x to t irrespective of whether or not the corresponding links are working. Thus defined, b_{ij} generally provides good lower bounds as long as there are very few failed links.

(2) Zero flow function. When estimated delay (see section 3.1 for further details) is used as a distance measure then

$$a_{ij} = \begin{cases} \text{average delay corresponding to link } ij \\ \text{including any processing delay at } i. \end{cases}$$

b_{ij} may be set to the average delay in the low intensity limit. Now, under appropriate assumptions (cf. section 3.1), the average delay of packets on a particular link is $1/(c-f)$ where c is the capacity of a link and f is the total flow in that link. When the flow tends to zero the transmission time tends to $1/c$; for any other flow, $f > 0$, the transmission time is greater. Thus, the limiting value $1/c$ provides a lower bound to the expected delay. With b_{ij} as defined, $h(x) = d^b(x, t)$ is the expected delay time for a packet to travel from x to t with congestion effects ignored completely. This will usually provide a fairly weak lower bound to $d(x, t)$, but may be effectively improved as described below (after example 2.14).

Centralised virtual circuit routing

Suppose now that virtual circuit routing is being employed and that routing calculations are performed centrally at a network routing centre (NRC). The calculations could be effected as follows. When the network is set up or the topology changes, perhaps through the addition of extra links or nodes, the values of $d^b(x, y)$ are calculated for each pair (x, y) and stored at NRC. At some time during the operation of the network a request, for a virtual circuit from node r to node t, is sent from node r to NRC. NRC calculates a shortest route from r to t using algorithm (N) with $h(x) = d^b(x, t)$. The NRC then sends information to the nodes on this route (virtual circuit) sufficient for packets of data to be routed correctly. It may also be noted that the set-up phase of algorithm (N) requires $dist(x)$ to be set up for every node whether or not that node ever enters set *CAND*. This is clearly wasteful and further enhancement is obtained by using Perko's device for restricting the number of nodes *explicitly* labelled (cf. Perko 1983, 1986).

Example 2.14 For the network in figure 2.23a find a shortest route from node 19 to node 8 when:

    (1) number of hops is used as distance measure;

    (2) link 10-15 is currently failed but all other links are working.

Solution Figure 2.23b shows the tree generated by algorithm (N), and figure 2.23c shows the corresponding tree generated by Dijkstra's algorithm. □

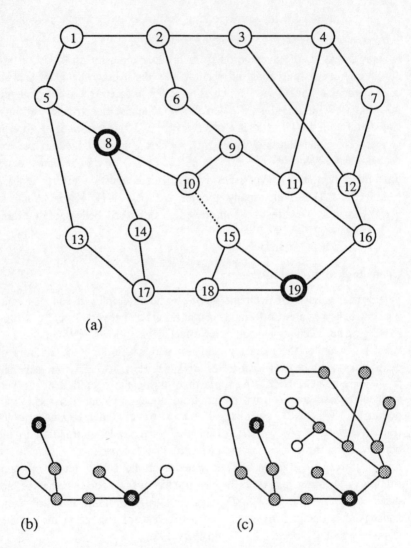

(a)

(b)   (c)

Figure 2.23 The link 10-15 is removed from the network of (a) and algorithm (N) applied to find the shortest route from node 19 to node 8 (cf. example 2.14). The resulting shortest distance tree is shown in (b) in which permanently labelled nodes are shaded. The corresponding tree obtained using Dijkstra's method is shown in (c) for comparison.

The zero flow function could have been used to define h but would generally lead to $h(x)$ being a weak lower bound to $d(x, t)$. However, two points may be noted:

(1) the link delay a_{ij} at the time of virtual circuit determination would generally provide an excellent lower bound, but the calculations to obtain $h(x)$ would not be justified;

(2) when a virtual circuit has to be computed and set up the values of the link delays will have changed. That is, the virtual circuit corresponds to the shortest path from r to t relative to data that was correct at some previous time but will now be only approximately so! Consequently the path found is only an approximate shortest path. It seems sensible to relax the strict condition that $b_{ij} \leq a_{ij}$. Based on these observations, a possible scheme for setting up a virtual circuit quickly would be for NRC periodically to calculate the shortest distances $d(x, t)$ for every pair (x, t) using the latest available a_{ij}. Then when a call for a virtual circuit to be set up is received by NRC, Nemhauser's algorithm is used employing the appropriate lower bounds $h(x) = d(x, t)$. (If somewhat more caution is felt to be necessary then

$$h(x) = \theta \times (\text{low intensity value of } d(x, t)) + (1 - \theta) \times (\text{latest value of } d(x, t))$$

could be used for some θ in the range $0 < \theta < 1$.)

2.6 FINDING ALTERNATIVE PATHS

Algorithms such as those presented so far provide a single (shortest) path along which flow is to be routed. It is, though, often desirable to have more than one path available. This may be the case when:

(1) the possibility of link failure is to be accounted for;

(2) a subnet is heavily used so that it is best not to send flow from origin r to destination t via any *single* path from r to t. (This is trivially seen to be so in the extreme case in which the demand D_{rt} exceeds the capacity of each link out of r; to stand any chance of accommodating it, more than one path from r to t must be used.)

When k (greater than one) paths from r to t are required it may seem sensible to use the 'best' k paths available, thus giving rise to what will be

termed the *unrestricted k-shortest path problem*. However, because of
the nature of computer network routing, it is relevant to consider the *restricted k-shortest path problem* which requires the following k paths to
be found:

$\pi_1 = ru_1...t$, a shortest path from r to t;

$\pi_2 = ru_2...t$, a shortest path from r to t such that u_2 does not coin -
cide with u_1;

$\pi_3 = ru_3...t$, a shortest path from r to t such that u_3 does not coincide with either u_1 or u_2; etc.

It turns out that the restricted k-shortest path problem is considerably
simpler than the unrestricted one and from now on we shall consider
only the former. Before developing a solution method it is convenient to
study a refinement of the label-setting algorithm (algorithm L-S).

If it is desired that a full shortest path calculation should not be
performed every time a virtual circuit is to be set up then the following
scheme could be used. Node routing tables are set up as for datagram
routing but with the following modification. At each node, x, the entry
corresponding to a particular destination, t, contains

(1) the preferred next link en route to t,
(2) one (or more) alternative next links.

When setting up a virtual circuit a message is sent from the origin node
using preferred links as far as possible. If the message reaches t then the
desired route has been found. If not, the designated alternative link is
taken at the point at which the message is blocked, and then the message
continues using preferred links as far as possible. This is extended with
alternative links only being used if a preferred link is not available. In
this way, either a route to t is found or the absence of a suitable route
(ie. consisting of preferred and alternative links only) is established.

To make use of this outlined scheme it is necessary to have available
a method for solving a *restricted k*-shortest path problem (at least for
$k = 2$) in which each of the k selected routes must have *different* initial
links.

Recently, Topkis (1988) developed an algorithm for solving the restricted k-shortest path problem. His algorithm is an effective one
whose complexity is equivalent to that of applying Dijkstra's algorithm
to the same network k times; indeed it degenerates to Dijkstra's algorithm when $k = 1$.

Perhaps the most obvious weakness of the Topkis algorithm is the large amount of initialisation that needs to be performed with approximately $deg(x)+1$ labels having to be set at every node x where $deg(x)$ is the number of nodes that are neighbours of x. Nor is it clear that Perko's device can be employed satisfactorily. Consequently, it seems that it might be worthwhile seeking an alternative algorithm. In the following, one such attempt will be described for the case of $k = 2$.

The approach consists of two phases:

Phase (1): first, for each node x, determine shortest paths *from* every other node.

Phase (2): for each node x, find the restricted second shortest path *to* every other node.

Phase (1) may be effected by using a Dijkstra-like algorithm or, preferably, a label-correcting algorithm based on deques (Gallo and Pallottino, 1986) applied for each node x. Alternatively, an integrated scheme may be used (cf. section 2.4).

Whatever the overall scheme used, the effort of finding all first shortest paths must be embedded somewhere in the calculations. There does, however, seem to be scope for utilising the information thus gained to reduce the effort of finding second shortest paths. A description of how this might be attempted will now be given.

First, the set of nodes $X - \{r\}$ is partitioned into sets $F(j)$, with one for each neighbour j of r, such that x belongs to $F(j)$ only if rj is the first link on a shortest route from r to x. Figure 2.24 shows the situation with $r = 17$ and *one* possible partitioning

$F(13) = \{1, 2, 5, 13\}$
$F(14) = \{6, 8, 9, 10, 14\}$
$F(18) = \{3, 4, 7, 11, 12, 15, 16, 18, 19\}$.

For nodes in the set $F(j)$ the second shortest path may be found by applying a shortest path algorithm from origin r with link rj removed (or its length set to ∞). It would be wasteful to use Dijkstra's algorithm for this as much computation may be involved with there being one application for each link from r.

Note that if link rj does not provide the shortest path from r to j (that is, $j \notin F(j)$) then the shortest path calculations from r with rj removed are redundant and may be omitted. It is, therefore, assumed from now on that rj is the first shortest path from r to j. Then j becomes, in a sense, the most 'inconvenienced' node when link rj is removed. This is formalised in theorem 2.12.

Theorem 2.12 $d_2(r,j) - d_1(r,j) \geq d_2(r,x) - d_1(r,x)$, for all $x \in F(j)$, where $d_m(a,b)$ denotes the length of the m-th best restricted path from node a to node b.

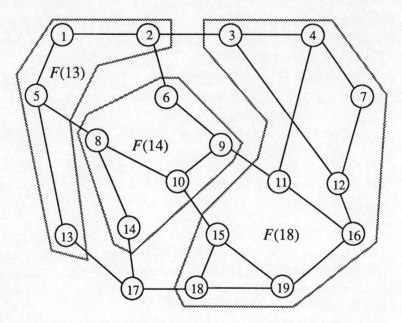

Figure 2.24 This network is the same as that of figure 2.23a but with link 10-15 reinstated.

Proof By the definition of $F(j)$,

$$d_1(r,x) = d_1(r,j) + d_1(j,x). \tag{2.11}$$

The second restricted shortest path from r to j followed by the shortest path from j to x provides a path from r to x which is not the designated first shortest path. Hence

$$d_2(r,x) \leq d_2(r,j) + d_1(j,x) \tag{2.12}$$

The desired result follows immediately from (2.11) and (2.12). □

Consider now the application of Nemhauser's algorithm from origin r with a consistent function h defined by $h(x) = d^a(x, j)$ for all x (that is, $b_{ij} = a_{ij}$ all $ij \in A$ in the notation of theorem 2.11). The algorithm is terminated as soon as a node u satisfying

$$h(u) < d_1(u, r) + d_1(r, j) \tag{2.13}$$

is selected for scanning.

Theorem 2.13 With u as specified by (2.13), $d_2(r, j) = dist(u) + h(u)$.

Proof When Nemhauser's algorithm is terminated, $dist(u)$ is the length of a shortest path π_1 from r to u not using link rj, and $h(u)$ is the length of a shortest path π_2 from u to j. The path $\pi = \pi_1\pi_2$ is a shortest path from r to j **via** u. Moreover, π does not contain link rj since otherwise π_2 would end with rj and have length $h(u) = d_1(u, r) + a_{rj} = d_1(u, r) + d_1(r, j)$ contradicting (2.13). Consequently, $d_2(r, j) \le dist(u) + h(u)$.

To establish the inequality, assume π^* is a shortest path from r to j which does not contain link rj. Then π^* must contain a temporarily labelled node, v say, and

$$d_2(r, j) = \text{length of } \pi^* \le dist(v) + h(v).$$

Now since u is the node selected for scanning, not v, it follows that

$$d_2(r, j) = d(v) + h(v) \ge dist(u) + h(u)$$

and the desired result follows immediately. $\qquad\square$

When Nemhauser's algorithm is terminated in this way, it is unlikely that j will have been labelled and the number of nodes scanned will often be *very* small. Under reasonable conditions it may be shown that the computational effort required in phase (2) is essentially quadratic in the number of nodes in the network; that is, the calculation is *asymptotically* dominated by phase (1).

Example 2.15 For the network of figure 2.24, find the restricted second shortest path from node 17 to node 14.

Solution After nodes 13 and 18 have been added to the emerging SD-tree node 5 is selected for scanning. Now $d_1(5,17) = dist(5) = 2$ and $h(5) = 2$. Consequently

$$h(5) < d_1(5, 17) + d_1(17, 14).$$

It can be concluded from theorem 2.13 that the restricted second shortest path from node 17 to node 14 is via the first shortest path 17-13-5 from 17 to 5 followed by the first shortest path 5-8-14 from 5 to 14. $\qquad\square$

What of the other nodes in $F(14)$?   It may be seen from the next theorem that there is no need to repeat the application of Nemhauser's algorithm.

Theorem 2.14 Let *CAND* be the set of temporarily labelled nodes when application of Nemhauser's algorithm is terminated by condition (2.13). Then, for all $x \in F(j)$

$$d_2(r, x) = \min_{v \in CAND}(dist(v) + d_1(v, x)). \tag{2.14}$$

Proof Let w be any value of v for which the minimum of (2.14) occurs with the restriction that if there is a tie and u minimises (2.14) then $w = u$. Now suppose there is a shortest path π from w to x via r. Firstly, w cannot be equal to u for then

$$
\begin{aligned}
d_1(u, x) &= d_1(u, r) + d_1(r, x) & & r \text{ is on } \pi \text{ and } w = u \\
&= d_1(u, r) + d_1(r, j) + d_1(j, x) & & x \in F(j) \\
&> d_1(u, j) + d_1(j, x) & & \text{by (2.13)} \\
&\geq d_1(u, x) & & \text{by the triangle property}
\end{aligned}
$$

which is impossible. Hence, $w \neq u$ and

$$
\begin{aligned}
dist(u) + d_1(u, x) &> dist(w) + d_1(w, x) \\
&= dist(w) + d_1(w, r) + d_1(r, x) \\
&= dist(w) + d_1(w, r) + d_1(r, j) + d_1(j, x) \\
&\geq dist(w) + d_1(w, j) + d_1(j, x) \\
&\geq dist(u) + d_1(u, j) + d_1(j, x) \quad \text{(by definition of } u) \\
&\geq dist(u) + d_1(u, x).
\end{aligned}
$$

But this is a contradiction and therefore no shortest path from w goes via r and the desired result is established. $\square$

Example 2.16 Find the restricted second shortest paths from node 17 to all nodes in $F(14)$ for the network of figure 2.24.
Solution When Nemhauser's algorithm terminates $CAND = \{5, 15, 19\}$ (cf. the solution of example 2.15)

$$d_2(17, 6) = \min (2+3, 2+3, 2+4) = 5, \qquad \text{path is } 17\text{-}13\text{-}5\text{-}1\text{-}2\text{-}6$$
$$\text{or } 17\text{-}18\text{-}15\text{-}10\text{-}9\text{-}6$$
$$d_2(17, 8) = \min (2+1, 2+2, 2+3) = 3, \qquad \text{path is } 17\text{-}13\text{-}5\text{-}8$$

$d_2(17, 9) = \min (2+3, 2+2, 2+3) = 4$, path is 17-18-15-10-9

$d_2(17, 10) = \min (2+2, 2+1, 2+2) = 3$, path is 17-18-15-10. □

2.7 EXERCISES

2.1 With reference to the network of figure 2.25, 20 kbps of flow enter at node *a* and leave at node *g*. Verify that the flow is conserved. Determine an equivalent set of path and circuit flows.

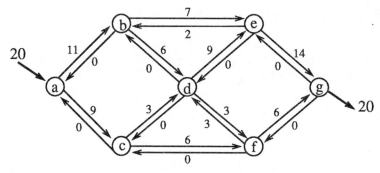

Figure 2.25 The number beside each arc *ij* is the flow in that arc in kbps.

2.2 For the network of 2.25 and the arc flows given, calculate the *average* number of hops traversed when a packet is sent from *a* to *g*. By what percentage can this be reduced by redirecting flow?

2.3 The traffic demand matrix corresponding to the network of figure 2.26a is given below. If routing is by minimum number of hops calculate the flow in each of the links of the network.

$$
\begin{bmatrix}
- & 3 & 2 & 0 & 2 & 3 & 4 & 1 \\
  & - & 2 & 5 & 3 & 5 & 0 & 1 \\
  &   & - & 0 & 2 & 2 & 1 & 0 \\
  &   &   & - & 1 & 2 & 4 & 2 \\
  &   &   &   & - & 3 & 0 & 2 \\
  &   &   &   &   & - & 1 & 2 \\
  & \text{symmetric} &   &   &   &   & - & 3 \\
  &   &   &   &   &   &   & - \\
\end{bmatrix}
$$

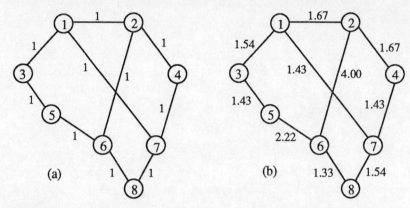

Figure 2.26 (a) link length = 1 for all *ij*; (b) link length = $20/(20 - x_{ij})$.

2.4 Use Dijkstra's algorithm to find the shortest path from node *r* to node *t* in the network of figure 2.27 below.

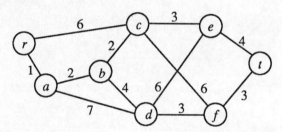

Figure 2.27

2.5 Repeat exercise 2.4 using algorithm (LC-Q).

2.6 If h_1 and h_2 are consistent functions on a network $N = (X, A)$ (with respect to finding shortest paths to 'goal node' *t*), determine which of the following are also consistent.

(1) ch_1, $0 \leq c \leq 1$

(2) $h_1 + h_2$

(3) $h_1 * h_2$

(4) $(1-\alpha)h_1 + \alpha h_2$

(5) $h_1 - k$ where *k* is a constant

(6) $h_1 - h_2$.

2.7   Using the link flows resulting from question 2.3 and link lengths given by $a_{ij} = 20/(20 - x_{ij})$ where x_{ij} is the flow in ij from i to j, calculate, by inspection if you wish, the shortest distances $h(k) = d(k, 7)$ from every node k to node 7. Suppose link 6-8 now fails; use the function h and Nemhauser's algorithm to find a new shortest route from node 6 to node 8.

2.8 A network satisfies the following conditions:

    (1) no node has more than D connecting links;

    (2) for each working link i-j the link length a_{ij} at all times lies in some interval $min_{ij} \le a_{ij} \le max_{ij}$ for which $max_{ij} \le K \times min_{ij}$;

    (3) for each link i-j there is a path from node i to node j which has no more than e links and does *not* contain i-j.

If D, K and e are constants independent of the network, prove that phase (2) of the algorithm of section 2.6 for finding alternative routes from node i to all other nodes can be carried in $O(n)$ calculations.

Chapter 3

Congested Flow

It was seen in the previous chapter how packets of information may be routed, simply and optimally, when conditions are such that link capacities are large enough for congestion effects to be negligible. As the intensities of traffic in links increase, however, congestion effects become more and more important as a result of interference between packets on different routes, retransmissions, etc. The way in which link delay is affected by congestion is explored in section 3.1 where relevant queuing theory concepts are developed.

If, in the absence of link failure, packets belonging to any particular OD pair are constrained to follow a single path, then the choice of an optimal set of routes is a far from trivial combinatorial problem. This is termed 'discrete route assignment' and is treated in section 3.6 where the important concept of Lagrangean relaxation is introduced. As congestion increases, so more tends to be gained by spreading packets belonging to a given OD pair over more than one route. Such *bifurcated* flows are introduced in section 3.2 together with some theoretical results that are useful in later sections. The following section is concerned with ways of finding bifurcated flows optimal to within a specified tolerance including the use of the PARTAN technique for improving the convergence of the Frank-Wolfe iterative method.

Although optimal bifurcated flows provide a useful and convenient tool for designing networks, they have not found favour as a means of routing in practice. One reason for this is that packets can arrive out of order at their destination (or at least at the exit node from the subnet) thus needing to be resequenced; another weakness is that conditions typically vary with time so that an optimal solution at one particular time is likely to become suboptimal soon after. *Adaptive* routing, described in sections 3.4 and 3.5, aims to overcome this latter difficulty.

3.1 QUEUING AND DELAY ANALYSIS

Consider the (exceptional) case in which a switching node, i, has only a single active outgoing link, ij say, and a single active incoming link. Between a packet being received at i and being received at j there are various delays (cf. figure 3.1).

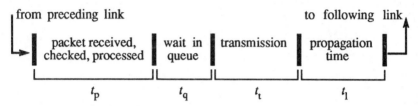

Figure 3.1 Delay at node i and on link ij.

These delays are:

(1) a *processing* delay, t_p, resulting from various operations performed on the packet (relating to error detection, routing, ...) before being placed in the appropriate output queue.

(2) a *queuing* delay, t_q, while packets ahead of the given one are transmitted. If link ij is free when a given packet enters the queue, then $t_q = 0$. Otherwise t_q depends on the queuing discipline in operation. If this is FCFS (First-Come-First-Served), also called FIFO, then the packet must wait its turn:

   (i) while transmission is completed for the packet currently being sent, and

   (ii) while any other packets already in the queue ahead of the given one are transmitted.

(3) a *transmission* delay, t_t, which is the time between the first bit of the packet leaving i and the last bit leaving. This depends only on the size (number of bits) of the packet and the *capacity* of the link ij in bps.

(4) a *propagation* delay, t_l, which is the time between the (last) bit leaving i and arriving at j. This depends on the physical length of the link. [Note that it is appropriate to include propagation for a single bit only, as bits other than the last are propagated over the link during the transmission time.]

The total delay associated with link ij is thus

$$W = (t_p + t_l) + (t_q + t_t).$$

Now the propagation delay t_l is usually negligible (unless a satellite link is being used) and t_p unimportant if the node has adequate processing power (that is, packets can be processed as fast as they are received and no queuing is involved at this stage). In any case t_l, and to a lesser extent t_p, is effectively independent of packet length and may be added if desired at the end of the calculation.

Suppose now that link ij has capacity c bps (that is, ij can handle up to c bps but no more) and that, on average, each packet has $1/\mu_f$ bits. Then, on average, $\mu = c\mu_f$ pps (packets per second) can be transmitted and $t_t = 1/\mu$.

Even at this level of generality some conclusions can be made. First, if λ is the average number of packets received per second then

(1) if $\lambda > \mu$, bits are coming into node i faster than they can be sent out along link ij and the queue, in principle, builds up indefinitely. [In practice, of course, this could not happen because of flow and congestion control, and finite buffer size.]

(2) if $\lambda < \mu$, link ij has sufficient capacity to cope with the *average* incoming traffic and the system is stable; queues may build up from time to time though, because of temporarily high traffic rates.

Thus, a general requirement for stability is that

$$\rho = \lambda/\mu < 1,$$

where ρ is known as the *utilisation factor*.

Next define

L_q = average number of packets in the queue.

L_s = average number of packets in the system (waiting or being transmitted).

W_q = average time spent in the queue. This corresponds to t_q.

W_s = average time a packet spends in the system (waiting and being transmitted). This corresponds to $t_q + t_t$.

The following result, known as Little's Theorem relates these quantities.

Theorem 3.1 (Little) $L_s = \lambda W_s$ and $L_q = \lambda W_q$.

This result will not be proved here but will be illustrated by an example.

Example 3.1 Six packets, containing 2000, 800, 2000, 2000, 800 and 2000 bits respectively, arrive for transmission over a 50 kbps link during a 200 ms period; arrivals are at times 8, 24, 56, 80, 112 and 128 ms from the start of the period respectively, and the system is initially empty. Figure 3.2 illustrates the situation distinguishing, for each packet, between transmission and waiting time in the queue whilst other packets are being transmitted. Transmission times are multiples of 400/50000 s = 0.008 s, and arrivals occur at multiples of 0.008 s after the start of the period. Consequently, it is convenient to split the period into 25 *time slots* each of length 0.008 s (cf. figure 3.2).

As there are 15 shaded areas in figure 3.2, the total waiting time in the queue for all six packets is $\Sigma t_q = 120$ ms giving $W_q = 0.12/6 = 0.02$ s. This total may however be computed in a different way by adding up the numbers of packets waiting in each time slot; the result is that $6 W_q = 0.008 \times \Sigma l_q = 0.008 \times 15 = 0.12$ s. The average number of packets waiting in the queue, L_q, is $15/25 = 0.6$. The arrival rate is $\lambda = 6/0.02 = 30$ pps and so $\lambda W_q = 30 \times 0.02 = 0.6$ also. The equality is true since L_q and λW_q both correspond to the total of the shaded areas (packet wait times) in figure 3.2. From this observation it is clear that $L_q = \lambda W_q$ more generally; in fact it is true in a wide range of circumstances and will be accepted without question from now on. That $L_s = \lambda W_s$ is also true may be seen by similar arguments. □

To proceed further, more information is needed on the distributions of arrivals and packet lengths. A model which is much used is the one in which packets of random lengths arrive randomly and are transmitted on a FCFS basis. More precisely, the packet arrival and packet transmission times are Poisson processes (cf. appendix A for definition) and this model is an example of an (M/M/1) queue. It is a standard result (derived in appendix A) that this assumption leads to interarrival times and packet transmission times that correspond to (negative) exponential probability distribution functions. Let these be f and g say, then

$$f(t) = \left\{ \begin{array}{ll} 0 & t \leq 0 \\ \lambda \exp(-t\lambda) & t > 0 \end{array} \right. \qquad g(t) = \left\{ \begin{array}{ll} 0 & t \leq 0 \\ \mu \exp(-t\mu) & t > 0 \end{array} \right.$$

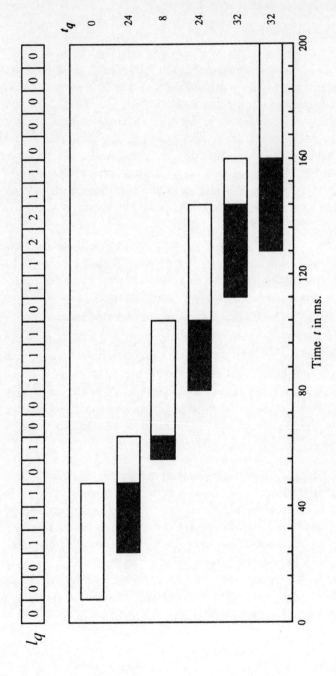

Figure 3.2 The interval of time each packet of example 3.1 spends queuing and being transmitted; queuing time is distinguished by shading. t_q, for each packet, is the total time (in ms) spent queuing; l_q, for each time slot, is the number of packets in the queue.

where λ is the average number of packets arriving per unit time and $1/\mu$ is the average time for a packet to be transmitted. Now the negative exponential distribution is *memoryless* (cf. appendix A): the time to the next arrival is independent of the time of any previous arrival, and the remaining time for completion of packet transmission is independent of the time when transmission started. Since arrival and transmission are *independent* processes it follows that the *state* of the queue at a particular instant is completely described by the number of packets in the system, counting 1 for the packet being transmitted (if there is one); the further development of the system depends only on this state and not on how it was arrived at. This process is conveniently illustrated by means of the *state transmission diagram* of figure 3.3.

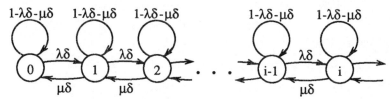

Figure 3.3 The states of an (M/M/1) queue are shown as circles containing the number of packets in the (queueing) *system*. The arcs show the possible transitions that may be made over a small instant of time, δ, together with the transition probabilities.

Let $\pi_i(t)$ be the probability of being in state i at time t, and let p_{rs} be the probability of a transition from state r to state s in the time interval $(t, t+\delta)$. Then, for all $i > 0$ and to first order in δ

probability of transmission completion $= p_{i,i-1} \pi_i(t) = \mu\delta\,\pi_i(t)$,

probability of arrival $= p_{i-1,i} \pi_{i-1}(t) = \lambda\,\delta\,\pi_{i-1}(t)$.

For the queue to be in a steady state $\pi_i(t) = \pi_i$ for all i, and $P_{i,i-1} = P_{i-1,i}$ (since otherwise queues would tend to build up or shorten). This gives

$$\pi_i = \rho\pi_{i-1} \quad \text{for } i = 1, 2, \ldots$$

that is, $\pi_n = \rho^n\pi_0$. Now, since the system must be in some state, $\sum\pi_i = 1$ leading to $\pi_0 = 1 - \rho$, and hence

$$\pi_n = \rho^n(1 - \rho).$$

From this, the average number in the system, L_s, may be derived:

$$L_s = \sum_n n\pi_n = (1 - \rho)\sum_n n\rho^n = \rho(1 - \rho)/(1 - \rho)^2 = \rho/(1 - \rho).$$

By using Little's theorem,

$$W_s = L_s/\lambda = 1/(\mu - \lambda).$$

Also, since the average transmission time is $1/\mu$,

$$W_q = W_s - 1/\mu = \rho/(\mu - \lambda),$$

and, again by Little's theorem,

$$L_q = \lambda W_q = \rho^2/(1 - \rho). \tag{3.1}$$

Example 3.2 Arrival of packets to a link of capacity c kbps is Poisson with, on average, λ packets arriving per second; the lengths of the packets are exponentially distributed with a mean of $1/\mu_f$ bits per packet. Calculate L_q and W_q if

(1) $c = 64$ kbps, $\lambda = 30$ pps, $1/\mu_f = 213$ bits;

(2) $c = 16$ kbps, $\lambda = 10$ pps, $1/\mu_f = 1440$ bits.

Also, for each case, calculate π_0 and the probability, p_{20}^*, that there are more than 20 packets in the system.

Solution   (1) $\rho = \lambda/c\mu_f = 30 \times 213/64000 = 0.1$. Substitution into the expression (3.1) gives $L_q = 0.011$ packets, and by Little's theorem $W_q = 0.011/30 = 0.0004$ s. $\pi_0 = 1 - \rho = 0.9$. The probability of there being in excess of 20 packets in the system is

$$p_{20}^* = \pi_{21} + \pi_{22} + \pi_{23} + ...$$
$$= \rho^{21}[\pi_0 + \pi_1 + \pi_2 + ...]$$
$$= \rho^{21} = 10^{-21}.$$

(2) $\rho = \lambda/c\mu_f = 10 \times 1440/16000 = 0.9$. $L_q = 8.1$ pkts and $W_q = 0.81$ s; $\pi_0 = 0.1$ and $p_{20}^* = 0.11$.

The number in the system (or queue) depends only on the utilisation factor ρ; figure 3.4 shows L_s plotted against ρ. For small ρ, $L_s \approx \rho$ and the average number of packets in the system increases approximately linearly as ρ increases. For larger ρ, however, L_s increases more rapidly and when ρ is nearly 1, $L_s \approx 1/(1 - \rho)$. In (1) of example 3.2, $\rho = 0.1$ is small and the queue will rarely contain more than a few packets. The small value of ρ suggests that buffer space for up to 10 packets to queue is more than adequate. On the other hand, for case (2), ρ at 0.9 is high and the system is becoming congested. More buffer space is required and with buffer space for up to 50 packets there is still a chance of about 1 in 200 of a packet being lost. □

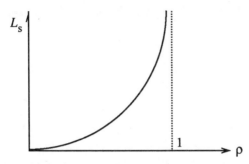

Figure 3.4 L_s as a function of ρ for an (M/M/1) queue.

Networks of queues

Consider now queues at two successive links *ij* and *jk*, with arrival of packets at *ij* according to a Poisson process with parameter λ pps and with packet lengths exponentially distributed with mean length $1/\mu_f$ bits. After the packets are received at *j* they are sent along link *jk*. Suppose, for simplicity, that the two links have the same capacity *c*. Then, neglecting retransmissions (resulting from errors and lost packets) it is clear that the arrival rates for the two queues are the same and, since packet lengths do not change, the service rates are the same.

The first queue is (M/M/1) and the distribution of packets leaving it is Poisson (this is a result of the 'memoryless' property of the exponential distribution). Packets, whose lengths have not changed, arrive at the second queue in the same order as to the first so that service for the second queue is exponentially distributed with the same mean $1/\mu_f$ bits. Is the second queue also (M/M/1)? The answer is no, because the arrivals and service times are not independent! To see this, consider a very long packet; this will take a (relatively) long time to be transmitted from *i* to *j* so there must be a large inter-arrival time between the previous packet and the current one as seen by the second queue. That is, long packets can only follow long inter-arrival times and so service times (packet lengths) and inter-arrival times are correlated.

On the other hand if packets were permitted to 'magically' change their lengths then arrivals and services would not be correlated and the second queue would be (M/M/1). Thus the two queues could be treated as two *independent* (M/M/1) queues with the probability of occupancy of the combined states

$$\pi_{i,j} = \text{Prob [queue 1 is in state } i \text{ and queue 2 is in state } j]$$

being given by

$$\pi_{i,j} = [\rho_1^i(1 - \rho_1)][\rho_2^j (1 - \rho_2)]$$

which for our situation ($\rho_1 = \rho_2 = \rho$) reduces to $\rho^{i+j}(1 - \rho)^2$.

In reality, some packets will need to be retransmitted thus reducing the correlation somewhat. More importantly, in a network of queues nodes may have more than one incoming link and/or more than one outgoing link, and packets may start and terminate at a node. All this has a 'randomising effect' and simulation and actual experiments have shown that treating the queues as isolated (M/M/1) queues is a fairly good approximation; this is the so-called *Independence Assumption* (Kleinrock, 1964).

When λ is in pps and $1/\mu_f$ is the number of bits per packet, then $x = \lambda/\mu_f$ is the arrival rate in bps. From now on we shall assume this conversion to bps (or kbps or Mbps as appropriate) and formulae will be in terms of x, c and $\rho = x/c \, (= \lambda/c\mu_f)$.

3.2 BIFURCATED FLOWS

In the previous section it was seen how randomness can result in extra delay. Also, under the Kleinrock Independence Assumption, the average delay $W_{ij}(x_{ij})$ and total delay $F_{ij}(x_{ij})$, resulting from queuing and transmission for link ij may be expressed as

$$W_{ij}(x_{ij}) = 1/(c_{ij} - x_{ij}) \tag{3.2}$$

$$F_{ij}(x_{ij}) = x_{ij}/(c_{ij} - x_{ij}) \tag{3.3}$$

where x_{ij} is the flow in bps along link ij and c_{ij} is the capacity of the link, also in bps. The form of this *delay function*, W_{ij}, was shown in figure 3.4. Whether or not the Independence Assumption is a true reflection of reality, the delay function may be expected to possess the following properties: $W_{ij}(x_{ij})$ is approximately $1/c_{ij}$ for very low flow intensities; $W_{ij}(x_{ij})$ becomes very large as the flow intensity approaches the capacity of the link; $W_{ij}(x_{ij})$ increases smoothly as the flow increases, and the rate of increase also increases. These conditions will now be assumed and may be expressed mathematically as:

(W_1) *Low intensity limit:* $W_{ij}(x_{ij}) \rightarrow 1/c_{ij}$ as $x_{ij} \rightarrow 0$;

(W_2) *High intensity limit:* $W_{ij}(x_{ij}) \rightarrow \infty$ as $x_{ij} \rightarrow c_{ij}$;

(W_3) *Continuity:* $W_{ij}(x_{ij})$ is continuous for $0 \leq x_{ij} < c_{ij}$;

(W_4) *Monotonicity:* $\partial W_{ij}(x_{ij})/\partial x_{ij} > 0$ for $0 < x_{ij} < c_{ij}$;

(W_5) *Convexity:* $\partial^2 W_{ij}(x_{ij})/\partial x_{ij}^2 > 0$ for $0 < x_{ij} < c_{ij}$.

The function of (3.2) satisfies these five properties. In any case, the methods that follow are applicable if conditions (W_1) - (W_5) are satisfied whatever the detailed form of W_{ij}.

Example 3.3 Four nodes A, B, C and D are connected via full-duplex links whose capacities, in kbps, are shown in figure 3.5; the traffic demand matrix is also given. What will be the total delay per unit time (on average) if routing is based on low intensity link delays? Suggest ways in which routing may be improved in the light of these results.

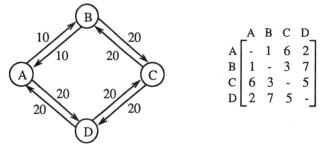

Figure 3.5 Network and traffic demand matrix for the problem of example 3.3.

Solution The delay depends on routing, whether or not congestion is taken account of. As suggested, the length d_{ij} of ij will be taken to be the limiting value of $W_{ij}(x_{ij})$ as $x_{ij} \to 0$, that is $1/c_{ij}$. Solving the appropriate shortest distance problem (cf. sections 2.2, 2.54) leads to the routing pattern shown in table 3.1.

Table 3.1 Routing for the network of figure 3.5 with link lengths based on the low intensity limit.

O-D pair	D_{ij}	Route	O-D pair	D_{ij}	Route
A - B	1	*A - B*	*B - A*	1	*B - A*
A - C	6	*A - D - C*	*C - A*	6	*C - D - A*
A - D	2	*A - D*	*D - A*	2	*D - A*
B - C	3	*B - C*	*C - B*	3	*C - B*
B - D	7	*B - C - D*	*D - B*	7	*D - C - B*
C - D	5	*C - D*	*D - C*	5	*D - C*

Table 3.2 The flow and average packet delay corresponding to the routing of table 3.1.

Arc	Traffic (kbps)	ρ_{ij}	$\rho_{ij}/(1 - \rho_{ij})$
AB, BA	1	0.1	0.111
BC, CB	10	0.5	1.000
CD, DC	18	0.9	9.000
DA, AD	8	0.4	0.667
Totals		1.9	10.778

The total delay per second is $2 \times 1.9 = 3.8$ s in the linear approximation and $2 \times 10.778 = 21.56$ s using (3.3). The high value for the actual delay arises because the link *CD* is heavily congested and so it is desirable to reduce its load. Traffic between *B* and *D* uses this link but could be sent via *A* instead of via *C*. Suppose just 1 kbps of flow from *B* to *D* is diverted along *B - A - D* (with a similar redirection of flow from *D* to *B* along *D - A - B*) the remainder following its previous course. Then flows in *AB, BC, CD* and *DA* become 2, 9, 17 and 9 kbps respectively giving much reduced total delay of 15.11 s. Results of diverting further traffic between *B* and *D* via *A* are as given below.

It is seen that, at first, great gains are made but the rate of gain decreases until a point is reached at which the increasing congestion on links *AB* and *AD* outweighs the effect of decreasing congestion on *BC* and *CD*. Thus, if it is assumed that there is no penalty incurred by splitting traffic for an OD pair between two (or more) routes, then the optimal amount of traffic to divert from *B-C-D* to *B-A-D* (and from *D-C-B* to *D-A-B*) is around 4 kbps (more precisely, 3.9 kbps). On the other hand, if all traffic for an OD pair must follow a single route then it is better to switch all 7 kbps of traffic from *B-C-D* to *B-A-D* (and from *D-C-B* to *D-A-B*). □

Traffic directed via A (in kbps)	Total network delay per second (in secs)
0	21.56
1	15.11
2	12.19
3	10.85
4	10.52
5	11.09
6	12.83
7	16.80

Splitting and bifurcated flows

It has been seen from example 3.3 that there may be advantages in adopting a *splitting flow* in which the traffic for a given OD pair is split between two or more routes. Such a flow may be described by a set of probabilities $\{p_{ij}^{rt}\}$ where p_{ij}^{rt} is the probability that a packet from origin r to destination t will, when at node $i \neq t$, be sent to j as the next node. This does not say that r-t flow must pass through a given node i, but that *if it does* then it gives the probabilities with the aid of which the next link is chosen. Of course, if no r-t flow can reach i it is irrelevant what value is assigned to p_{ij}^{rt}.

Since the delay is a function of the *total* link flow it is clear that packets at node $i \neq t$ may be treated in the same way whatever their origin. Correspondingly, we may set

$$p_{ij}^{rt} = p_{ij}^{t} \text{ for all } t, \text{ all } i \neq t, \text{ and all } j.$$

A splitting flow for which this relation is true will be called a *bifurcated flow*, and the set $\{p_{ij}^{t}\}$ will be termed the *bifurcation pattern* at node i. A network flow in which flow is not split for any OD pair may be regarded as a special case of a bifurcated flow with

$$p_{ij}^{t} = \begin{cases} 1 & \text{if } j = k \\ 0 & \text{otherwise} \end{cases}$$

where k is a particular neighbour node of node i.

Example 3.4 There are two parallel links from node a to node b, each capable of carrying up to 10 kbps (cf. figure 3.6). Packet arrival is a Poisson process with mean arrival rate of 8 kbps. Find an optimal bifurcated flow.

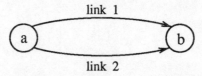

link 1

link 2

Figure 3.6 Node a is linked to node b by two parallel 10 kbps links.

Solution   Call the links 'link 1' and 'link 2' and let the corresponding utilisation factors be ρ_1 and ρ_2 respectively.   If all flow goes via link 1, then $\rho_1 = 0.8$, $\rho_2 = 0$ yielding a total delay of $F = 0.8/(1-0.8) + 0/(1-0)$ $= 4$ s.   Similarly, if all flow is via link 2.

It is intuitively obvious, and may easily be verified rigorously, that the optimal bifurcated flow is obtained by sending 4 kbps along each of the two links giving a total delay of $2 \times [0.4/(1-0.4)] = 1.333$ s.   However, with the random assignment of packets to the two links it may happen that link 1 is idle, link 2 is busy, and a packet at a is assigned to link 2. This is clearly wasteful. An alternative scheme is to keep a single queue at a and to assign packets from the front of the queue to either link 1 or link 2 depending on which becomes available first.   This is an example of an (M/M/2) queuing system for which the total average delay per unit time is given by $4\rho/(4 - \rho^2)$ (cf. exercise 3.1).   [ρ is here the combined arrival rate divided by the capacity of each of the two links and so is 0.8 for this example.]   That is, the total delay per second is on average 0.95 s, which is better than for the best bifurcated flow.   Somewhat similar, but not quite as good, is to maintain two separate queues but to assign an incoming packet to the shorter queue as measured by buffer occupancy at the time of arrival.   The TRANSPAC network is organised along these lines (Schartz, 1987).   ☐

From now on the discussion will be restricted to bifurcated flows.

A nonlinear least cost flow problem

The question arises as to how to determine an optimal bifurcated flow. That is, if the Independence Assumption is invoked, to find an optimal solution to the nonlinear multicommodity flow problem (cf. section 2.2).

minimise $\sum_i \sum_j \dfrac{x_{ij}}{c_{ij} - x_{ij}}$

subject to

$$x_{ij} = \sum_r \sum_t x_{ij}^{rt} \tag{3.4}$$

$$\sum_i x_{ij}^{rt} - \sum_k x_{jk}^{rt} = \begin{cases} -D_{rt} & j = r \\ 0 & j \neq r, t \\ D_{rt} & j = t \end{cases} \tag{3.5}$$

$$x_{ij}^{rt} \geq 0 \tag{3.6}$$

$$x_{ij} \leq c_{ij}. \tag{3.7}$$

This mathematical program has some interesting and useful mathematical properties, which will be developed via a sequence of definitions and theorems. The reader should endeavour to understand the meanings of the results, at least in intuitive terms.

Definition 3.1 A set X is *convex* if for any two points a and b in X, $(1-\theta)a + \theta b$ also belongs to X for all θ satisfying $0 < \theta < 1$.

In words: a convex set is such that for every pair of points a and b in the set, all points intermediate between a and b are also in the set (cf. figure 3.7).

Theorem 3.2 The set of feasible flows $F = \{ x \mid x$ satisfies (3.4) - (3.7)$\}$ is a convex set.
Proof Let x^1 and x^2 be distinct feasible flows. Setting

$$x_{ij}^{rt} = (1-\theta)x_{ij}^{1rt} + \theta x_{ij}^{2rt}$$
$$x_{ij} = (1-\theta)x_{ij}^1 + \theta x_{ij}^2$$

it is readily verified that, for $0 < \theta < 1$, the sets $\{x_{ij}^{rt}\}$ and $\{x_{ij}\}$ satisfy (3.4) -(3.7) and so define a feasible flow. $\qquad\square$

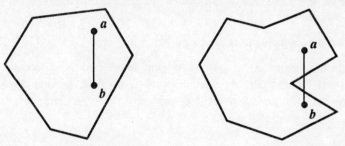

Figure 3.7 The set on the left is convex. The set on the right is not convex since not all points intermediate between *a* and *b* belong to the set.

Definition 3.2 A function *f* is *convex* on the convex set *X* if, for any two distinct points *a* and *b* in *X*

$$f((1-\theta)a + \theta b) \le (1-\theta)f(a) + \theta f(b) \quad \text{for all } \theta \text{ such that } 0 < \theta < 1$$

and it is *strictly convex* if

$$f((1-\theta)a + \theta b) < (1-\theta)f(a) + \theta f(b) \quad \text{for all } \theta \text{ such that } 0 < \theta < 1.$$

A function *g* is *concave* (*strictly concave*) if -*g* is convex (strictly convex).

The interpretation of this is that a convex function is overestimated by the linear function fitted through the points $(a, f(a))$ and $(b, f(b))$.

Theorem 3.3 A twice differentiable function *f* of a single variable *x* is convex on the (convex) set $a \le x \le b$ if

$$\frac{\partial^2 f}{\partial x^2} \ge 0.$$

Proof This standard result will not be proved formally; instead we rely on the reader's geometric intuition.   □

Theorem 3.4 The function $x_{ij}/(c_{ij} - x_{ij})$ is convex on the set $0 \le x_{ij} \le b$ where $0 < b < c_{ij}$.

Proof The function is twice differentiable and

$$\frac{\partial^2 f}{\partial x_{ij}^2} = \frac{2c_{ij}}{(c_{ij} - x_{ij})^3} > 0$$

for $0 \le x_{ij} \le b$.   □

Theorem 3.5 The function $F(x) = \sum_i \sum_j x_{ij}/(c_{ij} - x_{ij})$ is convex on the set $0 \le x_{ij} \le b_{ij}$ where $0 \le b_{ij} < c_{ij}$.

Proof Each term $x_{ij}/(c_{ij} - x_{ij})$ is convex and it is readily shown from definition 3.2 that the sum of convex functions is again convex. ☐

Definition 3.3 A function f has a *local minimum* at ξ if there is a number $\varepsilon > 0$ such that $f(x) - f(\xi) \ge 0$ for all x satisfying $d(x,\xi) < \varepsilon$. [$d(x,\xi)$ here denotes the 'distance between vectors x and ξ'.]

This says that there is no point x for which $f(x) < f(\xi)$ provided x is 'sufficiently close' to ξ.

Definition 3.4 A function f has a *global minimum* at ξ if $f(x) - f(\xi) \ge 0$ for all x.

Clearly, a global minimum is also a local minimum but the converse is not in general true (cf. figure 3.8). Thus a global minimum is best among all local minima. Local and global maxima are defined in an analogous way.

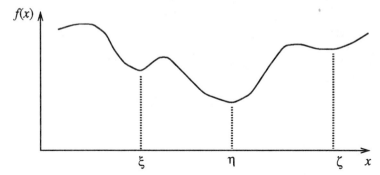

Figure 3.8 The function f of a single variable x has local minima at each of ξ, η and ζ. The global minimum is at η.

Definition 3.5 An *extreme point* of a convex set X is one which cannot be represented as $(1-\theta)a + \theta b$ where a and b are distinct points in X and $0 < \theta < 1$.

Definition 3.6 A set X is a *polytope* if it has a finite subset $\{a_1, ..., a_n\}$ of extreme points a_i, $i = 1, ..., n$, and X comprises precisely those points which can be expressed as a linear combination

$$x = \Sigma_i \alpha_i \, a_i \quad \text{where} \quad \alpha_i \geq 0 \quad \text{for all } i \text{ and } \Sigma_i \alpha_i = 1.$$

Theorem 3.6 Let f be a convex function defined on a convex set X. Then

(1) every local minimum of f is a global minimum;

(2) there is a global maximum at an extreme point of X if X is a polytope.

Proof (1) Let ξ be any local minimum of f which is not a global minimum, and η a global minimum. Since ξ is a local minimum there exists $\varepsilon > 0$ such that

$$f(x) \geq f(\xi) \quad \text{if } d(x,\xi) < \varepsilon. \tag{3.8}$$

Now let $x = (1-\theta)\xi + \theta\eta$, $0 < \theta < 1$ be any point satisfying $d(x,\xi) < \varepsilon$; then by convexity of f,

$$
\begin{aligned}
f(x) &\leq (1-\theta)f(\xi) + \theta f(\eta) \\
&< (1-\theta)f(\xi) + \theta f(\xi) \quad \text{since } \eta \text{ is a global minimum and } \xi \text{ is not} \\
&= f(\xi). \tag{3.9}
\end{aligned}
$$

From (3.8) and (3.9) it follows that $f(\xi) < f(\xi)$, but this is a contradiction and so the desired result is established.

(2) Suppose that there is a global maximum at η. Since X is a polytope, there is a set $\{ a_1, ..., a_n \}$ of extreme points of X such that $\eta = \Sigma_i \alpha_i a_i$ with $\alpha_i \geq 0$ for all i and $\Sigma_i \alpha_i = 1$. It is readily verified, by induction (cf. exercise 3.2), that the convexity of f implies

$$f(\eta) \leq \Sigma_i \alpha_i f(a_i). \tag{3.10}$$

Let k be that index i for which $f(a_i)$ is maximal subject to $\alpha_i \neq 0$. Then from (3.10)

$$
\begin{aligned}
f(\eta) &\leq \Sigma_i \alpha_i f(a_i) \\
&\leq \Sigma_i \alpha_i f(a_k) \\
&= (\Sigma_i \alpha_i) f(a_k) \\
&= f(a_k).
\end{aligned}
$$

Consequently, a_k is an extreme point which is also a global maximum. □

Corollary If g is a concave function defined on the convex set X, then

(1) every local maximum of f is a global maximum;

(2) there is a global minimum at an extreme point of X if X is a polytope.

Returning to the problem (3.4) - (3.7), the set of feasible flows forms a convex set X (theorem 3.2), the objective function is convex (theorem 3.5) and consequently every local minimum is also a global minimum. Hence any *descent method* which starts with a feasible flow and continually adjusts it so as to reduce the objective will (under reasonable conditions) lead, in the limit, to an optimal flow. The next section shows how this may be achieved.

3.3 FLOW DEVIATION

By theorems 3.5 and 3.6 it is sufficient to find a point x for which no small change in flow pattern will lead to decreased total delay. Consequently, the approach of example 3.3 looks promising; there, flow from B to D (and from D to B) was redirected via A and 3.9 kbps was found to be the optimal amount to divert. The process could be repeated, each time for an OD pair different from the previous one, thus reducing further and further the total delay. We now look at one way of effecting such a repeated improvement method.

Repeated linear approximation

Consider any function Φ of the network flow which depends only on the *total* flow in each of the links and is of the form

$$\Phi(x) = \sum_i \sum_j \Phi(x_{ij}) \qquad (3.11)$$

$$x_{ij} = \sum_r \sum_t x_{ij}^{rt}$$

If $x(0)$ is a given feasible solution and x any other 'nearby' feasible solution, then expanding $\Phi(x)$ in a Taylor series about $x(0)$ (cf. Courant, 1934) gives

$$\Phi(x) = \Phi(x(0)) + \sum_i \sum_j [x_{ij} - x_{ij}(0)] \left[\frac{\partial \Phi}{\partial x_{ij}}\right]_{x_{ij} = x_{ij}(0)} + \varepsilon$$

where ε is of second order in the displacements $x_{ij} - x_{ij}(0)$. If quadratic and higher terms are ignored (the linear approximation) then, by (3.11),

$$\Phi(x) = K(0) + \sum_i \sum_j d_{ij} x_{ij}$$

where

$$K(0) = \Phi(x(0)) - \sum_i \sum_j d_{ij} x_{ij}(0) \quad \text{and} \quad d_{ij} = \left[\frac{\partial \Phi}{\partial x_{ij}}\right]_{x_{ij} = x_{ij}(0)}.$$

Since $K(0)$ is constant, $\Phi(x)$ is minimised when $\sum_i \sum_j d_{ij} x_{ij}$ is minimised. With the conservation constraints imposed to ensure feasibility this gives the problem

SP(0):   minimise $\sum_i \sum_j d_{ij} x_{ij}^{rt}$

   subject to

$$x_{ij} = \sum_r \sum_t x_{ij}^{rt}$$

$$\sum_i x_{ij}^{rt} - \sum_k x_{jk}^{rt} = \begin{cases} -D_{rt} & j=r \\ 0 & j \neq r, t \\ D_{rt} & j=t \end{cases} \qquad (3.12)$$

$$x_{ij}^{rt} \geq 0.$$

There are also capacity constraints $x_{ij} \leq c_{ij}$, but these will be omitted as they are implicitly taken account of in a different way (see below). SP(0) is just the minimal cost multicommodity problem of section 2.2, and is solved easily by finding, for each OD pair, a shortest path from origin to destination.

Of course, the above linear problem is based on an approximation which is only 'good near to $x(0)$'. If the optimal solution to SP(0) is $x^*(0)$ say, then as x moves from $x(0)$ towards $x^*(0)$, $\Phi(x)$ does decrease initially, though it may begin to rise again later (cf. the transfer of flow in example 3.3). This suggests performing a *1-dimensional search* (or *line search*) along the line segment from $x(0)$ to $x^*(0)$. Expressed mathematically, it is required to solve

LS(0):   minimise $\Phi((1-\theta)x(0) + \theta x^*(0))$
   subject to $0 \leq \theta \leq 1$.

Note that when θ takes the values 0 and 1, x takes the values $x(0)$ and $x^*(0)$ respectively. Also, because $\Phi \to \infty$ as $x_{ij} \to c_{ij}$ the optimal solution $x(1) = (1-\theta_m)x(0) + \theta_m x^*(0)$ satisfies the capacity constraints via the minimisation, even if $x^*(0)$ does not (see the following example). Now $x(1)$ is unlikely to be an optimal solution even if the line search were to be carried out exactly, but it can be asserted that it is better than $x(0)$. It seems sensible therefore to start at this new approximation to the optimal flow and to obtain a further improved solution by solving corresponding shortest distance and line search problems SP(1) and LS(1) respectively, and so on. [Note that this method can be applied to other nonlinear problems with linear constraints (Frank and Wolfe, 1956). It is known as the Frank-Wolfe or *flow deviation* method, and will also be called algorithm (FW) in this text.]

Example 3.5 The capacities of links *at, am, mt, bm, bt* of the network of figure 3.9 are 20, 25, 25, 20 and 20 kbps respectively. There is 15 kbps of traffic from *a* to *t* and 10 kbps of traffic from *b* to *t*. If the traffic conditions are steady, find a flow pattern which leads to minimum total delay.

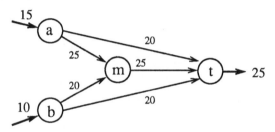

Figure 3.9 Network for example 3.5. The numbers beside arcs are the corresponding capacities.

Solution The (M/M/1) delay function $x/(c-x)$ may be expressed as the infinite series

$$x/(c-x) = (x/c)(1-x/c)^{-1}$$
$$= (x/c)[1 + (x/c) + (x/c)^2 + \ldots].$$

In order to simplify the calculations therefore the total delay will, for each *ij*, be approximated by

$$\Phi_L = \sum_i \sum_j [(x_{ij}/c_{ij}) + (x_{ij}/c_{ij})^2]$$

or, written out in full,

$$\Phi_L(x) = \Phi_L(x_{at}, x_{am}, x_{mt}, x_{bm}, x_{bt}) \tag{3.13}$$

$$= 0.05x_{at} + 0.0025x_{at}^2 + 0.04x_{am} + 0.0016x_{am}^2 + 0.04x_{mt} +$$
$$0.0016x_{mt}^2 + 0.05x_{bm} + 0.0025x_{bm}^2 + 0.05x_{bt} + 0.0025x_{bt}^2.$$

$$(3.14)$$

from which

$$d_{at} = 0.05 + 0.005x_{at}$$
$$d_{am} = 0.04 + 0.0032x_{am}$$
$$d_{mt} = 0.04 + 0.0032x_{mt}$$
$$d_{bm} = 0.05 + 0.005x_{bm}$$
$$d_{bt} = 0.05 + 0.005x_{bt}.$$

Initially, nothing is known about how congested the various links will be, and so to get an initial feasible solution, $d = (d_{ij})$ is evaluated at a flow of zero giving $d = (0.05, 0.04, 0.04, 0.05, 0.05)$, where the components of d are given with the same link order as in (3.13). With respect to these cost coefficients, solving the appropriate shortest path problem yields a starting solution in which all flow from a and b goes directly to t, that is $x(0) = (15, 0, 0, 0, 10)$ and, from (3.14), $\Phi_L(x(0))$ = 2.0625 compared to the true value $\Phi(x(0)) = 4.000$. The value of d for this feasible flow is $(0.125, 0.04, 0.04, 0.05, 0.10)$. Using these co-efficients in SP(0) leads to the shortest paths from a to t and b to t being a-m-t and b-m-t respectively; sending all flow along these paths corresponds to the solution $x^*(0) = (0, 15, 25, 10, 0)$. Note that this is not a feasible flow since it requires a flow of 25 kbps in link mt and with the unapproximated delay function leads to infinite delay, though all other points x_θ on $x(0)$-$x^*(0)$ do correspond to feasible flows.

Substituting gives

$$x_\theta = (1-\theta)x(0) + \theta x^*(0) = (15-15\theta, 15\theta, 25\theta, 10\theta, 10-10\theta)$$

leading, after some manipulation, to

$$\Phi_L(x_\theta) = 2.0625 - 0.775\theta + 2.4225\theta^2.$$

The line search can now be performed analytically with the minimum being obtained when

$$\frac{\partial \Phi_L}{\partial \theta} = -0.775 + 4.845\theta = 0$$

or $\theta = 0.160$. Using this value gives the next approximation

$x(1) = 0.840x(0) + 0.160x^*(0) = (12.6, 2.4, 4.0, 1.6, 8.4)$

$\Phi_L(x(1)) = 2.001$

$\Phi(x(1)) = 2.810$

$d = (0.113, 0.048, 0.053, 0.055, 0.092).$

Solving SP(1) it is found that the shortest paths from a to t and b to t are a-m-t and b-t respectively; thus

$x^*(1) = (0, 15, 15, 0, 10)$

with $x_\theta = (12.6 - 12.6\theta, \ 2.4 + 12.6\theta, \ 4.0 + 11.0\theta, \ 1.6 - 1.6\theta, \ 8.4 + 1.6\theta)$, LS(1) solves to give $\theta = 0.110$ and

$x(2) = (11.214, 3.786, 5.210, 1.424, 8.576)$
$\Phi_L(x(2)) = 1.9902$
$\Phi(x(2)) = 2.5454$

and so on with the values of $x(i)$ and $\Phi_L(x(i))$ converging, as i tends to infinity, to the optimal flow and the optimal flow value respectively. (Further terms in these sequences may be derived from table 3.3.)   □

Table 3.3 Convergence of the Frank-Wolfe method for example 3.5. (Flows are given for a-t and b-t only.)

i	$x(i)$	$\Phi_L(x(i))$	$d(i)$	$x^*(i+1)$	$\theta(i)$
0	(15, 10)	2.063	(0.045, 0.010)	(0, 0)	0.160
1	(12.6, 8.4)	2.001	(0.013, -0.019)	(0, 10)	0.110
2	(11.214, 8.576)	1.990	(-0.003, -0.021)	(15, 10)	0.179
3	(11.892, 8.827)	1.987	(0.006, -0.015)	(0, 10)	0.056
4	(11.226, 8.893)	1.984	(-0.002, -0.017)	(15, 10)	0.118
....		.....			
∞	(11.053, 10.000)	1.974			

Geometric interpretation

It is helpful to interpret the course of the solution of example 3.5 in geometrical terms. Since five flow variables $x_{at}, \ x_{am}, \ x_{mt}, \ x_{bm}, \ x_{bt}$ are involved it might appear that the interpretation would require a 5-dimensional space. This is not so, since once x_{at} and x_{bt} are known the values of x_{am}, x_{mt}, and x_{bm} can be determined from the conservation of flow equations

$$x_{am} = 15 - x_{at}, \quad x_{mt} = 25 - x_{at} - x_{bt}, \quad x_{bm} = 10 - x_{bt}.$$

Substitution into (3.14) leads to

$$\Phi_L(x) = 3.71 - 0.158x_{at} - 0.170x_{bt} + 0.0057x_{at}^2 + 0.0032x_{at}x_{bt} + 0.0066x_{bt}^2.$$

The lines of constant objective value, that is $\Phi_L(x) = constant$, are thus ellipses some of which are shown in figure 3.10. The initial point chosen is $x(0) = (15, 10)$ at the top right hand corner of the feasible region. Linearising at this point

$$d_{at} = \left[\frac{\partial \Phi_L}{\partial x_{at}} \right]_{x_{at} = x_{at}(0)} = -0.158 + 0.0114x_{at} + 0.0032x_{bt}$$

$$d_{bt} = \left[\frac{\partial \Phi_L}{\partial x_{bt}} \right]_{x_{bt} = x_{bt}(0)} = -0.170 + 0.0032x_{at} + 0.0132x_{bt}.$$

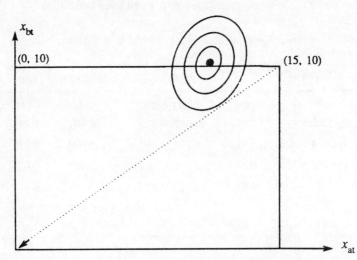

Figure 3.10 Level contours associated with the problem of example 3.5. The diagonal of the rectangle indicates the initial search direction.

The gradient vector is thus $d = (0.045, 0.010)$. To minimise Φ_L we should move to an extreme point as far as possible in the direction $-d$.

This gives the point $x^*(0) = (0, 0)$. Performing the line search gives the expression

$$\Phi_L(x_\theta) = 3.71 - 4.07(1-\theta) + 2.4225(1-\theta)^2$$

and, as before, $\theta = 0.160$, yielding

$x(1) = (12.6, 8.4),$
$\Phi_L(x(1)) = 2.001,$
$\Phi(x(1)) = 2.810.$

Some further terms in the sequences for $x(i)$ and $\Phi_L(x(i))$ are given in table 3.3 in which $d(i)$ and $\theta(i)$ denote the values of d and θ at iteration i.

From figure 3.11 it is seen that the feasible directions chosen become increasingly nearer to being at right angles to the direction of steepest descent $-d$. This is because the feasible direction is always chosen to be *towards a vertex of the feasible region*. This feature results in slow convergence as optimality is approached. [This is a general feature of the Frank-Wolfe method and is not peculiar to flow problems; it is treated further later in this section.]

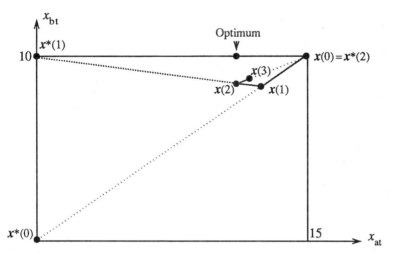

Figure 3.11 Successive search directions and values of $x(i)$. See also figure 3.10.

Before leaving this problem, some general points are in order. First, since the network has been dispensed with when reducing to two variables, the linear problem to be solved is no longer an explicit shortest distance problem. Second, since Φ_L is a quadratic function, it is easy to find the exact solution to the unconstrained problem by solving

$$\frac{\partial \Phi_L}{\partial x_{at}} = \frac{\partial \Phi_L}{\partial x_{bt}} = 0,$$

that is, by solving the pair of simultaneous equations

$$-0.158 + 0.0114 x_{at} + 0.0032 x_{bt} = 0$$
$$-0.170 + 0.0032 x_{at} + 0.0132 x_{bt} = 0.$$

It is easily verified that the optimal solution is

$$x_{at} = 10.993, \quad x_{bt} = 10.214,$$

but this violates the capacity constraint $x_{bt} \leq 10$. Intuition suggests (cf. figure 3.10) that the optimal solution will have $x_{bt} = 10$ giving $\Phi_L(x) = 2.67 - 0.126 x_{at} + 0.0057 x_{at}^2$, from which $x_{at} = 11.053$. By invoking the conservation constraints, the full solution is then completed by

$$x_{am} = 3.947, \quad x_{mt} = 3.947, \quad x_{bm} = 0.$$

with $\Phi_L(x) = 1.974$.

It is interesting to note how 'shallow' the minimum is; $\Phi_L(x)$ is within 1% of its optimum value at $x(2)$ even though $x(2)$ is some way off the optimal solution.

Using PARTAN

An advantage of the Frank-Wolfe method for centralised routing is that it is only necessary to store *total* link flows. This is barely apparent from example 3.5 in which only link *mt* can carry flow for more than one OD pair. However, consider iteration $i = 1$ of the solution for which

$$x(1) = (12.6, 2.4, 4.0, 1.6, 8.4).$$

It is not necessary to know that x_{mt} comprises flows of $x_{mt}^{at} = 2.4$ from a to t and $x_{mt}^{bt} = 1.6$ from b to t. $x^*(1)$, is constructed to satisfy the conservation constraints, and so it follows that $(1-\theta)x(1) + \theta x^*(1)$ must also satisfy the conservation constraints for all $0 \le \theta \le 1$ (cf. theorem 3.2). As observed earlier, capacity constraints are taken care of implicitly once an initial feasible solution has been found. Clearly, these observations generalise to the case of any iteration for a larger network in which a single link may carry flow for many OD pairs.

If only the *total* link utilisation corresponding to an optimal routing is required, as may be the case when *designing* a network (cf. chapter 5), then the output from the Frank-Wolfe algorithm is clearly sufficient. Consequently, it is worth investigating ways in which the convergence of this algorithm may be improved. However, before tackling this it is appropriate to consider first the minimisation of a convex quadratic function f of two variables x and y over the whole of the x-y plane; without loss of generality this function may be taken to be $f(x, y) = x^2/a^2 + y^2/b^2$. The contours of $f(x, y) = constant$ are concentric ellipses (cf. figure 3.12). The Frank-Wolfe algorithm modified by omitting the conservation constraints becomes the well known *steepest descent* algorithm (see for example, Walsh, 1975) in which successive line searches are performed in the direction opposite to that of the gradient vector at the point at which linearisation takes place. Let $x(0)$ be some starting point and l_0 the line tangential to the contour through $x(0)$. If also the first two line searches are along lines l_1 and l_2 and the corresponding minima are $x(1)$ and $x(2)$ the situation is as shown in figure 3.13.

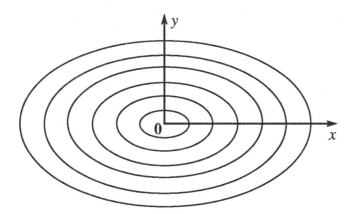

Figure 3.12 Concentric ellipses $x^2/a^2 + y^2/b^2 = constant$.

Theorem 3.7 (Parallel tangents theorem) Lines l_o and l_2 of figure 3.13 are parallel, and the line L through $x(0)$ and $x(2)$ passes through the centres of the ellipses.

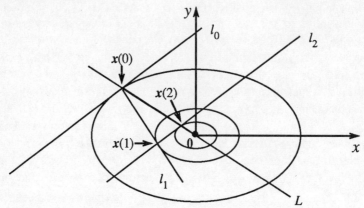

Figure 3.13 Illustration of the 'parallel tangents' theorem.

Proof Since the gradient vector at any point x is perpendicular to the tangent to the ellipse through x it follows that l_1 is perpendicular to l_o and l_2 is perpendicular to l_1. Consequently, l_2 is parallel to l_o as required. To prove the second result, consider the projective transformation which increases the scale in the y direction by the factor a/b. This transforms the ellipses into concentric circles (figure 3.14).

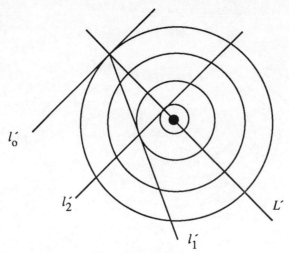

Figure 3.14 A projection of figure 3.13.

Since parallelism is not destroyed by such a projective transformation, l_2' is parallel to l_0' and hence L' passes through the centre of the circles. The desired result then follows by considering the inverse transformation to return to figure 3.13. □

From the above result it follows that the minimum of an unconstrained quadratic function of two variables may be obtained by two line searches (along l_1 and l_2) followed by a single 'PARTAN' search (along L). For a quadratic function of m variables it is sufficient to make an initial line search followed by m-1 line search / PARTAN search pairs (cf. Walsh, 1975).

Example 3.6 Investigate the use of PARTAN for the problem of example 3.5.

Solution The equivalent version of the problem will be employed in which only the two variables x_{at} and x_{bt} are used. Consider a PARTAN search along the line $x(i)$ and $x(i+2)$. Let

$$x_\varphi = (1 - \varphi)x(i) + \varphi x(i+2).$$

Clearly $\varphi \geq 0$ is required, but what of the upper limit? Successively substituting for $x(i+2)$ and $x(i+1)$ gives

$$x_\varphi = (1 - \varphi)x(i) + \varphi x(i+2)$$

$$= (1 - \varphi)x(i) + \varphi[(1 - \theta(i+1))x(i+1) + \theta(i+1)x^*(i+1)]$$

$$= (1 - \varphi)x(i) + \varphi[(1 - \theta(i+1))[(1 - \theta(i))x(i) + \theta(i)x^*(i)]$$

$$+ \theta(i+1)x^*(i+1)]$$

and, after rearrangement of terms,

$$x_\varphi = [(1 - \varphi) + \varphi(1 - \theta(i+1))(1 - \theta(i))]x(i) + \varphi(1 - \theta(i+1))\theta(i)x^*(i)$$

$$+ \varphi\theta(i+1)x^*(i+1).$$

Since the feasible region for the flow problem is convex it follows that x_φ is feasible if the coefficients of $x(i)$, $x^*(i)$ and $x^*(i+1)$ are all in the range 0 to 1. The latter two are satisfied automatically; for the first it is required that

$$(1 - \varphi) + \varphi(1 - \theta(i))(1 - \theta(i+1)) \geq 0,$$

or equivalently that

$$\varphi \leq 1/[\theta(i) + \theta(i+1) - \theta(i)\theta(i+1)].$$

As an example consider $i = 1$ and a PARTAN search along the direction from $x(1)$ to $x(3)$. Recalling that

$x(1) = (12.6, 8.4), \quad x(3) = (11.892, 8.827)$
$\theta(1) = 0.110, \quad \theta(2) = 0.179,$

leads to

$\varphi \leq 1/[\theta(1) + \theta(2) - \theta(1)\theta(2)]$
$\quad = 1/[0.110 + 0.179 - 0.110*0.179] = 3.713.$

The PARTAN search would then maximise $\Phi_L(x_\varphi)$ for $0 \leq \varphi \leq 3.713$. In fact the maximum will be achieved at the upper limit $\varphi = 3.713$, that is at the point

$x_\varphi = 0x(1) + 3.713(0.110)(0.821)x^*(1) + 3.713(0.179)x^*(2)$
$\quad = 0.335x^*(1) + 0.665x^*(2)$
$\quad = (1 - \alpha)x^*(1) + \alpha x^*(2)$

where $\alpha = 0.335$. Hence, as expected, x_φ is a point on the feasible region (viz (9.975, 10)) and is quite close to the optimal solution.   □

There are other methods for solving problems of this type, for example: Bertsekas and Gafni (1982), Lupi (1986) and Florian et al (1987).

3.4 ADAPTIVE ROUTING (1)

Ideally, a routing algorithm should be
- simple
- adaptive
- stable
- free from looping
- optimal.

How do the algorithms developed thus far measure up to these ideals?

Comparison of routing approaches

Virtual circuit (v.c.) routing involves fairly simple algorithms. While for a particular v.c. the route is fixed, packets for different v.c.s corresponding to the same OD pair can follow different routes, thus tending to 'even out' the flow. Since v.c.s are calculated every time a new session is established there is some adaptiveness. Stability is not really a problem. Looping is also not a problem as a v.c. cannot contain a loop. Routing by means of v.c.s has experienced considerable popularity with network designers.

For datagram routing the label-correcting and label-setting algorithms of section 2.4 are relatively simple. They do not require excessive amounts of calculation at a node particularly if calculations are performed centrally. Adaptiveness is limited unless updates are performed very frequently in which case computational and communication overheads may become excessive. Instability may be experienced since flow for any OD pair may, between updates, 'follow a single route only'; this can lead to oscillation between routes at successive updates. Worse still, the routes oscillated between can be poor ones as the example below shows. Datagram routing is often not optimal in the sense that there is a theoretically better bifurcated routing. Temporary looping may occur after an update but a packet will usually 'get out of the loop' before long.

Example 3.7 Investigate, for the network of figure 3.15, the effect on the routing pattern of the introduction of flows of 3 from node 6 to

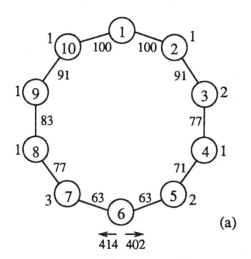

(a)

Figure 3.15 Ten nodes are connected in a ring by links of capacity 16. The flow per unit time between node i and node 1 (and between node 1 and node i) is shown beside node i for $i \neq 1, 6$. There is no flow for any other OD pair. The length of each link is shown beside that link. The numbers beneath node 6 indicate the distances from node 6 to node 1 in the two possible directions.

node 1 and from node 1 to node 6. It may be assumed that the (M/M/1) queuing approximation is applicable and that the length of each link ij is $1000/(16-x_{ij})$; the factor of '1000' is included merely to avoid fractions.

Solution In the following discussion only flows *to* node 1 will be discussed explicitly, it being understood that flows *from* node 1 follow the corresponding reverse paths. Initially, packets from nodes 2, ..., 5 flow counterclockwise, and packets from nodes 7, ..., 10 flow clockwise (cf. figure 3.15). The distance from node 6 to node 1 is 414 by the clockwise route and 402 by the conterclockwise route. Thus, when the extra flow from node 6 is introduced it will initially be routed via node 5. At the next update, link lengths will change to those shown in figure 3.16a, and this time packets from nodes 2, ..., 5 flow counterclockwise, and those from other nodes flow clockwise. That is, the flow from node 6 switches direction.

At the next update, flow from both nodes 6 and 7 switches direction (cf. figure 3.16b). At the following two updates flow from nodes 4, 5, 6 and 7 first switches to the clockwise direction (figure 3.16c) then switches back to the counterclockwise direction (figure 3.16d); after this, the flow pattern oscillates between these two patterns (neither of which is very good!). □

The relatively complicated bifurcated flows are, in a sense, optimal. The computational burden of calculating them is, however, considerable so that only relatively infrequent updates could conceivably be entertained; that is, bifurcated routing is not very adaptive. By their nature bifurcated flows lead to stable routing. Looping is not a problem.

Information requirements for routing

Typically, a considerable proportion of traffic to (and from) a node 'originates at' (and is 'destined for') a nearby node; in any case, traffic from (or to) a remote node must pass via nearby nodes. Therefore, a routing algorithm should work with accurate information on local conditions, though it is acceptable for data on more remote parts of the network to be less precise. Moreover, it is preferable that the response to local changes should be rapid, thus suggesting that routing calculations should be distributed. Other properties of distributed calculations that are beneficial are: the spreading of the computational burden; the extra reliability in the face of link failures (in the sense that an isolated part of a network could still function to a limited extent).

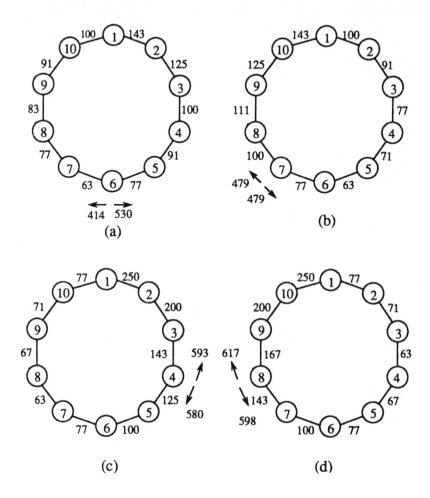

Figure 3.16 The flow round the ring network of figure 3.15 after successive updates is indicated in (a) - (d). Note that the tie in (b) is resolved in favour of the counterclockwise direction (as would be seen to be the case had the link lengths been calculated to greater numerical accuracy).

One possibility for organising a distributed routing system is, periodically,

> to send, from each node x to every node w adjacent to x, the current estimates $D(x,y)$ of the shortest distances from x to every other node y of the network.

In this way a node u receives the values $D(v, y)$ for every node y and every neighbouring node v of u. In order to show how such a scheme may be taken advantage of, the Bellman-Ford algorithm will first be introduced.

The Bellman-Ford algorithm

In the notation of section 2.4, the set of shortest distances $\{d(x, y)\}$ must satisfy

$$d(x, x) = 0, \quad \text{for all } x$$
$$d(x, y) = \min_{i \neq x} \{a_{xi} + d(i, y)\}, \quad \text{for all } x \neq y. \tag{3.15}$$

That a subpath of a shortest path must itself be a shortest path between its endpoints is an expression of 'The Principle of Optimality' of *dynamic programming*. (Dynamic programming is described further in section 6.1.) The Bellman and Ford method starts with *estimates* $D(x, y)$ of $d(x, y)$, for all x and y; it then repeatedly updates these until the equations in (3.15) are satisfied.

Algorithm (DP(∞))

{A dynamic programming method for finding all shortest paths with '∞' for the initial estimates.

Input: the matrix of link lengths $\{a_{ij}\}$.}

    Set $D^{(0)}(x, x) = 0$ and $D^{(0)}(x, y) = \infty$ for all x, y with $x \neq y$.

    Set $k = 0$.

    while there is possibility of further changes and $k < n\text{-}1$

    begin

        Set $k \leftarrow k+1$.

        for each node x **do**

        begin

         for all y **do**

          begin

           if $y = x$

           then $D^{(k)}(x, y) = 0$

           else $D^{(k)}(x, y) = \min_{i \neq x} \{a_{xi} + D^{(k-1)}(i, y)\}$

         end

        end

    end

{Output: $D^{(k)}(x, y)$ is the shortest distance from x to y.}

Note that paths can be determined in a straightforward way by keeping pointers. Also, if there is the possibility of negative length cycles the restriction '$k<n$' is removed from the **while** loop; a negative length cycle is detected if k reaches the value n (in which case the algorithm is terminated).

Example 3.8 Use algorithm DP(∞) to find the shortest distances between every pair of nodes in the network of figure 3.17.

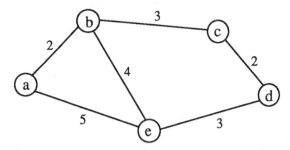

Figure 3.17 A five node network; the numbers beside links indicate current lengths.

Solution Initially the matrix of distance estimates is

$$(D^{(0)}(x,\ y)) = \begin{bmatrix} 0 & \infty & \infty & \infty & \infty \\ \infty & 0 & \infty & \infty & \infty \\ \infty & \infty & 0 & \infty & \infty \\ \infty & \infty & \infty & 0 & \infty \\ \infty & \infty & \infty & \infty & 0 \end{bmatrix}$$

At iteration 1, the following calculations are performed corresponding to origin node a.

$$D^{(1)}(a,a) = 0$$
$$D^{(1)}(a,b) = \min \{ a_{ab} + D^{(0)}(b,\ b),\ a_{ae} + D^{(0)}(e,\ b) \}$$
$$= \min \{ 2+0,\ 5+\infty \} = 2$$
$$D^{(1)}(a,c) = \min \{ a_{ab} + D^{(0)}(b,\ c),\ a_{ae} + D^{(0)}(e,\ c) \}$$
$$= \min \{ 2+\infty,\ 5+\infty \} = \infty$$
$$D^{(1)}(a,d) = \min \{ a_{ab} + D^{(0)}(b,\ d),\ a_{ae} + D^{(0)}(e,\ d) \}$$
$$= \min \{ 2+\infty,\ 5+\infty \} = \infty$$
$$D^{(1)}(a,e) = \min \{ a_{ab} + D^{(0)}(b,\ e),\ a_{ae} + D^{(0)}(e,\ e) \}$$
$$= \min \{ 2+\infty,\ 5+0 \} = 5.$$

For node b the updated estimates are:

$$D^{(1)}(b, a) = \min \{a_{ba} + D^{(0)}(a, a), \, a_{bc} + D^{(0)}(c, a), \, a_{be} + D^{(0)}(e, a)\}$$
$$= \min \{2 + 0, \, 3 + \infty, \, 4 + \infty\} = 2$$
$$D^{(1)}(b, b) = 0$$
$$D^{(1)}(b, c) = \min \{a_{ba} + D^{(0)}(a, c), \, a_{bc} + D^{(0)}(c, c), \, a_{be} + D^{(0)}(e, c)\}$$
$$= \min \{2 + \infty, \, 3 + 0, \, 4 + \infty\} = 3$$
$$D^{(1)}(b, d) = \min \{a_{ba} + D^{(0)}(a, d), \, a_{bc} + D^{(0)}(c, d), \, a_{be} + D^{(0)}(e, d)\}$$
$$= \min \{2 + \infty, \, 3 + \infty, \, 4 + \infty\} = \infty$$
$$D^{(1)}(b, e) = \min \{a_{ba} + D^{(0)}(a, e), \, a_{bc} + D^{(0)}(c, e), \, a_{be} + D^{(0)}(e, e)\}$$
$$= \min \{2 + \infty, \, 3 + \infty, \, 4 + 0\} = 4.$$

Performing similar calculations with the other three nodes as origins leads to the updated matrix of distance estimates

$$\begin{bmatrix} 0 & 2 & \infty & \infty & 5 \\ 2 & 0 & 3 & \infty & 4 \\ \infty & 3 & 0 & 2 & \infty \\ \infty & \infty & 2 & 0 & 3 \\ 5 & 4 & \infty & 3 & 0 \end{bmatrix}$$

Performing the second iteration $(k = 2)$ leads to the updated matrix of distance estimates

$$\begin{bmatrix} 0 & 2 & 5 & 8 & 5 \\ 2 & 0 & 3 & 5 & 4 \\ 5 & 3 & 0 & 2 & 5 \\ 8 & 5 & 2 & 0 & 3 \\ 5 & 4 & 5 & 3 & 0 \end{bmatrix}$$

After another iteration this becomes

$$\begin{bmatrix} 0 & 2 & 5 & 7 & 5 \\ 2 & 0 & 3 & 5 & 4 \\ 5 & 3 & 0 & 2 & 5 \\ 7 & 5 & 2 & 0 & 3 \\ 5 & 4 & 5 & 3 & 0 \end{bmatrix}$$

This is the matrix of true distances as is detected by there being no further changes at the next iteration.   □

For the above example, it is interesting to look at the calculations of $D^{(k)}(a, d)$ when $k = 1, 2, 3$. Initially, $D^{(0)}(a, d) = \infty$ as $a \neq d$. Then, $D^{(1)}(a, d) = \infty$ as a and d are not neighbours (that is, there is no path from a to d with only one link). Next,

$$D^{(2)}(a, d) = \min \{ a_{ab} + D^{(1)}(b, d), a_{ae} + D^{(1)}(e, d) \}$$
$$= \min \{ 2 + \infty, 5 + 3 \} = 8$$

corresponding to the path $a\text{-}e\text{-}d$ from a to d which contains two links. Finally,

$$D^{(3)}(a, d) = \min \{ a_{ab} + D^{(2)}(b, d), a_{ae} + D^{(2)}(e, d) \}$$
$$= \min \{ 2 + 5, 5 + 3 \} = 7$$

corresponding to the three link path $a\text{-}b\text{-}c\text{-}d$ from a to d comprising the link $a\text{-}b$ and the two link path $b\text{-}c\text{-}d$ that corresponds to $D^{(2)}(b, d)$. It seems that, at each iteration, paths with more and more links are being considered. This observation is formalised in the next theorem.

Theorem 3.8 Using algorithm DP(∞) for any network with n nodes and no negative length circuits:

(1) $D^{(k)}(x, y)$ is a monotonic decreasing sequence;

(2) $D^{(k)}(x, y)$ is the shortest distance from x to y using at most k links;

(3) $D^{(n-1)}(x, y) = d(x, y)$.

Proof Part (1) is trivial. For part (2), mathematical induction will be used with the general hypothesis

H_k: $D^{(k)}(x, y)$ is the shortest distance from x to y using at most k links.

Clearly H_0 is true. Suppose now that H_m is true, and π is a shortest path from x to y using at most $m+1$ links. Then if w is the first node on π from x

$$D^{(m+1)}(x, y) \leq a_{xw} + D^{(m)}(w, y). \tag{3.16}$$

The strict inequality cannot hold as this would imply $D^{(m)}(w, y)$ was not the shortest distance from w to y using at most m links, thus violating H_m. It follows that (3.16) must hold with equality, establishing H_{m+1}.

(3) is true since there is a shortest path from each x to each y with at most $n-1$ links. $\qquad\square$

An accelerated algorithm

It may be noted that in performing an update the latest estimate of a particular distance is not always used. To see this, consider the solution of example 3.8 after the first two rows of $D^{(1)}(x, y)$ have been calculated; thus

$$\begin{bmatrix} 0 & 2 & \infty & \infty & 5 \\ 2 & 0 & 3 & \infty & 4 \\ & & \text{<still to be calculated>} & & \\ & & & & \end{bmatrix}$$

Now, $D^{(1)}(c, a)$ was calculated from

$$D^{(1)}(c, a) = \min \{ a_{cb} + D^{(0)}(b, a),\ a_{cd} + D^{(0)}(d, a) \}.$$

However, as $D^{(1)}(b, a)$ is already available why not use that in place of $D^{(0)}(b, a)$ in the above formula? That is

$$D^{(1)}(c, a) = \min \{ a_{cb} + D^{(1)}(b, a),\ a_{cd} + D^{(0)}(d, a) \}$$
$$= \min \{ 3 + 2, 2 + \infty \} = 5.$$

This new estimate is now the correct shortest distance from a to c. After calculating the third row of the matrix $(D^{(1)}(x, y))$ the situation is

$$\begin{bmatrix} 0 & 2 & \infty & \infty & 5 \\ 2 & 0 & 3 & \infty & 4 \\ 5 & 3 & 0 & 2 & 7 \\ & & \text{<still to be calculated>} & & \end{bmatrix}$$

Now calculating $D^{(1)}(d, a)$ using the latest estimates

$$D^{(1)}(d, a) = \min \{ a_{dc} + D^{(1)}(c, a),\ a_{de} + D^{(0)}(e, a) \}$$
$$= \min \{ 2 + 5, 3 + \infty \} = 7.$$

The correct shortest distance from node d to node a has not yet been found, but the estimate is better than previously.

The complete matrix after the first iteration is

$$\begin{bmatrix} 0 & 2 & \infty & \infty & 5 \\ 2 & 0 & 3 & \infty & 4 \\ 5 & 3 & 0 & 2 & 7 \\ 7 & 5 & 2 & 0 & 3 \\ 5 & 4 & 5 & 3 & 0 \end{bmatrix}$$

The above minimisations, in which the most recently calculated distance estimates are used, may be better expressed as

$$D(x, y) \leftarrow \min_w \{ a_{xw} + D(w, y) \},$$

with an estimate being overwritten when a new estimate is obtained.

For the above problem it still takes three iterations before *all* the estimates are correct. This is because estimates corresponding to the 'early' nodes use less accurate data in the minimisations than do the 'later' nodes. An idea is to reverse the order in which nodes are considered at the second iteration; it is then found that two iterations are sufficient.

There are difficulties with using DP(∞) as it stands: the link lengths are constantly changing so that it cannot be assumed that the estimates $D^{(m)}(x, y)$ are indeed upper bounds on the true shortest distance from x to y. Also, it is implicitly assumed that data exchange is synchronous. The removal of these restrictions is discussed in the next section.

3.5 ADAPTIVE ROUTING (2)

Alternative starting conditions

An alternative initialisation for distance estimates is to set $D^{(0)}(x, y) = 0$ for all x and y. With this modification to step 1 of algorithm DP(∞) an algorithm, denoted by DP(0), is obtained.

Theorem 3.9   Using algorithm DP(0) for any network with n nodes which satisfies $a_{ij} \geq \beta > 0$ for all links ij:

(1) $D^{(k)}(x, y)$ is a monotonic increasing sequence;

(2) $D^{(k)}(x, y) \geq \min \{ d(x, y), k\beta \}$;

(3) $D^{(m)}(x, y) = d(x, y)$ for some finite m.

Proof Similar to that of theorem 3.8. □

The above theorems suggest the question of whether the initial distances can be set freely. Denote by DP(free) the modification of DP(∞) in which the initial estimates are set by

$D^{(0)}(x, x) = 0$ all x, and

$D^{(0)}(x, y) =$ any non-negative number if $x \neq y$.

Theorem 3.10 Using algorithm DP(free) for any network with n nodes and $a_{ij} \geq \beta > 0$ for all links ij:

$D^{(m)}(x, y) = d(x, y)$ for some finite m.

Proof If

$\underline{D}^{(k)}(x, y)$ is the value of $D^{(k)}(x, y)$ using algorithm DP(0), and

$\bar{D}^{(k)}(x, y)$ is the value of $D^{(k)}(x, y)$ using algorithm DP(∞),

then it is readily established, via mathematical induction, that

$\underline{D}^{(k)}(x, y) \leq D^{(k)}(x, y) \leq \bar{D}^{(k)}(x, y)$.

The desired result then follows immediately from theorems 3.8, 3.9. □

Example 3.9 Repeat the solution of example 3.8 but this time using algorithm DP(free) with the following matrix of initial distance estimates

$$(D^{(0)}(x, y)) = \begin{bmatrix} 0 & 3 & 6 & 6 & 4 \\ 3 & 0 & 5 & 5 & 6 \\ 6 & 5 & 0 & 1 & 4 \\ 6 & 5 & 3 & 0 & 3 \\ 4 & 6 & 4 & 3 & 0 \end{bmatrix}$$

The updated matrices of distance estimates $(D^{(k)}(x, y))$ for $k = 1, 2$ and 3 are

$$(D^{(1)}(x, y)) = \begin{bmatrix} 0 & 2 & 7 & 7 & 5 \\ 2 & 0 & 3 & 4 & 4 \\ 6 & 3 & 0 & 2 & 5 \\ 7 & 7 & 2 & 0 & 3 \\ 5 & 4 & 6 & 3 & 0 \end{bmatrix}$$

$$(D^{(2)}(x, y)) = \begin{bmatrix} 0 & 2 & 5 & 6 & 5 \\ 2 & 0 & 3 & 5 & 4 \\ 5 & 3 & 0 & 2 & 5 \\ 8 & 5 & 2 & 0 & 3 \\ 5 & 4 & 5 & 3 & 0 \end{bmatrix}$$

$$(D^{(3)}(x, y)) = \begin{bmatrix} 0 & 2 & 5 & 7 & 5 \\ 2 & 0 & 3 & 5 & 4 \\ 5 & 3 & 0 & 2 & 5 \\ 7 & 5 & 2 & 0 & 3 \\ 5 & 4 & 5 & 3 & 0 \end{bmatrix}$$

Notice that many estimates (13 in fact) are nearer their true values after the first iteration but three (for links a-c, b-d and d-b) have become worse.   □

In the above example it was implicitly assumed that updates are performed 'synchronously' for each node and that information exchanges are synchronous. This might not be easy to arrange in practice and might even not be desirable. For the case of asynchronous exchanges Bertsekas and Gallager (1987) make the following assumptions.

Assumption 1. There is a maximum period, τ, between updates at each node and between data exchanges.

Assumption 2. $D^{(0)}(x, y)=0$, for all x and y, at time 0.

Assumption 3. Out of date information is purged.

Assumption 4. The network remains strongly connected.

Theorem 3.11 Under assumptions 1 - 4,

$D^{(k)}(x, y) \rightarrow d(x, y)$ for all x and y as $k \rightarrow \infty$.

Proof See Bertsekas and Gallager (1987).   □

It should be noted that although this result establishes convergence the convergence may be very slow.

Gallager's method

As developed earlier, bifurcated flows could, at least in principle, be used for routing in slowly varying situations in which infrequent updates would suffice. Gallager (1977) put forward a method that would be applicable in more rapidly varying situations. As in section 3.3 the aim is to minimise the total delay

$$\Phi(x) = \Sigma_i \Sigma_j \Phi(x_{ij})$$

$$x_{ij} = \Sigma_r \Sigma_t x_{ij}^{rt}$$

whereas the aim of the adaptive scheme described earlier in this section was that each packet should be sent on a route minimising *that packet's delay*. These aims do not, in general, lead to the same solution even when traffic is constant (cf. exercise 3.6).

Gallager's algorithm is based on the idea that the bifurcation probabilities, p_{ij}^t, should be reduced on links ij which lead to relatively much congestion and reduced on links which lead to relatively little congestion. Specifically, the output probability p_{ij}^t is reduced by a small amount on all but that link ik, say, for which the marginal rate of change of congestion

$$\left[\frac{\partial \Phi}{\partial p_{ij}^t} \right]$$

is smallest; p_{ik}^t is increased by an amount which maintains normalisation $\Sigma_j p_{ij}^t = 1$. The Gallager algorithm is then, in outline,

Algorithm (G)
{Input: an initial loop free set of probabilities $\{p_{ij}^t\}$.
repeat
    begin Adjust probabilities by

$$p_{ij}^t \leftarrow \begin{cases} p_{ij}^t - \Delta_{ij}^t & \text{if } j \neq k \\ p_{ik}^t + \Sigma_{j \neq k} \Delta_{ij}^t & \text{if } j = k \end{cases}$$

    where ik is that outgoing link from node i for which the rate of change in congestion is minimal.
    end

The condition that $\{p_{ij}^t\}$ be 'loop free' means that there is no circuit i-j-k- ... -q-i with $p_{ij}^t > 0$, $p_{jk}^t > 0$, ..., $p_{qi}^t > 0$. This condition is essential for identifying 'downstream' nodes, thus facilitating the calculation of the rates of change in congestion (cf. example 3.10 below).

Increment determination

How is Δ_{ij}^t to be chosen? To answer this, first let T_i^t be the intensity of traffic at node i that is destined for node t. An increment ε in p_{ij}^t leads to an increment εT_i^t in the flow in link ij, and hence a *direct* increase in congestion on link ij of $\varepsilon F_{ij}' = \varepsilon(\partial\Phi/\partial x_{ij})$ (cf. section 3.3). If $j \neq t$ then this extra flow causes an increase in flow at downstream nodes equivalent to an increase of εT_i^t in the demand, D_{jt}, for OD pair (j, t) and hence to an increase of $\varepsilon T_i^t(\partial\Phi/\partial D_{jt})$. Thus

$$\frac{\partial\Phi}{\partial p_{ij}^t} = T_i^t \left(F_{ij}' + \frac{\partial\Phi}{\partial D_{jt}} \right).$$

By a similar argument

$$\frac{\partial\Phi}{\partial D_{jt}} = \sum_k p_{jk}^t \left(F_{ij}' + \frac{\partial\Phi}{\partial D_{kt}} \right).$$

We are now in a position to illustrate the determination of $\partial\Phi/\partial D_{jt}$ and hence $\partial\Phi/\partial p_{ij}^t$.

Example 3.10 Calculate $\partial\Phi/\partial p_{ij}^t$ for the network of figure 3.18 assuming (for simplicity) that

$$p_{ra}^t = 0.6, \quad p_{rb}^t = 0.4, \quad p_{ae}^t = 0.9, \quad p_{at}^t = 0.1, \quad p_{be}^t = 0.2,$$
$$p_{bt}^t = 0.8, \quad p_{et}^t = 1.0.$$

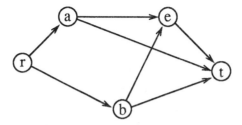

Figure 3.18 Network for example 3.10.

Solution

$$\frac{\partial \Phi}{\partial D_{tt}} = 0$$

$$\frac{\partial \Phi}{\partial D_{et}} = p_{et}^t \left(F_{et}' + \frac{\partial \Phi}{\partial D_{tt}} \right) = F_{et}'$$

$$\frac{\partial \Phi}{\partial D_{at}} = p_{ae}^t \left(F_{ae}' + \frac{\partial \Phi}{\partial D_{et}} \right) + p_{at}^t \left(F_{at}' + \frac{\partial \Phi}{\partial D_{tt}} \right)$$

$$= 0.9F_{ae}' + 0.9F_{et}' + 0.1F_{at}'$$

$$\frac{\partial \Phi}{\partial D_{bt}} = p_{be}^t \left(F_{be}' + \frac{\partial \Phi}{\partial D_{et}} \right) + p_{bt}^t \left(F_{bt}' + \frac{\partial \Phi}{\partial D_{tt}} \right)$$

$$= 0.2F_{be}' + 0.2F_{et}' + 0.8F_{bt}'$$

From these expressions

$$\frac{\partial \Phi}{\partial p_{ra}^t} = T_r^t \left(F_{ra}' + \frac{\partial \Phi}{\partial D_{at}} \right)$$

$$= T_r^t (F_{ra}' + 0.9F_{ae}' + 0.9F_{et}' + 0.1F_{at}').$$

Similarly

$$\frac{\partial \Phi}{\partial p_{rb}^t} = T_r^t (F_{rb}' + 0.2F_{be}' + 0.2F_{et}' + 0.8F_{bt}').$$

The values of F_{ij}' may be obtained by differentiating a theoretical function, such as that associated with an (M/M/1) queue, or by direct estimation. T_r^t may be obtained by monitoring traffic at r destined for t. ☐

The above process clearly generalises as long as the loop free condition is maintained. In the precise formulation of Gallager's algorithm this is indeed the case.

Finally, a reasonable possibility for Δ_{ij}^t would seem to be

$$\Delta_{ij}^t = \min \left\{ p_{ij}^t, \eta \left(\frac{\partial \Phi}{\partial p_{ij}^t} - \frac{\partial \Phi}{\partial p_{ik}^t} \right) \right\}.$$

Here η is merely a tuning parameter that is chosen on the basis of experiment. Gallager (1977) suggests dividing the second term in the minimisation by T_r^t. The reader is referred to Gallager (1977) for details of his method.

3.6 DISCRETE ROUTE ASSIGNMENT

Assigning a single route to each OD pair, or at least to each session, has the advantage of simplicity. However, the routing algorithms of chapter 2 do not explicitly take congestion into account. We now look at an alternative approach which does do this for cases in which demand is fairly steady. The requirement is that a single route for each possible OD pair (r, t) be determined beforehand in such a way that the overall network delay is minimised. For this *Discrete Routing Problem* (or DRP for short) it is convenient to introduce binary variables y_π, where $y_\pi = 1$ if π is the designated route for the OD pair corresponding to the endpoints of π, and is zero otherwise. With the (M/M/1) total delay function DRP may be formulated:

DRP: minimise $\sum_i \sum_j \dfrac{x_{ij}}{c_{ij} - x_{ij}}$

     subject to

$$x_{ij} = \sum_r \sum_t \sum_{\pi \in P_{rt}} \delta_{ij}^\pi y_\pi D_{rt} \quad \text{for all } i \text{ and } j \tag{3.17}$$

$$\sum_{\pi \in P_{rt}} y_\pi = 1 \qquad \text{for all } r \text{ and } t \tag{3.18}$$

$$0 \le x_{ij} \le c_{ij} \qquad \text{for all } i \text{ and } j \tag{3.19}$$

$$y_\pi = \{0, 1\} \qquad \text{for all } \pi \tag{3.20}$$

where P_{rt} is the candidate set of paths that are to be considered for OD pair (r, t) and

$$\delta_{ij}^\pi = \begin{cases} 1 & \text{if } ij \text{ is on } \pi \\ 0 & \text{otherwise.} \end{cases}$$

A general solution method for this problem requires the technique of branch-and-bound, but this is not introduced until section 4.3. Here, a method will be developed which leads to a (good) estimate of the optimal solution value and sometimes the optimal solution itself. It relies on the technique of Lagrangean relaxation which will now be outlined.

Lagrangean relaxation

Consider the general problem of the form

P: minimise φ

     subject to

$$\sum_j a_{ij} x_j \ge b_i, \quad i = 1, \dots, m \tag{3.21}$$

$$x = (x_1, \dots, x_n) \in \Omega.$$

Here the restriction that $x = (x_1, ..., x_n) \in \Omega$ covers all other constraints (equalities, inequalities, integrality, ...) that may be present.

It may happen that without the linear constraints (3.21), P would be (relatively) easy to solve. Accordingly, the associated problem Q_λ where $\lambda = (\lambda_1, ..., \lambda_n)$ and $\lambda_i \geq 0$ for all i, may be formed:

Q_λ: minimise $\{ \varphi - \sum_i \lambda_i (\sum_j a_{ij} x_j - b_i) \}$

   subject to

$$\sum_j a_{ij} x_j \geq b_i, \quad i = 1, ..., m$$
$$x \in \Omega.$$

If $v(R)$ denotes the optimal value of a problem R, then

$$v(Q_\lambda) \leq v(P) \tag{3.22}$$

since $\lambda \geq 0$ and $\sum_j a_{ij} x_j - b_i$ is constrained to be non-negative. If it happens that constraints (3.21) are all satisfied with equality then an optimal solution for P is at hand. On the other hand, when constraints (3.21) are not all satisfied with equality in an optimal solution of Q_λ, then we still have a lower bound $v(Q_\lambda)$ to the optimal solution *value* $v(P)$, and such information can be made use of in a branch-and-bound scheme (cf. section 4.3 for an example).

To solve Q_λ is likely to be just as difficult as solving P since the *'complexifying constraints'* (3.21) are still present. The next step is to relax these to get the problem, P_λ, called the *Lagrangean relaxation* of P (*with respect to constraint set* (3.21)):

P_λ: minimise $\{ \varphi - (\sum_i \lambda_i (\sum_j a_{ij} x_j - b_i)) \}$

   subject to $x \in \Omega.$

Not surprisingly, some multiplier vectors λ are better than others and this suggests an optimisation problem, LD, called the *Lagrangean dual* of P (with respect to the constraint set (3.21)):

LD: maximise$_{\lambda \geq 0} v(P_\lambda)$.

From (3.22) it is evident that, for an optimal solution $\lambda^* \geq 0$,

$$v(LD) = v(P_{\lambda^*}) \leq v(Q_{\lambda^*}) \leq v(P).$$

While the equality of v(LD) and v(P) often holds, there are many cases in which it does not, thus giving rise to a *duality gap* of v(P) - v(LD).

It should be noted that the above development applies to the case when (3.21) is an equality constraint, the only difference being that $\lambda \geq 0$ is no longer necessary.

To see how these ideas might be used in practice, we return to the discrete routing problem DRP.

Applying Lagrangean relaxation to DRP

The approach of Gavish and Hantler (1983) for applying Lagrangean relaxation to DRP will now be described. A perusal of the constraints (3.17) - (3.20) reveals that those of (3.17) are the only ones which involve *both* x and y variables, and so these are designated the complexifying constraints. With regard to the above discussion, Ω is the set of points $z = (x, y)$ which satisfy the constraints (3.18) - (3.20).

Incorporating the complexifying constraints into the objective with multipliers $\theta_{ij} \geq 0$, and letting P$\equiv$DRP and $\lambda \equiv \theta$, gives as the Lagrangean relaxation P_λ,

$$\text{DRP}_\theta: \quad \text{minimise} \sum_i \sum_j \frac{x_{ij}}{c_{ij} - x_{ij}} - \sum_i \sum_j \theta_{ij} \left(x_{ij} - \sum_r \sum_t \sum_{\pi \in P_{rt}} \delta_{ij}^\pi y_\pi D_{rt} \right)$$

subject to

$$\sum_{\pi \in P_{rt}} y_\pi = 1 \qquad \text{for all } r \text{ and } t \qquad (3.23)$$

$$0 \leq x_{ij} \leq c_{ij} \qquad \text{for all } i \text{ and } j \qquad (3.24)$$

$$y_\pi = \{0, 1\}. \qquad \text{for all } \pi \in P_{rt}. \qquad (3.25)$$

The objective φ may be split into two parts $\varphi = \varphi_1$ and φ_2 where

$$\varphi_1 = \sum_i \sum_j \left(\frac{x_{ij}}{c_{ij} - x_{ij}} - \theta_{ij} x_{ij} \right)$$

$$\varphi_2 = \sum_r \sum_t \sum_{\pi \in P_{rt}} a_\pi y_\pi$$

$$a_\pi = \sum_i \sum_j \theta_{ij} \delta_{ij}^\pi D_{rt} \quad \text{for all } \pi \in P_{rt}.$$

Thus the objective *separates* with φ_1 in terms of x_{ij} only and φ_2 in terms of y_π only. Also, the remaining constraints fall into two groups: (3.24) in terms of x_{ij} only and (3.23) and (3.25) in terms of y_π only. Consequently, the optimisation may be carried out independently for the x and

y variables. That is, DRP_θ may be decomposed into problems $DRP_{\theta x}$ and $DRP_{\theta y}$ where

$DRP_{\theta x}$: minimise $\varphi_1 = \sum_i \sum_j \left(\dfrac{x_{ij}}{c_{ij} - x_{ij}} - \theta_{ij} x_{ij} \right)$

subject to $0 \le x_{ij} \le c_{ij}$ for all i and j.

$DRP_{\theta y}$: minimise $\varphi_2 = \sum_r \sum_t \sum_{\pi \in P_{rt}} a_\pi y_\pi$,

subject to

$\sum_{\pi \in P_{rt}} y_\pi = 1$, for all r and t

$y_\pi = \{0,1\}$,   for all π.

These problems solve very simply. $DRP_{\theta x}$ further decomposes into separate problems, Q_{ij}, one for each link ij. Q_{ij} has objective $x_{ij}/(c_{ij} - x_{ij}) - \theta_{ij} x_{ij}$ which is a convex function over the convex region $0 \le x_{ij} \le c_{ij}$ so there is a unique minimal value by theorem 3.6. Differentiating the objective of Q_{ij} yields $c_{ij}/(c_{ij} - x_{ij})^2 - \theta_{ij} = 0$, and hence $DRP_{\theta x}$ is solved by setting $x_{ij} = \hat{x}_{ij} = c_{ij} - \sqrt{(c_{ij}/\theta_{ij})}$ if $c_{ij}\theta_{ij} > 1$ and $x_{ij} = \hat{x}_{ij} = 0$ if not. This may be written otherwise as

$\hat{x}_{ij} = \max \{0, c_{ij} - \sqrt{(c_{ij}/\theta_{ij})}\}$.

Substitution into φ_1 gives

$$v(DRP_{\theta x}) = - \sum_i \sum_j [\max \{0, (\sqrt{(c_{ij}\theta_{ij})} - 1)\}]^2.$$

$DRP_{\theta y}$ also decomposes, this time into problems Q_{rt} with one for each OD pair (r, t). Q_{rt} is solved by selecting the path $\pi \in P_{rt}$ for which a_π is minimal. That is,

$$\hat{y}_\pi = \begin{cases} 1 & \text{if } a_\pi = \min_{\tau \in P_{rt}} \{a_\tau\} \\ 0 & \text{otherwise.} \end{cases}$$

Collecting these results together gives

$$v(DRP_\theta) = - \sum_i \sum_j [\max \{0, (\sqrt{(c_{ij}\theta_{ij})} - 1)\}]^2 + \sum_r \sum_t \min_{\pi \in P_{rt}} \{a_\pi\}. \qquad (3.26)$$

It is thus seen that the Lagrangean relaxation DRP_θ is very easy to solve compared to DRP itself. The question remains however as to how to obtain a 'good' set of multipliers $\{\theta_{ij}\}$. Two general techniques which have been successful on other problems are *dual ascent* and *subgradient optimisation*; these are described further in sections 4.4 and 4.6 respectively.

Here, we will merely look at a particular numerical example.

A numerical problem

Example 3.11 Four nodes $a, ..., d$ are connected in a ring via 10 kbps lines (figure 3.19). Assuming links may reasonably be modelled by (M/M/1) queues, that the traffic demand matrix is

$$\begin{bmatrix} - & 3 & 2 & 1 \\ & - & 2 & 2 \\ & & - & 2 \\ \text{symmetric} & & & - \end{bmatrix}$$

and that packets for each OD pair (t, r) follow the reverse of the path followed by packets for OD pair (r, t), find an optimal discrete routing. Also use (3.26) to obtain a good lower to $v(P)$.

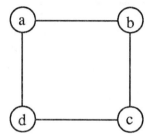

Figure 3.19 Ring network of example 3.11.

Solution Since there are only four feasible solutions the optimal one may be determined quite simply by enumerating all possibilities. It is found to be optimal to route all traffic between a and c along adc (or its reverse) and all traffic between b and d along bad (or its reverse). The value of the optimal solution is 5.833.

For each OD pair there are only two options: go clockwise and go counterclockwise. Based on this observation let

$$P_{ac} = \{abc, adc\}, \qquad P_{bd} = \{bcd, bad\}.$$

Finally, for pairs of adjacent nodes let

$$P_{ab} = \{ab\}, \quad P_{bc} = \{bc\}, \quad P_{cd} = \{cd\}, \quad P_{ad} = \{ad\}.$$

It is easily seen from (3.26) that $v(\text{DRP}_\theta) = 0$ for $\theta = 0$. This is of no help since it is obvious that the optimal solution must have a non-negative value!

Next, observe that increasing the value of θ_{ij} leads to an increase in $v(\mathrm{DRP}_{\theta y})$ but leaves $v(\mathrm{DRP}_{\theta x})$ unchanged as long as $(c_{ij}\theta_{ij}) \leq 1$, that is $\theta_{ij} \leq 1/c_{ij}$. Accordingly, set $\theta_{ij} = 1/c_{ij}$ for all ij giving $\theta = (0.1, 0.1, 0.1, 0.1)$, the components being in units of kbps^{-1}.

Immediately, $\hat{x}_{ij} = 0$ for all ij and $v(\mathrm{DRP}_{\theta x}) = 0$. The value of y_{π} is obtained by solving a shortest path problem in the network of figure 3.20.

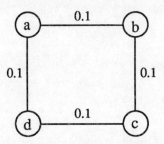

Figure 3.20 The shortest distance problem to find $v(\mathrm{DRP}_{\theta y})$.

For adjacent nodes, packets clearly use the single link between them; for opposite nodes the packets may go clockwise or counterclockwise. Then

$$v(\mathrm{DRP}_{\theta y}) = 2\{3(0.1) + 2(0.2) + 1(0.1) + 2(0.1) + 2(0.2) + 2(0.1)\} = 3.2$$

which is appreciably lower than $v(P) = 5.833$. It may be shown (cf. exercise 3.7) that this is the best that can be achieved if all θ_{ij} are constrained to be equal. If the restriction is removed, however, then the bound can be improved. It may be shown that the best value for θ is $(40/121, 40/169, 40/121, 40/169)$ (cf. exercises 3.8), for which

$$\hat{x}_{ab} = c_{ab} - \sqrt{(c_{ab}/\theta_{ab})} = 10 - \sqrt{(10/(40/121))} = 4.5 \text{ kbps.}$$

Similarly,

$$\hat{x}_{bc} = 3.5 \text{ kbps}, \hat{x}_{cd} = 4.5 \text{ kbps}, \hat{x}_{ad} = 3.5 \text{ kbps},$$

yielding $v(\mathrm{DRP}_{\theta x}) = -324/121 - 196/169$. For $\mathrm{DRP}_{\theta y}$ there is again a choice: y_{abc} or y_{adc} could be set to 1 and similarly for y_{bad} or y_{bcd}. This gives $v(\mathrm{DRP}_{\theta y}) = 720/121 + 560/169$ and hence $v(\mathrm{DRP}_{\theta}) = 396/121 + 364/169 = 5.427$. Since this is the maximal value for $v(\mathrm{DRP}_{\theta})$ there is a *duality gap* of $v(P) - v(\mathrm{DRP}_{\theta}) = 5.833 - 5.427 = 0.406$. $\square$

3.7 EXERCISES

3.1 An (M/M/2) queuing system has two identical servers and a single queue. 'Items' enter at the rear of the queue and are taken from the front of the queue by a server when it becomes free. The arrival pattern is Poisson with mean rate λ arrivals per unit time, and the service process is Poisson with *each* server having mean service rate μ. The state transition diagram is

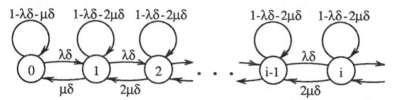

[Note that the rate from ⓪ to ① is only $\mu\delta$ since one server is idle when there is a single item is in the system!]

Let $\pi_i(t)$ be the probability of being in state i (that is, there are i items in the system). Show that, under steady state conditions

$$\pi_1 = \rho\pi_0, \text{ and } \pi_i = \rho\pi_{i-1}/2, \ i = 2, \dots ,$$

where $\rho = \lambda/\mu$. Deduce that $\pi_0 = (2 - \rho)/(2 + \rho)$, that the average number in the system is $L_s = 4\rho/(4 - \rho^2)$ and that the average waiting time is given by $W_s = 4/\mu(4 - \rho^2)$.

3.2 Prove that the sum, $h = f + g$, is convex (concave) if both f and g are convex (concave). What, if anything, can be said of $f - g$?

3.3 Prove that a twice differentiable function, f, of a single variable x is convex if $d^2f/dx^2 \geq 0$ for all x. Is the converse true? Give a corresponding criterion for a twice differentiable function of two variables x and y.

3.4 There are three links from node r to node t as shown in figure 3.21.

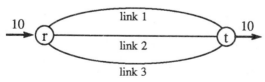

Figure 3.21

10 units of flow per unit time enter the network at r and 10 units of flow per unit time leave the network from t. The costs per unit flow along links 1, 2 and 3 are $10 + x$, $11 + y$ and $9 + 2z$, where x, y and z are the flows per unit time in links 1, 2 and 3 respectively. Consequently, the total cost per unit time is

$$\Phi = (10x + x^2) + (11y + y^2) + (9z + 2z^2).$$

Starting with the initial solution $(x, y, z) = (0, 0, 10)$ perform three iterations of the Frank-Wolfe algorithm. What would be the result if a PARTAN step is performed after the second iteration?

Noting that $z = 10 - x - y$ express Φ in terms of x and y only and hence find an *optimal* solution to this minimal cost flow problem. Draw a graph in x-y space and plot the progress of the above application of the Frank-Wolfe algorithm.

3.5 Apply algorithm DP(0) to the problem of finding all shortest paths in the network of figure 3.17.

3.6 In a road network a road user chooses a route to minimise his or her cost whereas in a computer network routing is under the control of the network and is typically with respect to minimisation of *total* cost. That is, a road user seeks a *user-optimal* solution whereas a computer network is designed with *system-optimality* in mind. To see that these concepts are different consider the network of figure 3.22.

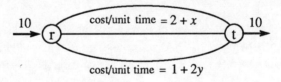

Figure 3.22

The total cost is $\Phi = (2x + x^2) + (y + 2y^2) = 210 - 39x + 3x^2$. Show that system optimality occurs when $x = 6.5$ (hence $y = 3.5$). This is not user-optimal though as the costs *per unit flow* along the two are $2 + x = 8.5$ and $1 + 2y = 8$ respectively. Find a user-optimal solution.

3.7 For the problem of example 3.11, show that $\theta_{ab} = \theta_{bc} = \theta_{cd} = \theta_{ad} = 0.1$ is an optimal set of multipliers if the extra condition that all θ_{ij} must be equal is imposed.

3.8 For example 3.11 it was found that when θ is (40/121, 40/169, 40/121, 40/169)

$$\hat{x}_{ab} = 4.5 \text{ kbps}, \; \hat{x}_{bc} = 3.5 \text{ kbps}, \; \hat{x}_{cd} = 4.5 \text{ kbps}, \; \hat{x}_{ad} = 3.5 \text{ kbps}, \quad (3.27)$$

and there are four solutions, $\hat{y}_1, ..., \hat{y}_4$, for $\hat{y}$ according as y_{abc} or y_{adc} is set to 1 and y_{bad} or y_{bcd} is set to 1. Find a linear combination

$$y^* = \alpha_1 \hat{y}_1 + ... + \alpha_4 \hat{y}_4 \text{ where } \alpha_1, ..., \alpha_4 \geq 0, \; \alpha_1 + ... + \alpha_4 = 1,$$

such that y^* yields the set of link flows of (3.27).

Chapter 4

Local Access Network Design

Attention will now be directed at network design in which it is required to specify the links that are to be established in a computer network and what their capacities should be. As noted in chapter 1, it is convenient to decompose the overall network design problem into two separate sub-problems: (1) the design of the local access networks; (2) the design of the communications subnet. The former problem will be considered first; this is because associated routing strategies are usually trivial since local access networks typically take the form of a tree or a ring.

This chapter opens, in section 4.1, by showing why trees are relevant with regard to local access networks and this is followed by a discussion of multipoint lines, constrained MSTs (Minimal Spanning Trees) and Branch-and-Bound. Concentrator location is dealt with in section 4.4 where the approach of 'dual ascent' is introduced. The important technique of *subgradient optimisation* is described in section 4.6 after a motivating development, in section 4.5, of a similar technique applied to differentiable functions. Capacitated concentrator location problems and design involving backup routes to provide for extra reliability are the subjects of section 4.7.

4.1 MINIMAL SPANNING TREES

For the first design situation to be considered it is assumed that:

(1) links are available in a single capacity only;
(2) capacities of links are such that congestion effects are negligible;
(3) it is required to determine which links are to be installed.

Here the topology is a variable but there is a fixed type of link and routing considerations are not important.

Formally, let $G = (X, E)$ be a connected graph with node set X, and let $\{d_{ij}\}_{ij \in E}$ be a set of strictly positive edge weights; d_{ij} will be termed the 'cost of establishing link ij'. Then it is required to solve the following minimal cost problem (called MSTP for reasons that will become clear later).

MSTP: Find a connected graph (X, F) with $F \subseteq E$

and such that $d(F) = \sum_{ij \in F} d_{ij}$ is minimal.

Although considerations other than cost may well be important when designing a network, it will be assumed for the moment that cost minimisation is paramount.

Theorem 4.1 If $d_{ij} > 0$ for all $ij \in E$ then the links of any optimal solution (X, F) of MSTP must form a tree.

Proof Suppose that an optimal solution (X, F) does not form a tree; then, since it must be a connected graph, it follows that it contains a cycle, γ say. By removing any link pq on γ, a strictly lower cost solution is obtained (since $d_{pq} > 0$). This contradicts the optimality of (X, F), and so the assumption that (X, F) is not a tree must be false. $\square$

Minimal spanning trees

For any connected network $G = (X, E)$ a connected 'subnetwork' (X, F) *spans* G if every node of X lies on at least one link in F. A tree (X, F) that spans G is termed a *spanning tree*. A *minimal spanning tree* (or MST for short) of G, relative to a set of weights $\{d_{ij}\}_{ij \in E}$, is a spanning tree (X, F) of G for which $d(F)$ is minimal.

Theorem 4.1 implies that, with respect to a set of strictly positive weights, MSTP is just the classical problem of finding an MST. This problem is, in fact, computationally very easy, it being solved by the following naive 'greedy' approach. The tree is 'grown' by starting with F empty and adding a least weight link of E to F, then a next least weight link and so on, an optimal solution (that is, an MST) resulting provided only that a potential link is not added to F if it would create a cycle when considered together with links already present. This is the essence of Kruskal's algorithm (Kruskal, 1956), which will now be stated formally.

Algorithm (K)

{Kruskal's algorithm to find an MST, (X, F), of a network (X, E).
 Input: a network (X, E) and a corresponding set of edge weights.}

    Set G_1 to be the graph with node set X and no edges.

    Set $i = 1$.

    while $i < n$ **do**

    begin

        Select a minimal weight edge, uv, in E.

        Discard uv from E (that is, $E \leftarrow E - \{uv\}$).

        If addition of uv to G_i would create a cycle

        then leave G_i as it is

        else add uv to G_i to form G_{i+1} and set $i \leftarrow i+1$.

    end

{Output: G_n is an MST.}

Example 4.1 It is planned to connect five cities by fibre optic cabling. The connections being considered, together with the corresponding lengths in km, are shown in figure 4.1. It is known that the total traffic entering the network will be no more than 1 Mbps (Megabits per second). How should the cities be connected if fibre optic cabling of capacity 10 Mbps is going to be used?

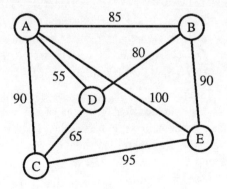

Figure 4.1 It is required to choose links, from among those shown, to connect the five cities at minimal cost.

Solution Since the total traffic is small compared to the capacity of the links to be installed, congestion is not a problem and an MST is sought.

Initially, $E = \{AB, AC, AD, AE, BD, BE, CD, CE\}$, G_1 consists of 5 isolated nodes, and i is 1.

At iteration 1, AD is the shortest link of E. Then AD is removed from E (that is, $E \leftarrow \{AB, AC, -, AE, BD, BE, CD, CE\}$). AD is added to G_1 to form G_2; i is incremented to 2.

At iteration 2, CD is the shortest link still in E; it is removed from E and added to G_2 to form G_3. i becomes 3.

At iteration 3, BD is the shortest link in E; it is removed from E and added to G_3 to form G_4. i becomes 4.

At iteration 4, AB is the shortest link in E. It is removed from E but not added to G_4 as it would create a cycle.

At iteration 5, AC is a shortest link in E. It is removed from E but not added to G_4 as it would create a cycle.

At iteration 6, BE is the shortest link in E; it is removed from E and added to G_4 to form G_5. i becomes 5.

The algorithm now terminates with $E = \{AE, CE\}$ and G_5 the MST (unique in this case). Its total weight is $55 + 65 + 80 + 90 = 290$ km. $\qquad \square$

The validity of algorithm (K) will be established later. It should be noted that Kruskal's algorithm is not the only algorithm for finding MSTs, but it is conceptually the simplest and is computationally competitive under the conditions of use that will be required by this text. [An alternative and *easy to implement* algorithm is that due to Prim (1956).]

Mathematical programming formulation

A *bipartition*, $<R, S>$, of a set X is a pair of sets R and S satisfying

$$R, S \subseteq X; \quad R \cap S = \emptyset; \quad R \cup S = X.$$

A bipartition $<R, S>$ of a set X is *proper* if neither R nor S is empty.

Suppose that all edge weights are strictly positive and that the graph (X, E) is connected. Then the problem MSTP may be formulated as the following mathematical program.

MSTP: minimise $(1/2)\sum_i \sum_j d_{ij} y_{ij}$

    subject to

$$\sum_{i \in R} \sum_{j \in S} y_{ij} \geq 1 \text{ for all proper bipartitions } <R, S> \text{ of } X \qquad (4.1a)$$

$$y_{ij} \in \{0, 1\}, \ y_{ij} = y_{ji} \text{ for all } i, j \in X. \qquad (4.1b)$$

Here, y_{ij} (and y_{ji}) = 1 if link ij is chosen; y_{ij} (and y_{ji}) = 0 otherwise. Note that the factor '1/2' is included in the objective to avoid 'double counting'. To restrict the possible links to a set E, each link $pq \notin E$ is assigned an infinite weight, the minimisation then automatically ensuring that $y_{pq} = 0$; in particular, d_{ii} is always set to infinity. When $d_{ij} > 0$ for all i, j the minimisation also ensures that no redundant links are included. This, together with the connectivity requirement (4.1a), implies that the resulting solution defines an MST.

    Constraint set (4.1a) is less convenient than the following equivalent set:

$$\sum_{i \in R} \sum_{j \in R} y_{ij} \leq 2(|R| - 1) \quad \text{for all } R \subseteq X \text{ with } |R| \geq 2 \qquad (4.2)$$

Theorem 4.2 Let (X, E) be a graph with $n > 1$ nodes and $\{y_{ij}\}$ a set of numbers each taking the value zero or one. Then if $\{y_{ij}\}$

    (a) is an optimal solution of MSTP then it satisfies (4.2),

    (b) satisfies (4.1b) and (4.2) then it also satisfies (4.1a).

Proof First, let $\{y_{ij}\}$ be a feasible solution to MSTP, then (4.2) is true as otherwise the graph would possess a cycle and so not be a tree.

    Conversely, suppose that $\{y_{ij}\}$ satisfies (4.1b) and (4.2). Then, for any proper bipartition $<R, S>$ of X,

$$2(n-1) \leq \sum_{i \in X} \sum_{j \in X} y_{ij} \qquad \qquad \text{by (4.2)}$$

$$= \sum_{i \in R} \sum_{j \in R} y_{ij} + \sum_{i \in R} \sum_{j \in S} y_{ij} +$$

$$\sum_{i \in S} \sum_{j \in R} y_{ij} + \sum_{i \in S} \sum_{j \in S} y_{ij}$$

$$\leq 2(|R| - 1) + 2(|S| - 1) + 2\sum_{i \in R} \sum_{j \in S} y_{ij} \qquad \text{by (4.2), (4.1b)}$$

$$= 2(n-2) + 2\sum_{i \in R} \sum_{j \in S} y_{ij}$$

and (4.1a) follows immediately.   □

Example 4.2 For the data given in example 4.1 use the connectivity constraints to find a lower bound to the weight of an MST.

Solution A lower bound, LB, may be obtained by relaxing constraints (4.2), and incorporating them into the objective with multipliers λ_R. Thus, with P_λ written in place of $MSTP_\lambda$

$$v(P_\lambda) = \min_{y_{ij} \in \{0,1\}} \{1/2 \Sigma_i \Sigma_j \, d_{ij} \, y_{ij} - \Sigma_R \lambda_R (\Sigma_{i \in R} \Sigma_{j \in R} y_{ij} - 2(|R|-1)) \}$$

$$= \Sigma_R 2\lambda_R (|R| - 1) + 1/2 \Sigma_i \Sigma_j \min (d_{ij} - 2 \Sigma_{R|ij \in R} \lambda_R, 0).$$

The Lagrange multipliers are now chosen as indicated by the following table.

R	$2\lambda_R$	$|R|$	$2\,\lambda_R(|R| - 1)$
$\{A, B, C, D, E\}$	55	5	220
$\{B, C, D, E\}$	10	4	30
$\{B, D, E\}$	15	3	30
$\{B, E\}$	10	2	10
			290

Since a feasible solution with weight 290 has been found, this provides an upper bound on the optimal solution value of UB = 290 km and so

$$LB = v(P_\lambda) = 290 \leq \text{value of optimal solution} \leq 290 = UB,$$

and hence the optimal value must be 290 km. That is, the solution found is an MST. □

Theorem 4.3 Algorithm (K) delivers an MST provided the initial graph (X, E) is connected.

Proof (Outline for the case when all the edge lengths are different.) Algorithm (K) clearly yields a spanning tree and hence an upper bound UB. A lower bound LB may be calculated as follows:

STEP 1 Set $R = X$ and μ_R = the length of the shortest link = $d^{(1)}$ say.
(Note that $\mu_R = 2\lambda_R$)
Reduce the lengths of all links by μ_R. Set $i = 2$.

Repeat step 2 for as long as possible.

STEP 2 Select the next unused link, in order of increasing length, which does not give rise to a cycle; let its length be $d^{(i)}$.
Let R be a maximal set whose nodes are not connected by a zero length edge. Reduce lengths of edges between nodes in R by
$\mu_R = d^{(i)} - d^{(i-1)}$. Set $i \leftarrow i+1$.

Now

$$LB = (n-1)\, d^{(1)} + (n-2)(d^{(2)} - d^{(1)}) + \ldots + (1)(d^{(n-1)} - d^{(n-2)}).$$
$$= d^{(1)} + d^{(2)} + \ldots + d^{(n-1)}.$$

The edges, with lengths $d^{(1)}$, $d^{(2)}$, ..., $d^{(n-1)}$, are clearly the edges that make up the tree produced by algorithm (K) and so UB is also equal to $d^{(1)} + d^{(2)} + \ldots + d^{(n-1)}$. The desired result follows immediately.   □

4.2 CENTRALISED NETWORKS

In a local access network, data may be received by a concentrator / multi-plexer from many independent terminals. To have a separate *point-to-point* line for each terminal would be unnecessarily costly and very likely infeasible. An alternative is to make use of *multipoint* lines, each of which may be shared between several terminals (cf. figure 4.2a).

The concepts to be discussed are applicable to any centralised system whether part of a larger system or not. Consequently the central site, whatever it may represent, will here be termed the *primary* node. The peripheral sites will often be termed *secondary nodes*, and may correspond to a single terminal or to several terminals regarded as constituting a single unit.

When a multipoint line is shared by several terminals there is clearly a need for an appropriate discipline to prevent more than one terminal transmitting at any one time. One solution is for a terminal to 'speak only when spoken to'; this is the approach of *polling* in which the primary node requests data from each terminal in turn. If a terminal has data to send when a request is received then it transmits; otherwise, the next terminal in turn is polled straight away. (Note that a problem does not exist with traffic *from* the primary node since all terminals 'listen all the time', and accept only those data destined for them.)

If cost were the only consideration then the MST solution of figure 4.2a would be optimal. However, this solution may be unsatisfactory because

    (1) the combined traffic from all 22 secondary nodes must travel along link 0-1 and may exceed the *capacity* of the type of line to be established;

    (2) the network is very *vulnerable* - if the link 0-1 were to fail then all 22 secondary nodes would be isolated from the primary node.

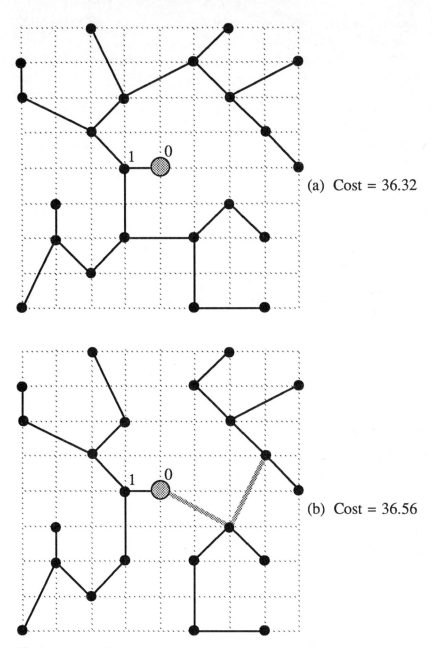

(a) Cost = 36.32

(b) Cost = 36.56

Figure 4.2 In (a) the secondary nodes are connected to the primary node (node 0) via a multipoint line (in the form of an MST) with total cost 36.32, where cost is taken to be the total line length in terms of the side of a small square as unit. (b) shows an alternative way of connecting the secondary nodes at an extra cost of 0.24; the thick shaded lines are the ones not in (a).

The very slightly costlier solution of figure 4.2b may well be preferable to the MST solution of figure 4.2a.

With regard to capacity considerations a problem that has been much considered in the literature is that of minimising the combined cost of the multipoint lines subject to the traffic in any line not exceeding a prescribed limit. (Note that this capacity constraint will tend to decrease vulnerability in general.) This problem will be termed the *Centralised Network Problem* (or CNP) and may be formulated as (cf. section 4.1)

CNP: minimise $(1/2) \sum_i \sum_j c_{ij} y_{ij}$ (4.3)
    subject to

$$\sum_i (y_{ij} + y_{ji}) \geq 2, \quad \text{for all } j \tag{4.4}$$

$$\sum_{i \in R} \sum_{j \in R} y_{ij} \leq 2(|R| - 1), \ R \subseteq \{0, ..., n\}, \ |R| \geq 2 \tag{4.5}$$

No terminal cluster demand can exceed *cap.*   (4.6)

$$y_{ij} \in \{0, 1\}, \ y_{ij} = y_{ji}, \quad \text{for all } i, j \tag{4.7}$$

where

$$y_{ij} = \begin{cases} 1 & \text{if } i \text{ and } j \text{ are linked} \\ 0 & \text{otherwise} \end{cases}$$

c_{ij} = cost of directly linking nodes i and j
Node 0 is the primary node.

It is usual to assume that lines are uniform throughout, in which case c_{ij} is independent of flow. The capacity constraint may be expressed by introducing flow variables x_{ij}. Such an approach was adopted by Gavish (1983). Here we prefer, for the time being, to leave it as it is.

The simplest strategy to adopt is first to solve MSTP (with c_{ij} in place of d_{ij}). If this is acceptable the optimal solution has been found. But if, as is likely to be the case, it is not acceptable then valuable information has still been obtained.

Theorem 4.4 If y^M defines an MST, and $v(y^M)$ is the associated cost, then

(1) $v(y^M)$ is a lower bound to the cost $v(y^*)$ where y^* is any optimal solution of CNP,

(2) there is an optimal solution y^* of CNP for which $y_{0j}^* \geq y_{0j}^M$, $j = 1, ..., n$.

Proof Part (1) is immediate. Part (2) is due to Chandy and Russell (1972). For an MST y^M, let J be the set of nodes adjacent to the primary node; that is, $y^M_{0j} = 1$ for all $j \in J$. For any optimal solution y^o, set $y^* = y^o$. If $y^*_{0j} \geq y^M_{0j}$, $j \in J$, is satisfied the desired result is true; otherwise y^* will successively be modified until it is true, all the while maintaining optimality.

Suppose that for solution y^* line $0i$ is used and let $V(i)$ denote the set of nodes which would be isolated from the primary node if line $0i$ were to fail. $V(i)$ will be called the *cluster* rooted at i (corresponding to solution y^*). If $y^*_{0j} \geq y^M_{0j}$, does not hold for $j \in J$, there is a cluster $V(i)$ and a node $k \in V(i)$, $k \neq i$ for which $y^*_{0k} = 0$ and $y^M_{0k} = 1$. Let π be the unique chain defined by y^* connecting nodes 0 and k. Then, for each link pq on π, $c_{0k} \geq c_{pq}$ (otherwise $0k$ would be in the solution y^* instead of pq). Moreover, $c_{0k} > c_{pq}$ cannot hold for **all** pq on the chain π since otherwise $0k$ could not be in the MST defined by y^M. Suppose uv is the *first* edge on π *from* node k for which $c_{0k} = c_{uv}$. y^* is now modified by setting $y^*_{0k} = 1$ and $y^*_{uv} = 0$ (cf. figure 4.3). Thus one violation of the set of conditions $y^*_{0j} \geq y^M_{0j}$ has been removed. Furthermore, if $uv = 0i$ then $c_{0i} = c_{0k} > c_{pq}$ for all pq on the π other than $0i$ and $0k$. Consequently, $y^M_{0i} = 1$ and no new violations have been introduced; hence the *number* of violations has been reduced by one. Continuing in this way the violations are removed one at a time until y^* satisfies the desired relations. □

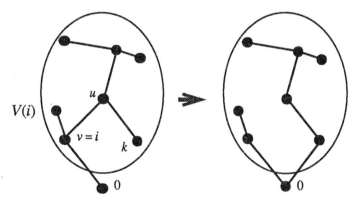

Figure 4.3 The tree on the left corresponds to the solution y^*; the chain π is here just $0iuk$. See text for further description.

A heuristic approach

The approach to be described is due to Esau and Williams (1966) and may be thought of as a 'greedy algorithm' since the best possible decision is made at each stage without regard to later decisions.

Algorithm (EW)
{Esau-Williams clustering algorithm.
  Input: the set of link costs $\{c_{ij}\}$.}
    Set $y_{0j} = y_{j0} = 1$ for $j = 1, ..., n$; $y_{ij} = y_{ji} = 0$ if $i, j \neq 0$;
    Set $C = \{1, ..., n\}$;
    Calculate $S_{ij} = (c_{0i} + c_{0j}) - (c_{ij} + c_{0j}) = c_{0i} - c_{ij}$ for all $i, j \in C$.
    while further merges possible **do**
    begin
        Let i^* and j^* be such that $S_{i^*j^*} = \max\{S_{ij} \mid i \in C, j \in C\}$.
        Add link i^*j^* and remove $0i^*$ provided capacity constraints not
        violated. $C \leftarrow C - \{i^*\}$.
    end
{Output: a set of clusters C_j.}

Example 4.3   A concentrator (node 0) and (groups of) terminals at six separate locations (nodes 1, ..., 6) are situated relative to each other approximately as indicated in figure 4.4. The internode distance matrix is shown alongside, with distances in km. The average traffic intensities associated with terminals 1, ..., 6 are (in bps and including overheads as appropriate) 390, 280, 250, 230, 160 and 350 respectively. 2.4 kbps lines are to be used, but to allow for statistical variation the value of *cap* is set at $0.3 \times 2400 = 720$ bps. Use the Esau-Williams heuristic method to find a low cost layout of lines.

Solution   It may easily be verified that the savings matrix (S_{ij}) is given by

$$(S_{ij}) = \begin{array}{c} \\ 0 \\ 1 \\ 2 \\ 3 \\ 4 \\ 5 \\ 6 \end{array} \begin{array}{c} \begin{array}{ccccccc} 0 & 1 & 2 & 3 & 4 & 5 & 6 \end{array} \\ \left[\begin{array}{ccccccc} - & \cdot & \cdot & \cdot & \cdot & \cdot & \cdot \\ \cdot & - & 6 & 37 & 15 & -7 & -14 \\ \cdot & -26 & - & -11 & 8 & -4 & -27 \\ \cdot & 15 & -1 & - & 13 & -14 & -16 \\ \cdot & -29 & -4 & -9 & - & -17 & -30 \\ \cdot & -47 & -12 & -32 & -13 & - & -2 \\ \cdot & -43 & -24 & -23 & -15 & 9 & - \end{array} \right] \end{array}$$

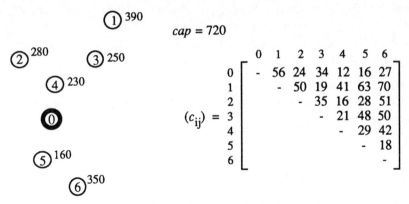

Figure 4.4 Six (groups of) terminals are situated at nodes 1, ..., 6 and are to be connected to the concentrator (node 0) by multipoint lines. The terminal demands are shown beside the nodes.

Initially, all nodes are connected directly via their own lines to node 0. The largest saving is $S_{13} = 37$. Link 1-3 is added to the network and 0-1 dropped to give a solution of value 169 - 37 = 132.

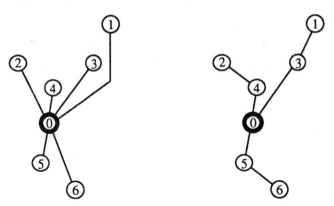

Figure 4.5 The figure on the left shows the initial network for example 4.3; the one on the right shows the network after the application of algorithm (EW).

Node 1 is now removed from C. The next best available saving is S_{14} but its addition would violate the capacity constraint. [Note that $S_{31} = 15$ but $1 \notin C$ and so is not admissible.] Similarly, link 3-4 is not added. The next best saving is $S_{65} = 9$. Add link 6-5, remove link 0-6 and remove node 6 from C.

Finally, $S_{24} > 0$ is the largest saving; link 2-4 is added, 0-2 removed and node 2 removed from C. No further merging is possible and the solution in figure 4.5 is obtained. It happens to be the optimal solution, but this is only known from other considerations (cf. section 4.3). Generally, the method is approximate though it tends to give reasonably good solutions.   □

A method similar to that of Esau and Williams is due to Clarke and Wright (1963) and is mentioned by Chou (1985) in relation to interconnecting rings.

4.3 CENTRALISED NETWORKS (B&B)

The usefulness of Theorem 4.4 is twofold in that given an MST:
- (1) the lower bound provided can be used to speed up the search for an optimal solution to CNP;
- (2) the links to the primary node in the MST can be used as a starting point for building an optimal solution.

Example 4.4 For the data of example 4.3 (reproduced in figure 4.6), find a minimum cost layout of lines.

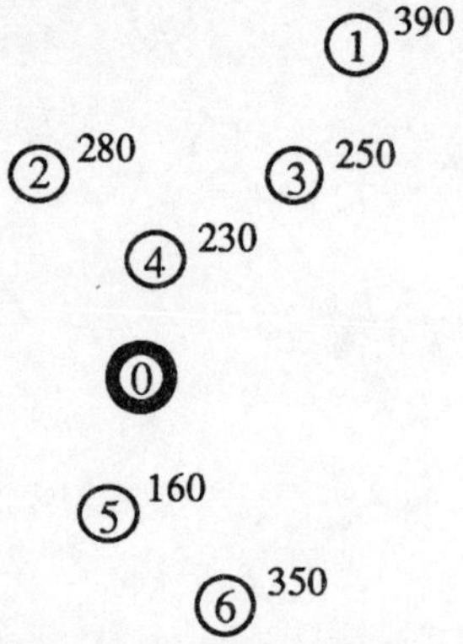

$①^{390}$ $cap = 720$

$②^{280}$ $③^{250}$
$④^{230}$
$⓪$
$⑤^{160}$
$⑥^{350}$

	0	1	2	3	4	5	6
0	-	56	24	34	12	16	27
1		-	50	19	41	63	70
2			-	35	16	28	51
3				-	21	48	50
4					-	29	42
5						-	18
6							-

Figure 4.6 Six (groups of) terminals are situated at nodes 1, ..., 6 and are to be connected to the concentrator at node 0 by multipoint lines. The terminal demands are shown beside the nodes. The internode distance matrix is shown on the right.

Solution The unique MST is shown in figure 4.7a; it employs two multipoint lines. From theorem 4.4 it may be asserted that the value, v^*, of the optimal solution to CNP for the given data, must satisfy

$$102 \le v^* \tag{4.8}$$

The theorem also permits the problem to be narrowed down by considering only those solutions of CNP which contain links 0-4 and 0-5. However the capacity constraint is violated for the MST solution by the line serving cluster $V(4) = \{1, 2, 3, 4\}$ since the combined traffic requirement is $390 + 280 + 250 + 230 = 1150$ bps (well in excess of the 720 bps maximum). In fact, for similar reasons, nodes 2, 3 and 4 could not be in the same cluster in any feasible solution. Consequently, as link 0-4 is constrained to be in the solution, it follows that 2-4 and 3-4 cannot both be present. Focusing on link 3-4, the set of all solutions, S_0, is partitioned into two subsets S_1 and S_2 where

S_1 comprises solutions **not** containing link 3-4
S_2 comprises solutions containing link 3-4.

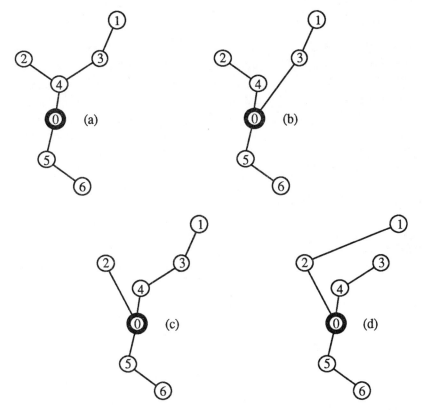

Figure 4.7 Diagrams (a) - (c) correspond respectively to the optimal solutions in the sets S_0, S_1, S_2 and S_3. See figure 4.8

The problem of finding an optimal solution in S_1 is the same as the original problem, except that c_{34} is set to infinity so that 3-4 is automatically excluded. The corresponding MST is shown in figure 4.7b. Its cost is 115 and, as it is feasible for CNP, it provides an *upper bound* on the optimal solution value. Thus

$$v^* \leq 115 \tag{4.9}$$

which together with (4.8) implies that

$$102 \leq v^* \leq 115.$$

For set S_2, link 3-4 is included, but since we know that this precludes link 2-4, c_{24} is set to infinity. The corresponding MST is shown in figure 4.7c. Its value is 110 but it is not feasible. As any solution better than that of figure 4.7b would have to belong to S_2 it follows that 110 $\leq v^*$ and hence by (4.9)

$$110 \leq v^* \leq 115.$$

Since nodes 1, 3 and 4 cannot be in the same cluster in any feasible solution and links 0-4 and 3-4 are constrained to be in all solutions so S_2 is split into S_3 and $S_4 = S_2 - S_3$ where S_3 is defined by the exclusion of both 1-3 and 1-4. For S_3, the MST is shown in figure 4.7d; its value is 141, and even though feasible, it is clearly of no use. S_4 contains no feasible solutions and hence it may now be asserted that S_0 does not contain any solution with value less than 115 so that $115 \leq v^*$, and this together with (4.9) implies that the solution of figure 4.7b is indeed optimal. $\qquad \square$

The solution method used above is a simple example of a technique known as *Branch-and-Bound* (or B&B for short). The course of the solution is illustrated by the *search tree* of figure 4.8, which shows how the set of solutions is successively split.

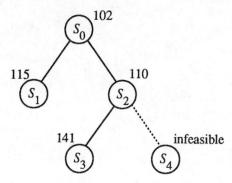

Figure 4.8 The search tree for the B&B solution of example 4.4.

Branch-and-Bound (B&B)

B&B may be described as a tree search algorithm. Let F be the set of feasible solutions for a given problem and $C \supseteq F$ some 'convenient' set of *candidate* solutions. Assuming, for simplicity, that C is finite, then all individual elements of C may be obtained (at least in principle) by successively partitioning C into smaller and smaller subsets provided that all partitions are proper. A *proper* partition of a set X is a collection $\{A_1, ..., A_p\}$ satisfying

$$X = A_1 \cup A_2 \cup ... \cup A_p, \text{ where } p > 1$$
$$A_i \cap A_j = \varnothing, \quad \text{for all } i \neq j$$
$$A_i \neq \varnothing, \quad \text{for } i = 1, ..., p.$$

This partitioning may be represented by a tree (as in figure 4.8) in which each subset, S with $|S| > 1$, is represented by a node and there is an edge from node S to node T if T belongs to the partition of S. Because of this tree analogy, the process of partitioning is called *branching*.

Example 4.5 Three large files are to be allocated to processors at three sites, one to each site. The volume of 'requests' to file i, $i = 1, 2, 3$ from site j, $j = 1, 2, 3$ is r_{ij}. Since *remote* requests necessitate communication between sites it is required to minimise $\sum_i \sum_j r_{ij}(1 - x_{ij})$ where

$$x_{ij} = \begin{cases} 1 & \text{if file } i \text{ is located at site } j \\ 0 & \text{otherwise.} \end{cases}$$

Solution Since the total activity $\sum_i \sum_j r_{ij}$ is a constant, $\sum_i \sum_j r_{ij} x_{ij}$ may equivalently be maximised, and so the problem is seen to be an example of the classical *Linear Assignment Problem* (cf. Christofides, 1975). Two points should be noted.

(1) This is a relatively crude model for file placement about which more is said in chapter 6.

(2) The Linear Assignment Problem is being used here merely for purposes of illustration; much more efficient solution methods are available (Christofides, 1975; Lawler, 1976).

Now define the sets F and C by

$$F = \{ (i, j, k) \mid i, j, k \in \{1, 2, 3\} \text{ and are distinct} \}$$
$$C = \{ (i, j, k) \mid i, j, k \in \{1, 2, 3\} \}.$$

F is seen to have $3\times2\times1 = 6$ elements whereas C has $3\times3\times3 = 27$ elements; that is, C contains 21 infeasible solutions. Initially, at level 0 (cf. figure 4.9) there is just one node corresponding to the set of all candidate solutions C. At the first branching, the set of all candidate solutions, C, is split into three subsets according as file 1 is allocated to site 1, 2 or 3 (thus generating level 1 of figure 4.9). At the next branching (to generate level 2 in figure 4.9) subsets are obtained by allocating file 2 to site 1, 2 or 3. The resulting tree is a *complete enumeration tree* since every feasible solution is represented by a unique 'terminal' node of the tree.

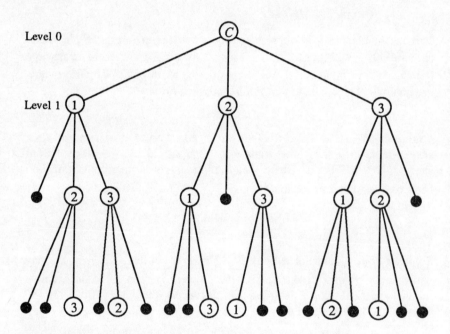

Figure 4.9 A complete enumeration tree for the problem of example 4.5. At level i, ⓙ is the subset obtained by allocating file i to site j. The solid circles indicate nodes whose corresponding solution set contains infeasible solutions only.

Notice that allocating both file 1 *and* file 2 to site 1 leads to infeasible solutions only. This is indicated in figure 4.9 by the leftmost solid circle at level 2. Such subsets, which contain only infeasible solutions, obviously need not be considered further and so are not branched from.   □

Reducing a complete enumeration tree merely by means of feasibility checks is only cutting out subsets of the set $C - F$; when $C = F$ there is no reduction at all. However, the second main feature of B&B, namely *bounding*, permits further (and often *very* substantial) saving in computational effort.

Assume that the problem under consideration is a minimisation one and suppose that, perhaps while generating the tree, a feasible solution, $\hat{x}$, is found. Then any solution whose objective value is worse than that of $\hat{x}$ cannot be optimal. This can be extended to any subset X of C. Let lb be a function from the set of subsets of C to the set of real numbers ($lb: 2^C \rightarrow \Re$) satisfying $lb(X) \leq f(x)$ for all $x \in X \cap F$. If $lb(X) > f(\hat{x})$ then

$$f(\hat{x}) < lb(X) \leq f(x) \text{ for all } x \in X \cap F \tag{4.10}$$

and so X cannot contain an optimal solution and may be eliminated; such elimination is termed *fathoming*. (Note that it is conventional to set $f(x) = \infty$ if $x \in C - F$.) If only *one* optimal solution is required, even though several may exist, then it suffices to replace the condition leading to the first inequality in (4.10) by $f(\hat{x}) \leq lb(X)$. Finally, for maximis - ation problems, *upper bounds* are relevant.

This covers the basic ideas of B&B but various extensions and variations are possible. A formal treatment of B&B is given in McKeown et al. (1991).

More on constrained minimal spanning trees

Now, it may be seen that the extent to which whole subsets of solutions are eliminated from consideration by fathoming is dependent on the quality or 'tightness' of the lower bounds and also on the upper bound as given by the value of the best solution to date (called the *incumbent* solution). In fact, practical experience has established the general principle that, with respect to overall computational effort, it is better to devote relatively more effort to generating good bounds so as to obtain relatively small search trees. The bounding rule, based on MSTs, that was used in example 4.4 is much too weak and it is only feasible to solve very small problems exactly in this way, even when using a powerful computer. A more sophisticated, Lagrangean relaxation approach due to Gavish (1985) will now be described.

The starting point is the formulation (4.3) - (4.7). Thus far, the capacity constraint (4.6) has been relaxed completely leaving an MST problem. This is now bettered somewhat, by replacing the capacity constraint by the condition

$$(1/2)\Sigma_j (y_{0j} + y_{j0}) \geq \lceil \Sigma_j t_j / cap \rceil = N_c \qquad (4.6^*)$$

where '$\lceil \ \rceil$' denotes rounding up to the nearest integer. This constraint states that at least N_c multipoint lines will be required. Certainly (4.6) implies (4.6*) but the converse is not generally true as will be seen shortly. The next step is to take constraint (4.6*) into the objective with multiplier $\lambda \geq 0$ to get

$$\min [(1/2)\Sigma_i \Sigma_j c_{ij} y_{ij} + \lambda(N_c - (1/2)\Sigma_j (y_{0j} + y_{j0}))]$$
$$= \lambda N_c + (1/2)\min \Sigma_i \Sigma_j c_{ij}^* y_{ij}$$

subject to

$$\Sigma_{i \in R} \Sigma_{j \in R} y_{ij} \leq 2(|R| - 1), \quad \text{for all } |R| \geq 2, \ R \subseteq \{0, ..., n\}$$

$$y_{ij} \geq 0, \quad y_{ij} = y_{ji} \quad \text{for all } i \text{ and } j.$$

This is just another MSTP but now with cost coefficients

$$c_{ji}^* = c_{ij}^* = c_{ij} - \lambda, \qquad \text{if } i = 0, j \neq 0$$
$$c_{ji}^* = c_{ij}^* = c_{ij}, \qquad \text{if } i, j \neq 0, \ j \neq i.$$

Example 4.6 For the problem of examples 4.3 and 4.4 obtain an improved initial lower bound using the revised formulation above.

Solution The bound obtained will clearly depend on the value of λ. For $\lambda = 0$, it will be 102 exactly as in example 4.4. Consider now what happens as λ increases slightly, to $\varepsilon > 0$ say. The MST will stay the same but the weights of the links 0-4 (and 4-0) and 0-5 (and 5-0) are 'reduced' to $12 - \varepsilon$ and $16 - \varepsilon$ respectively; the overall cost of the MST is thus reduced by 2ε. On the other hand, $\lambda N_c = 3\varepsilon$ is added to the objective leading to a net gain of ε.

Clearly the objective cannot be increased indefinitely in this way; at what point then does it cease to increase as ε increases? The answer is that as soon as the links incident to node 0 are reduced in weight sufficiently for three (or more) links to be in an MST, for then any extra reduction in MST value would be at least 3ε, offsetting the gain in λN_c which would be 3ε.

A little experimentation quickly shows that at $\lambda = 8$ there are two alternative MSTs as shown in figure 4.10. The initial lower bound has been raised to 110 which is considerably better than the previous 102.   □

The combined requirement of nodes 1, 3 and 4 is 390 + 250 + 230 = 870 bps, exceeding the specified limit of 720 bps. Hence there must be at least two links from the set $R = \{1, 3, 4\}$ to accommodate the desired traffic. That is,

$$(1/2)\Sigma_{i \notin R}\Sigma_{j \in R}(y_{ij} + y_{ji}) \geq \lceil \Sigma_{j \in R} t_j / cap \rceil = N_R \qquad (4.6^{**})$$

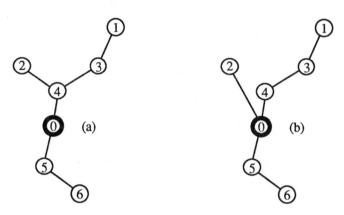

Figure 4.10 Two alternative MSTs both of weight 110.

Moreover (4.6^{**}) must hold for all subsets $R \subseteq \{1, ..., n\}$ with $|R| \geq 2$, and this set of constraints could be added to the formulation (4.3) - (4.7). However, this represents a very large number of constraints (more precisely $2^n - n - 1$), many of which will be satisfied automatically. A better strategy is to add constraints from this set *only as they are needed*. (This is termed *constraint generation*.)

Example 4.7 Continue the calculation of example 4.6 adding just the extra constraint of form (4.6^{**}) with $R = \{1, 3, 4\}$.
Solution The cluster $\{1, 3, 4\}$ was found to violate the capacity constraint and so the constraint

$$\Sigma_{i \notin R} \Sigma_{j \in R} (y_{ij} + y_{ji}) \geq 2$$

is generated and added to the formulation. This constraint is relaxed and incorporated into the objective with multiplier λ_R giving as the new objective

$$N_R + (1/2)\min \Sigma_i \Sigma_j c_{ij}^0 y_{ij}$$

with cost coefficients

$$c^o_{ji} = c^o_{ij} = c^*_{ij} - \lambda_R \qquad \text{if } i \in R, j \notin R$$

$$c^o_{ji} = c^o_{ij} = c^*_{ij} \qquad \text{otherwise.}$$

This has the effect of adding $\lambda_R N_R = 2N_R$ to the objective, the MST with calculations being made using the modified cost matrix

$$(c^o_{ij}) = \begin{bmatrix} - & 48-\lambda_R & 16 & 26-\lambda_R & 4-\lambda_R & 8 & 19 \\ & - & 50-\lambda_R & 19 & 41 & 63-\lambda_R & 70-\lambda_R \\ & & - & 35-\lambda_R & 16-\lambda_R & 28 & 51 \\ & & & - & 21 & 48-\lambda_R & 50-\lambda_R \\ & \text{symmetric} & & & - & 29-\lambda_R & 42-\lambda_R \\ & & & & & - & 18 \\ & & & & & & - \end{bmatrix}$$

obtained by reducing the weights of links between nodes 1, 3, 4 and nodes 0, 2, 5 and 6 by λ_R each. The new MST is shown in figure 4.10 and is seen to be the optimal solution to CNP since the associated lower bound is 115.   ☐

Before leaving this problem it is worth making some general points. First, branching has been avoided altogether using this *augmented Lagrangean* approach in which the formulation is augmented by appropriate constraints which are then incorporated into the objective in the usual way. However, more effort has been expended in obtaining an improved bound. This is a general feature, in that the effort of developing the B&B search tree can be reduced by putting more effort into generating stronger bounds. Moreover, the trade-off is such that it is generally more efficient in terms of overall computational effort to do this.

Secondly, the constraints (4.6**) are not always the tightest possible. For example, suppose that *cap* = 720 bps and that there are three nodes *a*, *b* and *c* each with requirement 450 bps. Then, letting $R = \{a, b, c\}$,

$$N_R = \lceil 3 \times 450 / 720 \rceil = \lceil 1350 / 720 \rceil = 2.$$

However, to use only two lines would require *two* of the nodes to be assigned to one of the lines thus violating the capacity constraint since $2 \times 450 = 900 > 720$. To overcome this deficiency, Gavish (1985) replaced

N_R by $\hat{N}_R$ where $\hat{N}_R$ is the least number of lines that would accommodate the demand $\sum_{j \in R} t_j$; such problems are called *packing problems*. Since $\hat{N}_R \geq N_R$, tighter constraints will result in general.

4.4 CONCENTRATOR LOCATION: A DUAL ASCENT ALGORITHM

It has been seen how it can be cost effective to serve a cluster of terminals using a single multipoint line. Consider now, the case of a system with a very large number of terminals spread over a wide area. Exclusive use of a multipoint line would imply a substantial proportion of lines serving clusters all of whose terminals are relatively remote (cf. figure 4.11). Each remote cluster could be approximated by a single 'superterminal' (or secondary node) at the centre of the cluster, and with traffic demand equal to the sum of the demands of the constituent terminals. In this model the secondary nodes are connected to a primary node via point-to-point lines. This is just the situation that was encountered before in a different guise, suggesting the possibility of grouping clusters into superclusters. A higher capacity line is of course required to serve a supercluster, implying a need for some form of multiplexor or concentrator (cf. figure 4.11b)). From now on, in this and subsequent sections, the term 'concentrator' is used to cover both these possibilities. Of course the cost of a concentrator, as well as the extra cost of the higher capacity lines, has to be taken into account, raising the following question. Where should concentrators be sited, to which terminals (or secondary nodes) should they be connected, and what should their sizes be?

Clustering

In the following, w_{max} is the maximum number of terminals that can share a multipoint line and d_{max} is a maximum distance parameter. The algorithm below is based on the paper of McGregor & Shen (1977).

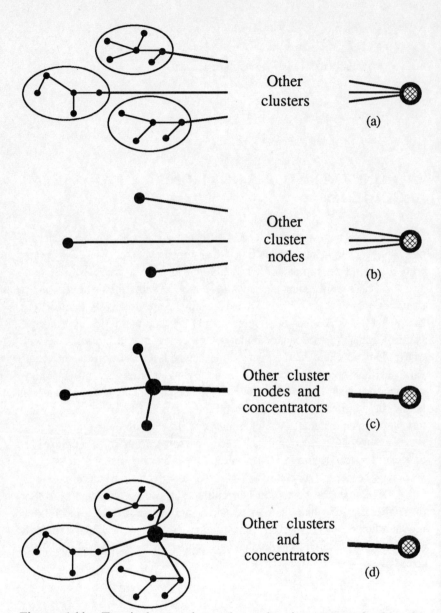

Figure 4.11 Terminals are clustered together into groups in (a) with each group being represented by a cluster node in (b). These are then connected to concentrators in (c). (d) shows the complete arrangement.

Algorithm (MGS)

{The McGregor-Shen clustering algorithm.

Input: $d_{max} > 0$, $w_{max} > 0$, and set of internode distances $\{d_{ij}\}$.}

Set $w_i = 1$ and $C_i = \{i\}$, $i = 1, ..., n$.

Set $CAND = \{(i, j) \mid d_{ij} = \min_{t \neq i} d_{it} \ \& \ d_{ij} \leq d_{max}\}$

while $CAND \neq \emptyset$ **do**

begin Select pair $(i, j) \in CAND$ for which d_{ij} is minimal.

Remove (i, j) from $CAND$, and also any pair (j, k) present.

If $w_i + w_j \leq w_{max}$

then reposition i at the centre of mass of i and j, and

set $w_i \leftarrow w_i + w_j$, $w_j \leftarrow \infty$, $C_i \leftarrow C_i \cup C_j$, $C_j \leftarrow \emptyset$;

recalculate d_{ri} for $r \in \{t \mid (t, i) \in CAND$ or $(t, j) \in CAND\}$

end

{Output: Each $C_i \neq \emptyset$ is a cluster containing no more than w_{max} terminals and satisfying the distance constraint implied by d_{max}.}

This procedure could be generalised quite straightforwardly by letting w_i be the average traffic generated by terminal i and w_{max} the maximum permitted in total.

McGregor & Shen (1977) first cluster terminals using the above approach, then approximate each cluster by a single node at the centre of mass.

Example 4.8 Twelve terminals are situated as shown in figure 4.12, the underlying grid indicating distances. Apply algorithm (MGS) with $d_{max} = 2.5$ and $w_{max} = 3$.

Solution First nodes 3 and 5 are combined, then the resulting node combined with node 6. [Note that an alternative is to group nodes 5 and 6 first.] Now the node forms a cluster since there are already $3 = w_{max}$ terminals in it. Other clusters are built up in a similar way. The final solution is shown in figure 4.12; there are five clusters even though, potentially, $12/3 = 4$ would have sufficed. ☐

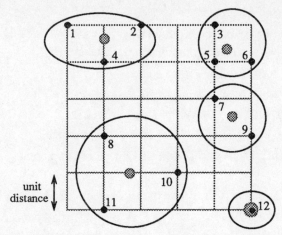

Figure 4.12 Clustering of nodes by algorithm (MGS) with cluster centres given by grey circles. Note that node 12 and its associated cluster centre coincide.

Mathematical formulation

The question of where best to locate concentrators will now be addressed. In what follows in this section, the word 'terminal' will be used to mean either a single physical terminal or a cluster such as might be obtained by using algorithm (MGS).

It will be assumed that a set of terminal locations, T, is given and a finite set, C, of potential concentrator sites specified. Also, initially it will be supposed that concentrators have sufficient capacity for capacity constraints not to be relevant; this restriction is relaxed in section 4.7.

The *(uncapacitated) Concentrator Location Problem* may now be formulated as

SLP: minimise $\sum_i \sum_j c_{ij} x_{ij} + \sum_i g_i y_i$
         subject to

$$\sum_i x_{ij} = 1 \qquad \text{for all } j \qquad (4.11)$$

$$x_{ij} \leq y_i \qquad \text{for all } i \text{ and } j \qquad (4.12)$$

$$x_{ij}, y_i \in \{0, 1\} \qquad \text{for all } i \text{ and } j \qquad (4.13)$$

where

$$x_{ij} = \begin{cases} 1 & \text{if terminal at } j \text{ is connected to a concentrator at } i \\ 0 & \text{otherwise.} \end{cases}$$

$$y_i = \begin{cases} 1 & \text{if there is a concentrator located at } i \\ 0 & \text{otherwise.} \end{cases}$$

c_{ij} = cost of connecting a terminal at j to a concentrator at i.

g_i = cost of establishing a concentrator at i (including cost of trunk line to primary node).

Constraint (4.11) requires that each terminal must be connected to some potential concentrator site, and constraints (4.12) permit such a connection only when a concentrator is actually established there.

This problem has been designated 'SLP' as it is abstractly identical to the *Simple Location Problem* that has received much attention in the Operations Research literature (eg. Erlenkotter, 1978, Korkel, 1989).

Now, incorporating constraints (4.11) and (4.12) into the objective with multipliers λ_j and $\mu_{ij} \geq 0$ gives the Lagrangean relaxation

$\text{SLP}_{\lambda, \mu}$:   minimise $\{ \Sigma_i \Sigma_j c_{ij} x_{ij} + \Sigma_i g_i y_i$

$$- \Sigma_j \lambda_j (\Sigma_i x_{ij} - 1) - \Sigma_i \Sigma_j \mu_{ij} (y_i - x_{ij})$$

subject to

$$x_{ij}, y_i \in \{0, 1\} \quad \text{for all } i \text{ and } j.$$

Rearranging,

$$v(\text{SLP}_{\lambda, \mu}) = \Sigma_j \lambda_j + \min_{x_{ij} \in \{0,1\}} \Sigma_i \Sigma_j (c_{ij} - \lambda_j + \mu_{ij}) x_{ij}$$

$$+ \min_{y_{ij} \in \{0,1\}} \Sigma_i (g_i - \Sigma_j \mu_{ij}) y_i.$$

This solves trivially to give

$$v(\text{SLP}_{\lambda, \mu}) = \Sigma_j \lambda_j + \Sigma_i \Sigma_j \min(0, c_{ij} - \lambda_j + \mu_{ij})$$

$$+ \Sigma_i \Sigma_j \min(0, g_i - \Sigma_j \mu_{ij}). \qquad (4.14)$$

An equivalence

Results will now be established showing that the search for good multiplier vectors may be restricted to a well defined region of λ - μ space.

Theorem 4.5 There are multipliers λ_j and $\mu_{ij} \geq 0$ maximising $v(\text{SLP}_{\lambda, \mu})$ and such that $\Sigma_j \mu_{ij} \leq g_i$ for all i.

Proof Suppose, for a particular index k, that $\sum_j \mu_{kj} = g_k + \varepsilon$, where $\varepsilon > 0$. Now let

$$\lambda_j^* = \lambda_j, \text{ for all } j; \quad (\mu_{ij}^* = \mu_{ij}, \text{ all } i \neq k, \text{ and } \mu_{kj}^* = \gamma \mu_{kj}) \text{ for all } j.$$

where $\gamma = g_k/(g_k + \varepsilon)$. The only terms of $v(\text{SLP}_{\lambda, \mu})$ affected by replacing (λ, μ) by (λ^*, μ^*) are those involving x_{kj} or y_k. Consequently, writing 'P' in place of 'SLP' for conciseness,

$$\Delta = v(P_{\lambda^*, \mu^*}) - v(P_{\lambda, \mu})$$

$$= [\sum_j \min(0, c_{kj} - \lambda_k^* + \mu_{kj}^*) - \sum_j \min(0, c_{kj} - \lambda_k + \mu_{kj})]$$

$$+ [\min(0, g_k - \sum_j \mu_{kj}^*) - \min(0, g_k - \sum_j \mu_{kj})].$$

Now,

$$\min(0, c_{kj} - \lambda_k^* + \mu_{kj}^*) = \min(0, c_{kj} - \lambda_k + \mu_{kj} - (1-\gamma)\mu_{kj})$$

$$\geq \min(0, c_{kj} - \lambda_k + \mu_{kj}) - (1-\gamma)\mu_{kj}.$$

and

$$\min(0, g_k - \sum_j \mu_{kj}^*) - \min(0, g_k - \sum_j \mu_{kj}) = \varepsilon.$$

Consequently,

$$\Delta \geq -(1-\gamma)\sum_j \mu_{kj} + \varepsilon = -(1 - g_k/(g_k+\varepsilon))(g_k+\varepsilon) + \varepsilon = -\varepsilon + \varepsilon = 0$$

and so $v(P_{\lambda^*, \mu^*}) \geq v(P_{\lambda, \mu})$; that is, to any solution one can be found which is at least as good and satisfies $\sum_j \mu_{ij} \leq g_i$ for all i. $\square$

Theorem 4.6 There are multipliers λ_j and $\mu_{ij} \geq 0$ maximising $v(\text{SLP}_{\lambda, \mu})$ and such that $c_{ij} - \lambda_j + \mu_{ij} \geq 0$ for all i and all j.

Proof Suppose there exist indexes k and l such that $c_{kl} - \lambda_k + \mu_{kl} = -\varepsilon < 0$ and let $\lambda_j^* = \lambda_j$ for all $j \neq k$, $\lambda_k^* = \lambda_k - \varepsilon$ and $\mu_{ij}^* = \mu_{ij}$ for all i and j; then

$$v(P_{\lambda^*, \mu^*}) - v(P_{\lambda, \mu}) = (\lambda_k^* - \lambda_k) + [\min(0, c_{kl} - \lambda_k^* + \mu_{kl}^*)$$

$$- \min(0, c_{kl} - \lambda_k + \mu_{kl})]$$

$$= -\varepsilon + [(0) - (-\varepsilon)] = 0. \qquad \square$$

From theorems 4.5 and 4.6 it follows that the constraints $\sum_j \mu_{ij} \leq g_i$ and $c_{ij} - \lambda_j + \mu_{ij} \geq 0$ may be added to the Lagrangean dual

LD: $\max_{\lambda \geq 0} v(P_{\lambda, \mu})$

to get

D: max $\sum_j \lambda_j$ (4.15)

    subject to

$$\sum_j \mu_{ij} \leq g_i, \quad \text{for all } i \tag{4.16}$$

$$\lambda_j \leq c_{ij} + \mu_{ij}, \quad \text{for all } i \text{ and } j \tag{4.17}$$

$$\lambda_j, \mu_{ij} \geq 0, \quad \text{for all } i \text{ and } j. \tag{4.18}$$

But this is just the linear programming dual of the original problem SLP with the integrality constraint relaxed to $x_{ij}, y_i \geq 0$ (cf. appendix B). This is not a coincidence but is an example of the *Integrality Property*. Before presenting the formal result it is necessary to establish some notation. P will denote the problem

P: minimise φ
    subject to

$$\sum_j a_{ij} x_j \geq b_i, \quad i = 1, ..., m$$

$$x = (x_1, ..., x_n) \in \Omega.$$

where Ω embodies linear and integrality constraints only, and $\bar{P}$ denotes the problem resulting from P when all integrality constraints are relaxed. $\bar{P}$ is a linear program and possesses a dual problem D. P_θ denotes the Lagrangean relaxation

P_θ: minimise $\varphi - \sum_i \theta_i (\sum_j a_{ij} x_j - b_i)$
    subject to

$$x = (x_1, ..., x_n) \in \Omega.$$

and $\bar{P}_\theta$ the problem P_θ with all integrality constraints relaxed. Finally LD denotes the Lagrangean dual

LD: $\max_{\theta \geq 0} v(P_\theta)$.

Theorem 4.7 (Integrality Property) If $v(P_\theta) = v(\bar{P}_\theta)$ for all $\theta \geq 0$ then $v(LD) = v(D)$.
Proof Geoffrion (1974).   □

The essence of this is that if the Integrality Property $(v(P_\theta) = v(\bar{P}_\theta)$

for all $\theta \geq 0$) holds then nothing more can be gained, in terms of optimal value, by solving the Lagrangean dual as opposed to the ordinary dual of the linear programming relaxation of P. It may, however, be convenient to work with the Lagrangean dual for other reasons.

Dual ascent

Since the problem D is a maximisation problem, the value of $v(P_{\lambda, \mu})$ for any $\lambda, \mu \geq 0$ must satisfy

$$v(P_{\lambda, \mu}) \leq v(LD) = \max{}_{\alpha \geq 0, \beta \geq 0} v(P_{\alpha, \beta}).$$

Thus, a lower bound to $v(SLP)$ is obtained by taking $v(P_{\lambda, \mu})$. A promising strategy is to solve D approximately by a computationally inexpensive routine which (hopefully) yields a strong lower bound for use in a B&B scheme. Such a scheme will now be described.

For a given value of μ_{ij}, λ_j may be chosen so that $\lambda_j \leq c_{ij} + \mu_{ij}$, and since the objective of D is max $\sum_j \lambda_j$, it is sensible to choose λ_j to be as large as possible subject to this condition holding for all i. Accordingly, set

$$\lambda_j = \min{}_i (c_{ij} + \mu_{ij}). \tag{4.19}$$

Now only the μ_{ij} need be determined. The algorithm starts with $\mu_{ij} = 0$ for all i and j and hence, from (4.19), $\lambda_j = \min{}_i (c_{ij})$. The aim is then to increase the λ_j, and hence $v(P_{\lambda, \mu}) = \max \sum_j \lambda_j$, by increasing the μ_{ij} subject to $\sum_j \mu_{ij} \leq g_i$. This is done as economically as possible by increasing as few μ_{ij} as possible at each step. A specific algorithm, based on the work of Bilde and Krarup (1977) and Erlenkotter (1978) will now be given.

Algorithm (BKE)

{To find a lower bound to SLP using the Bilde-Krarup-Erlenkotter method. Input: sets of costs $\{c_{ij}\}$ and $\{g_i\}$.}

    for each j, sort the coefficients c_{ij}; let M_j^k denote the k-th smallest.

    Set $\mu_{ij} = 0$, for all i, j; $\lambda_j = M_j^1$ for all j.

    Set *level* = 1 and *notfinished* = **true**.

while *notfinished* **do**
begin *notfinished* ← **false.**

    for $j = 1, 2, ..., m$ **do**
    begin

        Set $\delta_1 \leftarrow M_j^{\text{level}+1} - M_j^{\text{level}}$

        Set $\delta_2 \leftarrow \min (g_i - \sum_j \mu_{ij} \mid \text{for those } i \text{ for which } \lambda_j \geq c_{ij})$

        if $\delta = \min (\delta_1, \delta_2) > 0$

        then set *notfinished* ← **true;** and

            $\mu_{ij} \leftarrow \mu_{ij} + \delta$ for each i for which $\lambda_j \geq c_{ij}$, and $\lambda_j \leftarrow \lambda_j + \delta$.

    end
end

{Output: λ and μ together form a feasible solution of $P_{\lambda, \mu}$ and $v(P_{\lambda, \mu})$ $= \sum_j \lambda_j$.}

Example 4.9 (Modified from an example in Boffey, 1982, p103.)
A computer receives messages from terminals at five different sites. It is planned to establish one or more concentrators which will receive the data from terminals and forward it to the computer as required. Four candidate locations for concentrators are chosen with location i incurring a cost g_i. There is also a communication cost of c_{ij} per unit traffic sent from terminal j to a concentrator at i (including an allowance for the cost of forwarding from i, etc.). Where should concentrator(s) be sited so as to minimise the combined cost given the specific data in table 4.1?

Table 4.1

Location	g_i	Communication cost c_{ij}				
i		$j = 1$	2	3	4	5
1	7	7*	15	10	7*	10
2	3	10	17	4*	11	22
3	3	16	7*	6	18	14
4	6	11	7	6	12	8*

Solution Using algorithm (BKE) gives the following.

Step

1   *level* $= 1$. $\mu_{ij} = 0$.

    $\lambda_1 = M_1^1 = 7$, $\lambda_2 = M_2^1 = 7$, $\lambda_3 = M_3^1 = 4$, $\lambda_4 = M_4^1 = 7$,

    $\lambda_5 = M_5^1 = 8$. *notfinished* = **true.** *level* $= 1$.

2   *notfinished ← false.*

      $j=1$. $\delta_1 \leftarrow 10\text{-}7=3$, $\delta_2 \leftarrow$ min $(7\text{-}0)=7$, $\delta \leftarrow 3$, $\mu_{11} \leftarrow 3$.

      $\lambda_1 \leftarrow 10$. *notfinished ←* **true.**

      $j=2$. $\delta_1 \leftarrow 7\text{-}7=0$, $\delta_2 \leftarrow$ min $(3\text{-}0, 6\text{-}0)$, $\delta \leftarrow 0$.

      λ_2 remains at 7.

      $j=3$. $\delta \leftarrow$ min $(6\text{-}4, 3\text{-}0) = 2$, $\mu_{23} \leftarrow 2$.

      $\lambda_3 \leftarrow 6$.

      $j=4$. $\delta \leftarrow$ min $(11\text{-}7, 7\text{-}3) = 4$, $\mu_{14} \leftarrow 4$.

      $\lambda_3 \leftarrow 11$.

      $j=5$. $\delta \leftarrow$ min $(10\text{-}8, 6\text{-}0) = 2$, $\mu_{45} \leftarrow 2$.

      $\lambda_3 \leftarrow 10$.

2   *notfinished ← false.*

      $j=1$. $\delta \leftarrow 0$ since $\sum_j \mu_{1j} = 7 = g_1$.

      $j=2$. $\delta \leftarrow$ min $(15\text{-}7, 3\text{-}0, 6\text{-}2) = 3$, $\mu_{32} \leftarrow 3$, $\mu_{42} \leftarrow 3$.

      $\lambda_2 \leftarrow 10$.

      $j=3$. $\delta \leftarrow 0$.

      $j=4$. $\delta \leftarrow 0$.

      $j=5$. $\delta \leftarrow 0$.

2   *notfinished ← false.*

      $\delta = 0$ for $j = 1,..., 5$.

3   The solution is $\lambda = (10, 10, 6, 11, 10)$.

      $\mu_{ij} = 0$ except $\mu_{11}=3$, $\mu_{14}=4$, $\mu_{23}=2$, $\mu_{32}=3$, $\mu_{42}=3$, $\mu_{45}=2$.
      The value of the solution is $\sum_j \lambda_j = 47$.

Thus it has been found that 47 is a lower bound on the cost of an optimal solution to the given SLP. Now the multipliers will be used to generate a feasible solution for SLP. The μ_{ij} variables, $j = 1, ..., n$, may be thought of as that part of the fixed cost g_i for site i that is allocated to route i-j. Those sites i for which the whole of g_i has been allocated may be opened at 'zero extra cost' and are candidates for locating a concentrator. In example 4.9, $\sum_j \mu_{1j} = 7 = g_1$, $\sum_j \mu_{2j} = 2 < g_2$, $\sum_j \mu_{3j} = 3 = g_3$, $\sum_j \mu_{4j} = 5 = g_4$. Correspondingly, the solution $y = (1, 0, 1, 0)$ is tried and found to have a value of 47; this confirms that it is an optimal solution.

Alternatively, a duality interpretation may be given. For the given Lagrangean relaxation the Integrality Property holds (cf. exercise 4.7) so the multipliers will be interpreted as values of the dual variables, that is the problem D given by (4.15) - (4.18). Complementary slackness conditions require that (cf. appendix B)

$$x_{ij} (c_{ij} + \mu_{ij} - \lambda_j) = 0,$$

$$y_i (g_i - \sum_j \mu_{ij}) = 0,$$

$$\lambda_j (1 - \sum_i x_{ij}) = 0,$$

$$\mu_{ij} (y_i - x_{ij}) = 0.$$

The second set states, for optimal primal and dual solutions, that $y_i = 0$ if $\sum_j \mu_{ij} < g_i$; this is consistent with our earlier statement that sites i for which $\sum_j \mu_{ij} = g_i$ are candidates for having a concentrator located there. Generally an optimal solution need not require $y_i = 1$ for all i for which $\sum_j \mu_{ij} = g_i$. $\qquad \square$

4.5 MAXIMISING CONCAVE FUNCTIONS

The dual ascent approach illustrated in the last section can be remarkably effective but depends on the problem solver being able to tailor a suitable 'greedy-like' strategy to the structure of the problem in question. In the context of Lagrangean relaxation it is frequently required to find a maximum of a continuous concave function which is not everywhere differentiable. An appropriate, and often used, technique is that of *subgradient optimisation*. However, before discussing the technique explicitly, we prefer to set the scene by considering the maximisation of concave *differentiable* functions. This is then extended to the more general case in section 4.6.

A hill-climbing procedure

For differentiable functions a maximum can be obtained by finding a zero of the gradient function. However, it is convenient to develop first an alternative method which, although *less suitable for differentiable functions*, is useful for explaining the concepts of subgradient optimisation. Suppose that it is desired to find the maximum of a continuous function f of a single variable x, such as that whose graph is shown in figure 4.13. Let an initial estimate of the maximum point be $x = x^0$. Then, if the value $m = f(x^*)$ *were* known, a new estimate x^1 of x^* could be found by approximating the curve by the tangent at $(x^0, f(x^0))$:

$$x^1 = x^0 + t(m - f(x^0)) \bigg/ \left(\frac{df}{dx}\right)_{x=x^0} \qquad (4.20)$$

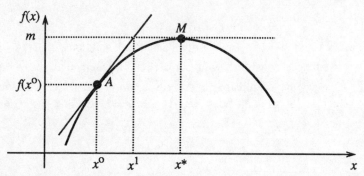

Figure 4.13 The curve is approximated by the tangent at A. This yields a new approximation x^1.

Theorem 4.8 If f is concave, differentiable, and possesses a unique maximum, then either a maximum occurs at x^0, or

$$|x^* - x^1| < |x^* - x^0| \text{ whenever } 0 < t < 2.$$

Proof If $(df/dx)_{x=x^0} = 0$, then x^0 is a maximum. Otherwise, suppose that this is not the case. If $x^0 < x^*$, then $(df/dx)_{x=x^0} > 0$ implying $x^1 > x^0$ (cf. figure 4.13). The concavity of f requires that

$$(f(x^*) - f(x^0))/(df/dx)_{x=x^0} \leq (x^* - x^0) \qquad (4.21)$$

and hence when $t = 1$ that $0 < x^* - x^1 < x^* - x^0$. If now, t is allowed to vary within the range $0 < t < 2$ then $x^0 < x^1 < x^* + (x^* - x^0)$ and hence again $|x^* - x^1| < |x^* - x^0|$. The same relation may be obtained in a similar way if $x^0 > x^*$ and the desired result follows immediately. $\qquad \square$

Theorem 4.9 Under the conditions of theorem 4.8, $x^k \to x^*$ as $k \to \infty$ where

$$x^{k+1} = x^k + t(m - f(x^k))/\left(\frac{df}{dx}\right)_{x=x^k} \tag{4.20a}$$

Proof Let $z^k = |x^* - x^k|$. By repeated application of theorem 4.8 it follows that $\{z^k\}$ is a monotonically decreasing sequence and, since $z^k > 0$ for all k, it must converge to some number $\alpha \geq 0$. Either $\alpha = 0$ and the desired result holds, or $\alpha > 0$ and there is no sequence point x^k in the interval $x^* - \alpha < x < x^* + \alpha$. The proof will consist of showing that the latter condition is impossible.

Convergence of $\{z^k\}$ implies that for any $\varepsilon > 0$, there exists an integer K, such that $0 < (x^* - \alpha) - x^k < \varepsilon$ or $0 < x^k - (x^* + \alpha) < \varepsilon$ for all $k > K$ and hence there is an infinite number of points x^k in (at least) one of these two intervals. For definiteness, suppose that there are an infinite number of sequence points in the 'left' interval $0 < (x^* - \alpha) - x^k < \varepsilon$ (the proof for the other case is similar). From (4.21)

$$(f(x^*) - f(x^* - \alpha)) \leq (x^* - (x^* - \alpha))d = \alpha d < 2\alpha d/t$$

where $d = (df/dx)_{x=x^*-\alpha}$. Since f is differentiable, and hence continuous, there exists $\varepsilon_0 > 0$ such that

$$(f(x^*) - f(x)) < 2\alpha d/t \quad \text{provided } x^* - \alpha - \varepsilon_0 \leq x \leq x^* - \alpha . \tag{4.22}$$

Then, if $0 < (x^* - \alpha) - x^k < \varepsilon_0$

$$\begin{aligned}
x^{k+1} &= x^k + t(f(x^*) - f(x^k))/(df/dx)_{x=x^k} \\
&< x^k + t(f(x^*) - f(x^k))/d \quad \text{since } (df/dx)_{x=x^k} \geq d \text{ by concavity of } f \\
&< x^* - \alpha + t(f(x^*) - f(x^k))/d \\
&< x^* - \alpha + 2\alpha \quad \text{by (4.22)} \\
&= x^* + \alpha. \tag{4.23}
\end{aligned}$$

Next,

$$\begin{aligned}
x^{k+1} &= x^k + t(f(x^*) - f(x^k))/(df/dx)_{x=x^k} \\
&= x^k + t(f(x^*) - f(x^k))/D \quad \text{where } D = (df/dx)_{x=x^k} \\
&> x^k + t(f(x^*) - f(x^* - \alpha))/D \\
&> x^* - \alpha - \varepsilon_0 + t(f(x^*) - f(x^* - \alpha))/D \\
&> x^* - \alpha. \tag{4.24}
\end{aligned}$$

provided ε_0 is chosen to satisfy $\varepsilon_0 < t(f(x^*) - f(x^* - \alpha))/D$ as well as (4.22). From (4.23) and (4.24) it follows that $x^* - \alpha < x^k < x^* + \alpha$ for some k as required. $\qquad\qquad\qquad\qquad\qquad\qquad\qquad\qquad\qquad\qquad\qquad$ □

If the condition of f having a *unique* maximum is dropped from theorems 4.8 and 4.9 there is a larger set of points to 'aim at' and so it might be expected that the results (suitably rephrased) would still hold; this is indeed the case (cf. exercise 4.6). Theorem 4.9 gives a possible strategy for maximising a differentiable concave function, f, namely

Procedure (HC)
{Hill climb procedure to find a maximum of f.
 Input: function f and an initial value x^0 of x. }
  Set *bestvalue* $= -\infty$.
  Set $k=1$, and specify a value of t such that $0 < t < 2$.
  while x^* has **not** been found to within a specified accuracy **do**
  begin
    Set $x^{k+1} = x^k + t(m - f(x^k))/(df/dx)_{x=x^k}$
    if $f(x^{k+1}) >$ *bestvalue* **then** set *best x* $= x^{k+1}$, *bestvalue* $\leftarrow f(x^{k+1})$
    Set $k \leftarrow k + 1$.
  end
{Output: *best x*, an approximate value of x maximising f.}

By theorem 4.9, $x^k \rightarrow x^*$ as $k \rightarrow \infty$. The only difficulty with this procedure is that it is the value of m that is being sought so it is not known for the update step. However, if an upper estimate m' of m is known then this could be substituted for m, and provided it was not too much different from m we might still hope for convergence.

Example 4.10 Apply the above procedure for the function f defined by

$$f(x) = 1 - x^2 + 6x,$$

given the information that the maximum, m, is no greater than 11. Start with $x^0 = 0$ and use $t = 1$.

Solution $f(x)$ may be re-expressed as $10 - (x - 3)^2$ from which the maximum is readily seen to occur for $x = 3$ and have the value 10; however, this will be ignored as the problem is being used solely for illustrative purposes.

Now $df/dx = 6 - 2x$ and

$$x^{k+1} = x^k + [10 + (x^k)^2 - 6x^k] / [6 - 2x^k].$$

Successive approximations are

$$x^0 = 0,$$
$$x^1 = x^0 + 10/6 = 1.667,$$
$$x^2 = 1.667 + 2.788 / 2.667 = 2.708.$$
$$x^3 = 4.568, \quad x^4 = 3.465, \quad x^5 = 2.158, \quad \ldots, \quad x^{12} = 2.992.$$

The values of x^k are shown graphically in figure 4.14 for $k = 1, \ldots, 12$. If x^{12} is accepted as being sufficiently near to optimal (the derivative df/dx is only 0.016) then the procedure terminates; if not, then it is not immediately clear that a better value will be found. ☐

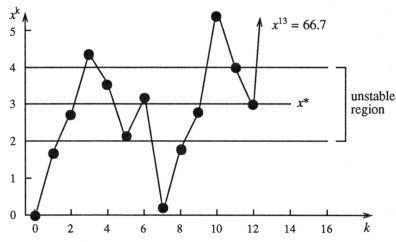

Figure 4.14 Successive approximations to max $f(x)$ are shown by solid circles.

It is seen that the optimal value, $x^*=3$, is approached at first; however, on closer inspection it may be noticed that whenever an approximation falls between 2 and 4 the next approximation is usually worse. Why should this be so? It is because m' is used in the update formula whereas the theorem proves convergence when $0 < t < 2$ and the increment $x^{k+1} - x^k$ is $t[m - f(x)]/[df/dx]$. Use of m' at a particular step corresponds to an *effective* value, t_{eff}, of t determined by setting $[m' - f(x)] = t_{eff}[m - f(x)]$.

That is

$$t_{\text{eff}} = [m' - f(x)] / [m - f(x)] = [1 + (x-3)^2] / (x-3)^2.$$

It is readily verified that $0 < t_{\text{eff}} < 2$ is satisfied unless $2 \le x \le 4$ which is precisely the region in which the algorithm is found to work badly! Such a region will be termed an *unstable region*.

A heuristic solution to overcome the lack of convergence as optimality is approached is to reduce the value of t (by a factor of 1/2 say) after p iterations have occurred without improvement in the best solution found so far.

Example 4.11 Find an approximation to the maximum of the function of example 4.10 starting with $t=1$ but halving the value of t when there has been no improvement after $p=2$ successive iterations. [It should be noted that the small value of p is chosen for illustrative purposes; in practice it is likely that a value in the range $7 \le p \le 15$ would be used.]

Solution The values of the first few x^k are shown in table 4.2 and in figure 4.15.

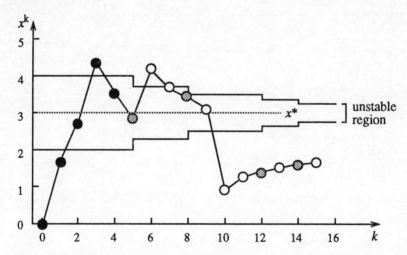

Figure 4.15 Successive approximations to $\max f(x)$ are shown: the first five (shown by solid circles) are the same as for figure 4.14; shaded circles are points at which t has just been reduced.

Notice that there is not now the same wild oscillation shown in figure 4.14, but that a new difficulty is encountered. It is that after x^9, which is very near to x^*, the next approximation is poor ($x^{10} = 0.879$). The

Table 4.2 Successive approximations x^k and $f(x^k)$ for example 4.11.

k	t	x^k	$f(x^k)$	f_{best}
0	1.0	0.000	1.000	1.000
1	1.0	1.667	8.222	8.222
2	1.0	2.708	9.915	9.915
3	1.0	4.568	7.540	...
4	1.0	3.465	9.873	...
5	0.5	2.812	9.965	9.965
6	0.5	4.188	8.588	...
7	0.5	3.681	9.536	...
8	0.25	3.412	9.830	...
9	0.25	3.058	9.997	9.997
10	0.25	0.879	5.500	...
11	0.25	1.203	6.770	...
12	0.125	1.350	7.278	...
13	0.125	1.491	7.722	...
14	0.0625	1.559	7.922	...
15	0.0625	1.625	8.110	...

value of t has been decreased to 0.25 so that x^k is only rising relatively slowly towards x^*. Because there are no improvements in best solution found the step length is halved every other iteration and x^k converges, but to a value less than x^*. From this example it is seen that t should decrease, though not too quickly. This suggests that an alternative way of determining step length is desired.   □

Often a function f is defined over an interval $a \le x \le b$ only. In this case the same update formula can be used except that derivatives at a and b are taken to be right and left derivatives respectively. Also, to avoid points outside the region $a \le x \le b$ the update step is modified to:

$$x^{k+1} = a \text{ if } x^k + t(f(x^*) - f(x^k))/(df/dx)_{x=x^k} < a$$

$$x^{k+1} = b \text{ if } x^k + t(f(x^*) - f(x^k))/(df/dx)_{x=x^k} > b.$$

This may be summarised by

$$x^{k+1} = P[x^k + t(f(x^*) - f(x^k))/(df/dx)_{x=x^k}]$$

where P denotes the operator projecting the argument to the nearest point in the desired region; in this case $a \le x \le b$.

A general result on convergenc of the sequence $\{x^k\}$ will now be given.

Theorem 4.10 Let f be a concave differentiable function defined on the interval $a \leq x \leq b$ and possessing a unique maximum, and let $\{x^k\}$ be a sequence determined by

$$x^{k+1} = P[x^k + \theta^k / d^k] \quad \text{where } d^k \text{ denotes } \left(\frac{df}{dx}\right)_{x = x^k}. \tag{4.25}$$

Then $x^k \rightarrow x^*$ if:

(i) $\theta^k \rightarrow 0$ as $k \rightarrow \infty$,

(ii) $\sum_k \theta^k = \infty$,

(iii) $df/dx \leq D$ for $a \leq x \leq b$.

Proof Let f^* be the maximum value of f over the interval concerned and define $R(\alpha) = \{ x \mid f(x) \geq \alpha \}$ for any $\alpha < f^*$. The desired result will follow if it can be shown that to each such α there exists a value of k for which $x^k \in R(\alpha)$; this will be established by contradiction.

Assume for $\alpha < f^*$ that there is no member of the sequence $\{x^k\}$ in $R(\alpha)$. Let $\delta > 0$ be such that $x \in R(\alpha)$ provided $|x - x^*| < \delta$ (such a δ existing since differentiability of f implies continuity).

Since $\theta^k \rightarrow 0$ as $k \rightarrow \infty$, there is an integer K such that for all $k \geq K$

$$|\theta^k / d^k| \leq \theta^k / d < \delta$$

where $d = \min \{ df/dx \mid x \in R(\alpha) \}$ \hfill (4.26)

Suppose, for definiteness, that $x^k < x^*$ for some $k \geq K$ (the case of $x^K < x^*$ is similar). Then $d^k > 0$,

$$x^{k+1} = P[x^k + \theta^k / d^k] = x^k + \theta^k / d^k$$

and $x^k < x^{k+1} < x^*$. Since $\theta^k / d \geq \theta^k / D$, it follows that

$$x^{k+m+1} - x^k \geq \sum_{i=0}^{i+m} \theta^i / D.$$

As $\{\theta^k\}$ is divergent it follows that $x^{k+m+1} > x^*$ for some m. Let m be the smallest value for which this is true, then

$$x^* - \delta < x^{k+m+1} < x^* + \delta$$

and $x^{k+m+1} \in R(\alpha)$ contrary to supposition. It follows that $x^k \rightarrow x^*$ as $k \rightarrow \infty$. $\qquad \square$

Again it is true that the restriction to a *unique* maximum is not necessary.

Before moving on to consider subgradients it should be mentioned that the above hill climb schemes can be extended to functions of more than one variable. Thus (4.20) is replaced by

$$x^1 = x^0 + t\,(m - f(x^0))\nabla f / |\nabla f|^2 \qquad (4.27)$$

where ∇f is the gradient of f at $x = x^0$. Also the update formula analogous to that given in theorem 4.10 is

$$x^{k+1} = P[x^k + \theta^k \sigma^k / |\sigma^k|] \quad \text{where } \sigma^k \text{ denotes } |\nabla f| \text{ at } x = x^k. \qquad (4.28)$$

4.6 SUBGRADIENT OPTIMISATION

Functions which have the desirable properties of being concave and continuous, but are not differentiable at all points at which the function is defined, arise naturally in connection with Lagrangean relaxation as example 4.12 below illustrates.

Maximising a not everywhere differentiable function

Example 4.12 Solve the 0-1 knapsack problem

P: minimise $\sum_j v_j x_j$
  subject to

$$\sum_j w_j x_j \geq W \qquad (4.29)$$
$$x_j \in \{0,1\} \quad \text{all } j$$

for the specific data set $v = (4, 1, 4, 3, 6, 3)$, $w = (6, 2, 5, 3, 7, 4)$, $W = 15$, by considering the solution $x = (1, 1, 0, 0, 1, 0)$.

Solution   The knapsack constraint (4.29) may be incorporated into the objective, with multiplier λ, yielding

P$_\lambda$:   minimise $[\sum_j v_j x_j - \lambda(\sum_j w_j x_j - W)]$
  subject to $x_j \in \{0,1\}$ for all j

which solves easily to give

$$f(\lambda) = v(P_\lambda) = \lambda W + \Sigma_j \min (0, v_j - \lambda w_j). \qquad (4.30)$$

To solve the Lagrangean dual requires finding $\lambda \geq 0$ for which $f(\lambda)$ is maximised. For the data set given, the graph of f is shown in figure 4.16 for $\lambda \leq 1.1$. It is seen that the graph is piecewise linear and the maximum occurs at $\lambda = 0.8$. To obtain the graph it may be noted from (4.30) that 'critical points' occur when $\lambda = v_j/w_j$, that is for $\lambda = 1/2$, 2/3, 3/4, 4/5, 6/7 and 3/3 = 1.

$0 \leq \lambda \leq 1/2, \quad f(\lambda) = 15\lambda + (0) + (0) + (0) + (0) + (0) + (0) = 15\lambda,$

$1/2 \leq \lambda \leq 2/3, \quad f(\lambda) = [15\lambda] + (1 - 2\lambda) = 1 + 13\lambda,$

$2/3 \leq \lambda \leq 3/4, \quad f(\lambda) = [1 + 13\lambda] + (4 - 6\lambda) = 5 + 7\lambda,$

$3/4 \leq \lambda \leq 4/5, \quad f(\lambda) = [5 + 7\lambda] + (3 - 4\lambda) = 8 + 3\lambda,$

$4/5 \leq \lambda \leq 6/7, \quad f(\lambda) = [8 + 3\lambda] + (4 - 5\lambda) = 12 - 2\lambda,$

$6/7 \leq \lambda \leq 1, \quad f(\lambda) = [12 - 2\lambda] + (6 - 7\lambda) = 18 - 9\lambda,$

$1 \leq \lambda, \qquad f(\lambda) = [18 - 9\lambda] + (3 - 3\lambda) = 21 - 12\lambda.$

The maximum value of f occurs at $\lambda = 0.8$ and is equal to

$$8 + 3(0.8) = 10.4 = 12 - 2(0.8).$$

Since the minimum value of $v(P)$ must be an integer, a better lower bound is obtained by rounding 10.4 up to 11. Now $x = (1, 1, 0, 0, 1, 0)$ is a feasible solution to P and has value 11; that is, 11 is also an upper bound on $v(P)$. Consequently, $(1, 1, 0, 0, 1, 0)$ is an optimal solution for problem P. $[(1, 0, 1, 0, 0, 1)$ is another.] $\qquad \square$

Applying the procedure (HC) with $m' = m = 10.4$, $t = 1$ and $\lambda^0 = 0$ leads to

$\lambda^0 = 0,$

$\lambda^1 = 0 + (10.4 - 0)/15 = 0.693,$

$\lambda^2 = 0.693 + (10.4 - 9.853)/7 = 0.771,$

$\lambda^3 = 0.771 + (10.4 - 10.314)/3 = 0.800.$

and the function has converged after only three iterations.

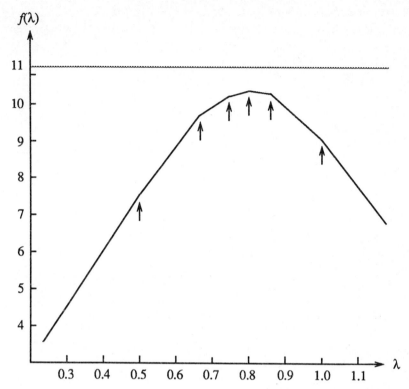

Figure 4.16 Graph of the function $f(\lambda)$ of example 4.12. (Note the false zero.) Points at which the function is not differentiable are indicated by means of arrows.

The function f satisfies all the conditions of theorems 4.8, 4.9 except that it is not differentiable at the points indicated in figure 4.16. Procedure (HC) worked because none of these points were encountered before convergence had taken place.

Of course, as earlier, the maximum value of the function f (ie. 10.4) would not be known beforehand. An upper bound could again be used but the same dangers, namely wildly oscillating behaviour and premature convergence, still present themselves; theorem 4.10 could be used however.

A difficulty that has been glossed over is that a sequence point, λ^k, may coincide with a point at which the derivative is not defined. Suppose that $\lambda^k = 2/3$ (cf. figure 4.17). Let $\varepsilon > 0$ be an arbitrarily small positive number. Then at $\lambda = 2/3 - \varepsilon$ the derivative of f is defined and equal to

13 whereas at $\lambda = 2/3 + \varepsilon$ the derivative of f is also defined but equal to 7. Intuition suggests that in place of the missing derivative at $\lambda = 2/3$ any value σ may be substituted subject only to $7 \leq \sigma \leq 13$. Such a number will be called a 'subgradient at $\lambda = 2/3$'.

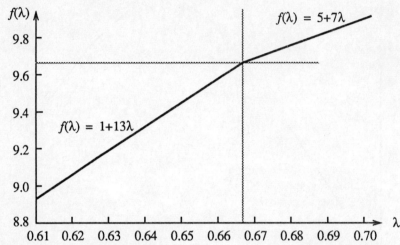

Figure 4.17 Part of the graph of figure 4.16 around the break point at (2/3. 9 2/3). Note the false zero.

In order to provide a more precise definition of 'subgradient' we first put forward an alternative definition of the gradient of a concave function, f, at a point x at which f is differentiable. Since

$$\frac{f(x+\varepsilon) - f(x)}{\varepsilon} \leq \left(\frac{df}{dx}\right) \leq \frac{f(x-\varepsilon) - f(x)}{-\varepsilon}$$

it follows that $f(x+\varepsilon) - f(x)$ and $f(x-\varepsilon) - f(x)$ are both less than or equal to $\varepsilon df/dx$ and tend to zero in the limit as $\varepsilon \to 0$. Then the alternative definition that we want for the *gradient* of the concave function f at the point x is a number d satisfying

$$f(x+\delta) - f(x) \leq d\delta$$

where δ is not restricted to being positive. Equivalently d must satisfy

$$f(x') \leq f(x) + d(x' - x).$$

This extends naturally to functions of several variables (ie. to functions of a vector quantity) by requiring the *gradient vector d* to satisfy

$$f(x') \leq f(x) + d.(x' - x).$$

Now let f be a continuous concave function defined over the convex region Ω. Then

Definition 4.1 A *subgradient* of f at the point $x \in \Omega$ is a vector σ satisfying $f(x') \leq f(x) + \sigma.(x' - x)$ for all points $x' \in \Omega$.

Note that at points $x \in \Omega$ at which f is differentiable there is a unique subgradient and it is equal to the gradient vector at x. Also, it may be seen that if f has a zero subgradient at x, then it has a maximum at x. Next, it will be shown how subgradients may be found for the type of function arising in connection with Lagrangean relaxation.

Theorem 4.11 The function f defined by

$$f(\lambda) = \min_{x \in \Omega} \{ \varphi(x) - \lambda.(Ax - b) \}$$

where φ is a function over the bounded discrete set Ω and $\lambda \geq 0$, is
    (1) piecewise linear;
    (2) continuous;
    (3) concave.

Proof   (1) Define $S(\xi) = \{ \lambda \mid f(\lambda) = \varphi(\xi) - \lambda.(A\xi - b) \}$ all $\xi \in \Omega$. Then every permissible λ belongs to *some* set $S(\xi)$ and f is linear on each $S(\xi)$ thus establishing piecewise linearity.

(2) Suppose $x(\lambda^1)$ and $x(\lambda^2)$ are points in Ω such that

$$f(\lambda^1) = \varphi(x(\lambda^1)) - \lambda^1.(Ax(\lambda^1) - b)$$
$$f(\lambda^2) = \varphi(x(\lambda^2)) - \lambda^2.(Ax(\lambda^2) - b).$$

Then

$$f(\lambda^1) - \lambda^2.(Ax(\lambda^2) - b) \leq \{\varphi(x(\lambda^2)) - \lambda^1.(Ax(\lambda^2) - b)\} - \lambda^2.(Ax(\lambda^2) - b)$$
$$= \{\varphi(x(\lambda^2)) - \lambda^2.(Ax(\lambda^2) - b)\} - \lambda^1.(Ax(\lambda^2) - b)$$
$$= f(\lambda^2) - \lambda^1.(Ax(\lambda^2) - b)$$

whence,

$$f(\lambda^1) - f(\lambda^2) \leq (\lambda^2 - \lambda^1).(Ax(\lambda^2) - b). \tag{4.31}$$

Similarly,

$$f(\lambda^2) - f(\lambda^1) \leq (\lambda^1 - \lambda^2).(Ax(\lambda^1) - b). \tag{4.32}$$

From (4.31) and (4.32) it follows directly that for any $\varepsilon > 0$ there exists a $\delta > 0$ satisfying $| f(\lambda^2) - f(\lambda^1) | < \varepsilon$ provided $| \lambda^2 - \lambda^1 | < \delta$ and so f is continuous.

(3) Let $f(\lambda^o) = \varphi(x(\lambda^o)) - \lambda^o.(Ax(\lambda^o) - b)$ where

$\lambda^o = (1-\theta)\lambda^1 + \theta\lambda^2$ and $0 \le \theta \le 1$.

From (4.31) with λ^2 replaced by λ^o, and (4.32) with λ^1 replaced by λ^o

$$f(\lambda^1) - f(\lambda^o) \le (\lambda^o - \lambda^1).(Ax(\lambda^o) - b) \qquad (4.33)$$

$$f(\lambda^2) - f(\lambda^o) \le (\lambda^o - \lambda^2).(Ax(\lambda^o) - b). \qquad (4.34)$$

Adding $(1-\theta)$ times inequality (4.33) and θ times inequality (4.34) yields

$$(1-\theta)f(\lambda^1) + \theta f(\lambda^2) - f(\lambda^o) \le [\lambda^o - (1-\theta)\lambda^1 - \theta\lambda^2].(Ax(\lambda^o) - b) = 0$$

by the definition of λ^o, and concavity of f is established. $\qquad \square$

Theorem 4.12 With the notation of theorem 4.11, $(b - Ax(\lambda^o))$ is a subgradient of the function f at the point λ^o.

Proof Let $\lambda^1 = \lambda$ and $\lambda^2 = \lambda^o$ in (4.31); then

$$f(\lambda) \le f(\lambda^o) + (\lambda^o - \lambda).(Ax(\lambda^o) - b)$$

$$= f(\lambda^o) + (\lambda - \lambda^o)(b - Ax(\lambda^o))$$

and the desired result follows. $\qquad \square$

Example 4.13 Consider the problem

minimise $x - 2y$
subject to

$$x - y \ge 0$$
$$x + y \le 3$$
$$x, y \in \{0,1\}.$$

Determine the Lagrangean relaxation obtained by taking both inequality constraints into the objective with multipliers λ, μ. Plot contours at intervals of 0.5 for $f(\lambda, \mu) = v(P_{\lambda, \mu})$ in the region $0 \le \lambda \le 2.5$, $0 \le \mu \le 1.5$. Find subgradients at the points $(\lambda, \mu) = (0.5, 1)$, $(1.5, 1.25)$, $(2, 1)$, $(1.5, 0.25)$ and $(1.5, 0.5)$. Apply subgradient optimisation with step lengths $\theta^k = 1$ for all k, and starting at the point $(\lambda, \mu)^o = (5, 1)$.

Solution The relaxation in question is

$P_{\lambda, \mu}$: $f(\lambda, \mu) = \min_{x, y \in \{0, 1\}} \{x - 2y - \lambda(x - y) - \mu(3 - x - y)\}$

$\qquad = \min \{-3\mu, -2 + \lambda - 2\mu, 1 - \lambda - 2\mu, -1 - \mu\}.$

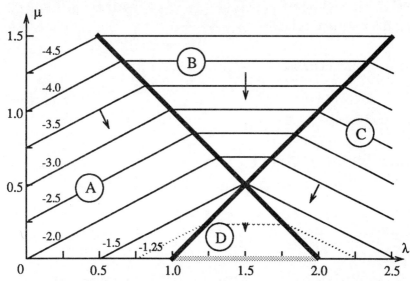

Figure 4.18 Contours are given at intervals of 0.5 with an extra contour at -1.25 being given. The heavy diagonal lines indicate the edges of the surface $z = f(\lambda, \mu)$. The maximum of f is attained at points in the interval: $1 \le \lambda \le 2$, $\mu = 0$.

Recalling that $\lambda, \mu \ge 0$, the required contours of the function $f(\lambda, \mu)$ are shown in figure 4.18, where A, B, C and D correspond to the regions for which $f(\lambda, \mu)$ is equal to $-2 + \lambda - 2\mu$, -3μ, $1 - \lambda - 2\mu$ and $-1 - \mu$ respectively. The directions of the first four subgradients required to be found are as shown at the respective points; their magnitudes are equal to four times the length of the arrows. The point (1.5, 0.5) lies on all four planes A, B, C, D and so $(1, -2)$, $(0, -3)$, $(-1, -2)$ and $(0, -1)$ are all subgradients at this point. □

The scope will now be widened somewhat to consideration of problems requiring f^* to be calculated where

$$f^* = \max f(\lambda)$$

and f is an arbitrary continuous concave function. Given an initial point λ^0, λ^n is defined recursively by

$$\lambda^{n+1} = \max(0, \lambda^n + \theta^n \sigma^n) \tag{4.35}$$

where σ^n is a subgradient of f at the point $\lambda = \lambda^n$, and $\{\theta^n\}$ a sequence of positive real numbers called *step lengths*.

Theorem 4.13 If the sequence $\{\theta^n\}$ of (4.35) satisfies

$$\theta^n = t_n (f(\lambda^*) - f(\lambda^n)) / |\sigma^n|^2 \tag{4.36}$$

where λ^* maximises f and $\varepsilon < t_n < 2 - \varepsilon$, $\varepsilon > 0$, then

$$|\lambda^{n+1} - \lambda^*| \leq |\lambda^n - \lambda^*|.$$

Proof $|\lambda^{n+1} - \lambda^*|^2 = |\lambda^n + \theta^n \sigma^n - \lambda^*|^2$

$$= |\lambda^n - \lambda^*|^2 + [(\theta^n \sigma^n)^2 + 2\theta^n(\lambda^n - \lambda^*).\sigma^n].$$

The desired result follows if the term in square brackets, which will be denoted by T, is negative. Now

$$T = (\theta^n \sigma^n)^2 + 2\theta^n(\lambda^n - \lambda^*).\sigma^n$$

$$\leq (\theta^n \sigma^n)^2 - 2\theta^n(f(\lambda^*) - f(\lambda^n)) \qquad \text{since } \sigma^n \text{ is a subgradient at } \lambda^n$$

$$= (t_n^2 - 2t_n)(f^* - f(\lambda^n))^2 / |\sigma^n|^2 \qquad \text{(substitution for } \theta^n)$$

and, since $(t_n^2 - 2t_n) = (t_n - 1)^2 - 1 \leq 0$ when $0 < t_n < 2$, it follows that $T < 0$ as required. $\qquad\qquad\qquad\square$

Theorem 4.14 If $f^* = \max f(\lambda)$ has a unique solution, $\lambda = \lambda^*$, then with the step size rule (4.36) $\lambda^n \to \lambda^*$ as $n \to \infty$.

Proof From theorem 4.13, $\{|\lambda^n - \lambda^*|\}$ is a monotonically decreasing sequence of non-negative numbers and so must converge to some number $\alpha \geq 0$. If $\alpha = 0$ the desired result is trivially true. Suppose then that $\alpha > 0$, and let

$$\Gamma = \{\lambda \mid |\lambda - \lambda^*| \geq \alpha\}$$

$s = \max_{\lambda \in \Gamma} |\sigma|$, where σ is a subgradient at λ

$\delta = \min_{\lambda \in \Gamma} (f^* - f(\lambda))$.

Then, from the proof of theorem 4.13,

$$T \leq (t_n^2 - 2t_n)(f^* - f(\lambda^n))^2 / |\sigma^n|^2 \leq (t_n^2 - 2t_n)\delta^2 / s^2 \leq (\varepsilon^2 - 2\varepsilon)\delta^2 / s^2$$

so that

$$|\lambda^{n+1} - \lambda^*|^2 - |\lambda^n - \lambda^*|^2 \leq (\varepsilon^2 - 2\varepsilon)\delta^2 / s^2.$$

Adding the inequalities for $n = 0, 1, \ldots$ leads to a contradiction (since the right hand side sums to $-\infty$) and hence α must be zero. $\qquad\square$

This result is in fact true more generally; it is not necessary for λ^* to be unique and λ may be restricted to some convex set (in which case it is necessary to apply the projection operator).

Example 4.14 Use subgradient optimisation to find the value of $f^* = \max f(\lambda, \mu)$ where

$$f(\lambda, \mu) = \min \{\lambda - 5, -\lambda - 2\mu + 45, -\lambda + 2\mu + 5\}.$$

Start at the point $(\lambda^0, \mu^0) = (17, 11)$ and use θ^n given by (4.36) with $t_n = 1$ for all n.

Solution The function f is illustrated in figure 4.19 over the rectangular region $7 \leq \lambda \leq 17$, $7 \leq \mu \leq 13$. Contours are shown at unit intervals.

$$f(\lambda^0, \mu^0) = f(17, 11) = \min (17 - 5, -17 - 22 + 45, -17 + 22 + 5) = 6.$$

Since the function f is differentiable at $(17, 11)$ there is a unique subgradient $\sigma^0 = (\partial h_2/\partial\lambda, \partial h_2/\partial\mu)$ where $h_2(\lambda, \mu) = -\lambda - 2\mu + 45$; that is $\sigma^0 = (-1, -2)$. From (4.36), $(\lambda^1, \mu^1) = (\lambda^0, \mu^0) + (1)(15 - 6)(-1, -2)/5 = (15.2, 7.4)$ and

$$f(\lambda^1, \mu^1) = \min (15.2 - 5, -15.2 - 14.8 + 45, -15.2 + 14.8 + 5) = 4.6.$$

Next, $\sigma^1 = (\partial h_3/\partial\lambda, \partial h_3/\partial\mu)$, where $h_3(\lambda, \mu) = -\lambda + 2\mu + 5$; that is, $\sigma^1 = (-1, +2)$. It may be verified that

$$(\lambda^2, \mu^2) = (13.12, 11.56), \quad (\lambda^3, \mu^3) = (11.872, 9.064), \text{ etc.}$$

The successive points (λ^n, μ^n) are plotted in figure 4.19. Notice that alternate points (after the first) lie on the lines $\lambda - 2\mu + 10 = 0$ and $\lambda + 2\mu - 30 = 0$. Also, the subgradient σ^i is alternately $(-1, -2)$ and $(-1, 2)$. This means that this particular problem is amenable to a technique of *acceleration* (of convergence).

Since subgradients are alternating it suggests that a better direction in which to head lies somewhere between. To express this, the subgradient σ^n is replaced by $\tau^n = \sigma^n + k\tau^{n-1}$ for some suitable constant k (τ^{-1} is taken to be the zero vector). Applying this to the problem in hand with $k = 0.6$ leads to the sequence of points illustrated in figure 4.20. It is

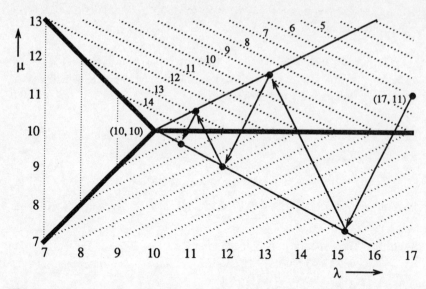

Figure 4.19 The function f of example 4.14 with contours drawn at unit intervals. The maximum value of 15 occurs at $(\lambda^n, \mu^n) = (15, 15)$. The very heavy lines indicate points at which the function is not differentiable. Points (λ^n, μ^n) [apart from the first] alternately lie on the lines $\lambda - 2\mu + 10 = 0$ and $\lambda + 2\mu - 30 = 0$ (shown by continuous lines).

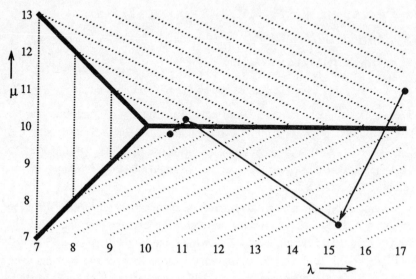

Figure 4.20 Illustration of subgradient optimisation with acceleration.

seen that in this case convergence is much more rapid. Of course, acceleration does not always work this well but it does seem generally to be beneficial. For more on acceleration see Camerini et al. (1975). □

Theorem 4.15 If the sequence $\{\theta^n\}$ of (4.35) satisfies

   (1) $\theta^n \to 0$ as $n \to \infty$,

   (2) $\sum_n \theta^n = \infty$,

then $\lambda^n \to \lambda^*$ as $n \to \infty$.

Proof The proof is somewhat similar to that of theorem 4.10 (see also Kennington and Helgason, 1980). □

This result also generalises to the case in which λ^* is not unique and λ is restricted to some convex region.

4.7 CAPACITATED CONCENTRATOR LOCATION

In the discussion of section 4.4, it was assumed that each concentrator had sufficient capacity to cope with anything that might be required of it. Of course, concentrators do not have infinite capacity. One approach would be to solve the uncapacited problem SLP, check whether any capacity constraints are violated and if not accept the solution - it is the optimal one. On the other hand, modifications would be required if any capacity constraint were violated. We now show how capacity constraints may be incorporated from the outset.

There is a fundamental difference between the uncapacitated and capacitated concentrator location problems. In the uncapacitated case it is clearly optimal to assign a terminal 'entirely' to a nearest concentrator; that is, the value of the objective cannot be improved by relaxing the constraint $x_{ij} \in \{0,1\}$ to $0 \le x_{ij} \le 1$ (or indeed to $x_{ij} \ge 0$). However, when concentrators have associated capacities it might be possible to obtain an improvement in objective value by using fractional assignments. To see this consider the artificial case of two concentrators, each with capacity C, and two terminals with traffic demands of $1.5C$ and $0.1C$. There is clearly *no feasible solution* when x_{ij} (in the notation of SLP - cf. section 4.4) is restricted to being an integer whereas there is a feasible fractional solution (for example, $x_{11} = 0.5$, $x_{12} = 0.0$, $x_{21} = 0.5$, $x_{22} = 1.0$).

Operations researchers have studied both uncapacitated location problems and capacitated location problems in which fractional assignment is possible. However, the problem of interest here - the capacitated location problem with integer assignments - has received relatively little attention until recently (cf. for example Klincewicz & Luss, 1986).

Kershenbaum approach

Kershenbaum (1987) supposed that there were K concentrator types available with type k having capacity cap_k, $k = 1, ..., K$. In order to avoid any concentrator being overloaded the constraint

$$\sum_j t_j x_{ij} \leq \sum_k cap_k y_{ik} \text{ for all } i$$

may be enforced where

$$x_{ij} = \begin{cases} 1 & \text{if terminal at } j \text{ is connected to a concentrator at } i \\ 0 & \text{otherwise} \end{cases}$$

$$y_{ik} = \begin{cases} 1 & \text{if a concentrator is located at } i \text{ and is of type } k \\ 0 & \text{otherwise} \end{cases}$$

$$t_j = \text{traffic generated per unit time by terminal } j.$$

Furthermore, to prevent more than one concentrator occupying any one site, Kershenbaum imposes

$$\sum_k y_{ik} \leq 1.$$

The full model KLP (which is almost identical to that of Kershenbaum) is then

KLP: minimise $x_o = \Sigma_i \Sigma_j c_{ij} x_{ij} + \Sigma_i \Sigma_k g_{ik} y_{ik}$
       subject to

$$\Sigma_i x_{ij} \geq 1 \qquad\qquad \text{for all } j$$

$$x_{ij} \leq \Sigma_k y_{ik} \leq 1 \qquad\qquad \text{for all } i \text{ and } j$$

$$\Sigma_j t_j x_{ij} \leq \Sigma_k cap_k y_{ik} \qquad \text{for all } i$$

$$x_{ij}, y_i \in \{0, 1\} \qquad\qquad \text{for all } i \text{ and } j$$

where

c_{ij} = cost of connecting a terminal at j to a concentrator at i
g_{ik} = cost of locating a concentrator of size k at i
t_j = amount of traffic produced at terminal j per unit time
cap_k = capacity of the kth type of concentrator.

Here we shall restrict discussion to the special case in which there is only one type of concentrator available ($K=1$). Then the KLP reduces to the *Capacitated (concentrator) Location Problem*

CLP: minimise $x_o = \Sigma_i \Sigma_j c_{ij} x_{ij} + \Sigma_i g_i y_i$
       subject to

$$\Sigma_i x_{ij} \geq 1 \qquad\qquad\qquad \text{for all } j \qquad\qquad (4.37)$$

$$x_{ij} \leq y_i \qquad\qquad\qquad\qquad \text{for all } i, j \qquad\qquad (4.38)$$

$$\Sigma_i t_j x_{ij} \leq cap_* y_i \qquad\qquad \text{for all } i \qquad\qquad (4.39)$$

$$x_{ij}, y_i \in \{0, 1\} \qquad\qquad\qquad \text{for all } i \text{ and } j. \qquad (4.40)$$

Note that since $K=1$, the subscript k is superfluous and has been omitted; the constraint $y_i \leq 1$ is redundant and has also been omitted.

Because of the similarity between CLP and the problem SLP an extension of the dual ascent method studied in section 4.4 looks promising. Incorporating constraints (4.38), (4.39) and (4.40) into the objective of CLP with multiplier vectors λ, μ and ν respectively, gives the Lagrangean dual problem

LD: maximise$_{\lambda, \mu, v}$ $v(P_{\lambda, \mu, v})$

where

$$v(P_{\lambda, \mu, v}) = \min_{x_{ij}, y_i \in \{0, 1\}} [\Sigma_i \Sigma_j c_{ij} x_{ij} + \Sigma_i g_i y_i$$
$$- \Sigma_j \lambda_j (\Sigma_i x_{ij} - 1) - \Sigma_i \Sigma_j \mu_{ij} (y_i - x_{ij})$$
$$- \Sigma_i v_i (cap * y_i - \Sigma_j t_j x_{ij})]$$
$$= \Sigma_j \lambda_j + \Sigma_i \Sigma_j \min (0, c_{ij} - \lambda_j + v_i t_j + \mu_{ij})$$
$$+ \Sigma_i \min (0, g_i - \Sigma_j \mu_{ij} - cap * v_i).$$

As for SLP, nothing is lost by enforcing the conditions that

$$\lambda_j \leq c_{ij} + v_i t_j + \mu_{ij} \qquad \text{for all } i \text{ and } j$$
$$\Sigma_j \mu_{ij} \leq g_i - cap * v_i \qquad \text{for all } i.$$

Note that for given v_i, $v(P_{\lambda, \mu, v})$ is just the relaxation of SLP with

$$c_{ij}{}^* = c_{ij} + v_i t_j \qquad \text{for all } i \text{ and } j$$
$$g_i{}^* = g_i - cap * v_i \qquad \text{for all } i.$$

A simplified dual ascent procedure may now be specified.

Solution Strategy (KDA)
{Dual ascent strategy for capacitated concentrator location model.}

STEP 1 (Setup) Set $\lambda = 0$, $\mu = 0$, $v = 0$.

STEP 2 (Ascent)
 Perform an SLP dual ascent using algorithm (BKE) (cf. section 4.4).

STEP 3 (Termination)
 For each concentrator, i, for which the capacity constraint is violated increase v_i by 'a small amount' ε_i and adjust λ_j and μ_{ij} as appropriate. Terminate.

Example 4.15 For the data of example 4.9 together with the extra information that $t = (3, 2, 3, 4, 5)$ and $cap = 10$, find an optimal allocation of concentrators to sites.

Solution Step 1 of algorithm (KDA) yields (cf. example 4.9).

$$\lambda = (10, 10, 6, 11, 10), \quad \Sigma_j \lambda_j = 47,$$

$\mu_{11} = 3$, $\mu_{14} = 4$, $\mu_{23} = 2$, $\mu_{32} = 3$, $\mu_{42} = 3$, $\mu_{45} = 2$.

$\Sigma_j \mu_{1j} = g_1$ and $\Sigma_j \mu_{3j} = g_3$ suggesting the solution $y = (1, 0, 1, 0)$ and hence

$$x_{11} = x_{32} = x_{33} = x_{14} = x_{15} = 1 \text{ with } x_{ij} = 0 \text{ otherwise.}$$

This solution satisfies all the constraints except that the traffic

$$t_1 + t_4 + t_5 = 3 + 4 + 5 = 12,$$

from the terminals assigned to the concentrator at site 1 exceeds the available capacity: $cap = 10$. Consider increasing v_1 (which corresponds to the violated constraint) by a small amount ε. This leads immediately to $\varepsilon * cap = 10\varepsilon$ being subtracted from the lower bound. The condition

$$\lambda_j \leq c_{ij} + v_i t_j + \mu_{ij}$$

now permits λ_1 to be increased by $\varepsilon t_1 = 3\varepsilon$, λ_4 to be increased by $\varepsilon t_4 = 4\varepsilon$ and λ_5 to be increased by $\varepsilon t_5 = 5\varepsilon$ for a total increase of 12ε. The net increase is thus $(12 - 10)\varepsilon = 2\varepsilon > 0$. It is thus beneficial to increase v_1, but by how much should it be increased?

Let $\varepsilon = 1/7$ and increase μ_{21}, μ_{24} and μ_{45} by 3/7, 4/7 and 5/7 to 3/7, 4/7 and 25/7 respectively. Then λ_1, λ_4 and λ_5 are increased by 3/7, 4/7 and 5/7 respectively, the lower bound becoming

$$v(P_{\lambda, \mu, v}) = \Sigma_j \lambda_j + \min (0, g_1 - \Sigma_j \mu_{1j} - cap * v_1)$$

all other terms being zero. Substitution gives

$$v(P_{\lambda, \mu, v}) = \Sigma_j \lambda_j - 1/7 \, cap = 48 \, 5/7 - 10/7 = 47 \, 2/7,$$

a net gain of 2/7.

At this point it may be observed that as the problem data is integral then so must be the value of an optimal solution; that is, the rounded value $\lceil 472/7 \rceil = 48$ is also a valid lower bound for $v(CLP)$ and, as will been seen later, it is in fact the optimal value. We shall attempt, however, to increase the value of $v(P_{\lambda, \mu, v})$.

It is tempting to increase v_1 to 1/5, μ_{45} by 1 and hence λ_5 to 11 (at which point further increase of μ_{45} is blocked as $\Sigma_j \mu_{4j} = g_4$); all other variables are unchanged. Then (cf. table 4.3)

$$v(P_{\lambda, \mu, v}) = \Sigma_j \lambda_j + \min (0, g_1 - \Sigma_j \mu_{1j} - cap * v_1)$$
$$= 49 + \min (0, 7 - 7 - 10/5) = 47.$$

Table 4.3

i	$c_{ij} + v_i\,t_j + \mu_{ij}$					$g_i - \sum_j \mu_{ij} - cap * v_i$
	1	2	3	4	5	
1	103/7	15	10	114/7	11	-10/5
2	103/7	17	6	114/7	22	0
3	16	10	6	18	14	0
4	11	10	6	12	11	0

This seems a retrograde step but the lower value results from wasteful use of the μ_{1j} as

$$\lambda_1 = 10\,3/7 < 103/5 = c_{11} + \mu_{11} + v_1$$
$$\lambda_4 = 114/7 < 11\,4/5 = c_{14} + \mu_{14} + v_1.$$

Correspondingly, μ_{11} and μ_{14} are reduced by $3/5 - 3/7 = 6/35$ and $4/5 - 4/7 = 8/35$ respectively, $\sum_j \mu_{1j}$ is reduced by $14/35 = 2/5$ and so

$$v(P_{\lambda,\mu,v}) = 49 + \min(0, 7 - 63/5 - 10/5) = 472/5.$$

It will now be shown that this solution is an optimal solution of the Lagrangean dual. From the above, it may be seen that to solve the relaxation $P_{\lambda,\mu,v}$, $\hat{y}_1 = 1$ and $\hat{y}_2$, $\hat{y}_3$ and $\hat{y}_4$ may be set to either 0 or 1. The x_{ij} variables may be set so that $\sum_i x_{ij} = 1$ is satisfied for all j. Hence $\hat{x}_{11}$ or $\hat{x}_{21}$ is 1 (but not both), $\hat{x}_{32}$ or $\hat{x}_{42}$, $\hat{x}_{23}$ or $\hat{x}_{33}$ or $\hat{x}_{43}$, $\hat{x}_{14}$ or $\hat{x}_{24}$, and $\hat{x}_{15}$ or $\hat{x}_{45}$ is 1. From among the possibilities two solutions 'A' and 'B' will be considered. Solution A is

$$y = (1, 0, 1, 0), \quad x_{11} = \hat{x}_{32} = \hat{x}_{33} = \hat{x}_{14} = \hat{x}_{15} = 1, \quad x_{ij} = 0 \text{ otherwise.}$$

This gives

$$\rho_A = (0, 0, 0, 0, 0) \text{ where } \rho_j = 1 - \sum_i x_{ij}, \quad j = 1,\dots,5.$$

$$\sigma_A = \begin{bmatrix} 0 & -1 & -1 & 0 & 0 \\ 0 & 0 & 0 & 0 & 0 \\ -1 & 0 & 0 & -1 & -1 \\ 0 & 0 & 0 & 0 & 0 \end{bmatrix} \text{ where } \sigma = x_{ij} - y_i \text{ for all } i \text{ and } j.$$

$$\tau_A = (2, 0, -5, 0) \text{ where } \tau_i = \sum_j t_j x_{ij} - cap * y_i \text{ for all } i \text{ and } j.$$

Solution 'B' is

$$y = (1, 0, 0, 1), \quad \hat{x}_{11} = \hat{x}_{42} = \hat{x}_{43} = \hat{x}_{14} = \hat{x}_{45} = 1, \quad \hat{x}_{ij} = 0 \text{ otherwise.}$$

This gives

$$\rho_B = (0, 0, 0, 0, 0)$$

$$\sigma_B = \begin{bmatrix} 0 & -1 & -1 & 0 & -1 \\ 0 & 0 & 0 & 0 & 0 \\ 0 & 0 & 0 & 0 & 0 \\ -1 & 0 & 0 & -1 & 0 \end{bmatrix}$$

$$\tau_B = (-3, 0, 0, 0).$$

Now combine 3/5 times ρ_A, σ_A and τ_A with 2/5 times ρ_B, σ_B and τ_B respectively, to get

$$\rho = (0, 0, 0, 0, 0)$$

$$\sigma = \begin{bmatrix} 0 & -1 & -1 & 0 & -2/5 \\ 0 & 0 & 0 & 0 & 0 \\ -3/5 & 0 & 0 & -3/5 & -3/5 \\ -2/5 & 0 & 0 & -2/5 & 0 \end{bmatrix}$$

$$\tau = (0, 0, -3/5, 0).$$

A move along the above subgradient (ρ, σ, τ) corresponds to

$$\lambda_j \leftarrow \max(0, \lambda_j + \theta\rho_j) \tag{4.41}$$

$$\mu_{ij} \leftarrow \max(0, \mu_{ij} + \theta\sigma_{ij}) \tag{4.42}$$

$$\nu_i \leftarrow \max(0, \nu_i + \theta\tau_i). \tag{4.43}$$

It is readily checked that all non-zero subgradient components are negative and the corresponding multipliers (λ_j, μ_{ij} or ν_i) are zero. Thus (4.41) - (4.43) result in no change in the Lagrange multipliers and the solution is optimal. $\qquad\square$

Pirkul's approach

Pirkul (1987) studied the simplified CLP described above except that t_j was replaced by a_{ij}; that is, the resource required by terminal j depends on which concentrator it is linked to. Here it will be assumed that a_{ij} is independent of i (and is hence replaced by t_j).

When finding lower bounds by relaxing constraints (whether incorporated into the objective or not) it might be expected that, generally, the more constraints that are relaxed the weaker the resulting bounds will tend to be. Pirkul relaxes only the *semi-assignment* constraints $\Sigma_i x_{ij} \geq 1$ obtaining

P_λ: $v(P_\lambda) = \Sigma_j \lambda_j + \min \Sigma_i \Sigma_j (c_{ij} - \lambda_j)x_{ij} + \Sigma_i g_i y_i$ (4.44)

subject to

$$x_{ij} \leq y_i \qquad\qquad \text{for all } i \text{ and } j \qquad\qquad (4.45)$$

$$\Sigma_j t_j x_{ij} \leq cap_* y_i \qquad \text{for all } i \qquad\qquad\qquad (4.46)$$

$$x_{ij}, y_i \in \{0, 1\}. \qquad\qquad \text{for all } i \text{ and } j \qquad\qquad (4.47)$$

Since there is no constraint connecting different concentrator sites the problem decomposes into

P_i: $v(P_i) = \min\ [\Sigma_j (c_{ij} - \lambda_j)x_{ij} + g_i y_i]$

subject to   (4.45) - (4.47).

Example 4.16 Apply the subgradient optimisation approach to the data of example 4.15 starting with $\lambda = (10, 10, 6, 11, 10)$.

Solution Problem P_1 is

P_1: minimise $-3x_{11} + 5x_{12} + 4x_{13} - 4x_{14} + 0x_{15} + 7y_1$

subject to

$$3x_{11} + 2x_{12} + 3x_{13} + 4x_{14} + 5x_{15} \leq 10$$

$$x_{ij} \leq y_i \qquad\qquad \text{for all } i \text{ and } j$$

$$x_{1j}, y_1 \in \{0, 1\}.$$

By inspection an optimal solution is $x_1. = (x_{11}, ..., x_{15}) = (1, 0, 0, 1, 0)$, $y_1 = 1$ and $v(P_1) = 0$. Similarly,

$x_2. = (x_{21}, ..., x_{25}) = (0, 0, 0, 0, 0)$, $y_2 = 1$ and $v(P_2) = 0$

$x_3. = (x_{31}, ..., x_{35}) = (0, 1, 1, 0, 0)$, $y_3 = 1$ and $v(P_3) = 0$

$x_4. = (x_{41}, ..., x_{45}) = (0, 0, 0, 0, 0)$, $y_4 = 0$ and $v(P_4) = 0$.

A subgradient is $\sigma = (\sigma_j) = (1 - \Sigma_i x_{ij}) = (0, 0, 0, 0, 1)$ and a new approximation for λ is $(10, 10, 6, 11, 10 + \theta)$ where θ is the chosen step length. If θ is selected to be 1 (which is in fact $(v(P) - 47)/|\sigma|$) then λ becomes $(10, 10, 6, 11, 11)$ and solutions for $P_1, ..., P_4$ are

$x_{1 \bullet} = (x_{11}, \ldots, x_{15}) = (1, 0, 0, 1, 0), \; y_1 = 1$ and $v(P_1) = 0,$

$x_{2 \bullet} = (x_{21}, \ldots, x_{25}) = (0, 0, 0, 0, 0), \; y_2 = 0$ and $v(P_2) = 0,$

$x_{3 \bullet} = (x_{31}, \ldots, x_{35}) = (0, 0, 0, 0, 0), \; y_3 = 0$ and $v(P_3) = 0,$

$x_{4 \bullet} = (x_{41}, \ldots, x_{45}) = (0, 1, 1, 0, 0), \; y_4 = 1$ and $v(P_4) = 0.$

Now $v(P_\lambda) = \Sigma_j \, \lambda_j = 48$. Since $y = (1, 0, 0, 1)$ leads to a feasible solution of value 48 it must be optimal.

Had the continuous approximation been used to solve the knapsack problem then the best that could have been achieved would have been 472/5 as with the dual ascent approach. The bound using Pirkul's relaxation will be at least as large as that using the Kerschenbaum relaxation (since fewer constraints are relaxed) and may in fact be strictly larger as demonstrated by the example above. However, it should not be inferred from a single example that the Pirkul approach will necessarily lead to an optimal solution with less *computational effort*. □

Secondary cover

In some situations, reliability of the network and the availability of its services to the terminal user are extremely important (cf. section 5.5). Pirkul et al. (1988) cite the cases of an air traffic system and a national weather service. For this reason they extend the 'classical' concentrator location problem of section 4.4 so that each terminal has to be assigned to *two* concentrators; one for *primary use* and the other for *secondary* (or *backup*) purposes when the primary one is unavailable. The Pirkul formulation of what will here be called the *Backup Location Problem* (or BLP) is

BLP: minimise $x_0 = \Sigma_i \Sigma_j \, (c_{ij} \, x_{ij} + d_{ij} z_{ij}) + \Sigma_i \, g_i \, y_i$

subject to

$$\Sigma_i \, x_{ij} = 1 \qquad \text{for all } j$$

$$\Sigma_i \, z_{ij} = 1 \qquad \text{for all } j$$

$$\Sigma_j \, (t_j \, x_{ij} + s_j \, z_{ij}) \leq cap * y_i \qquad \text{for all } i$$

$$x_{ij} + z_{ij} \leq y_i \qquad \text{for all } i \text{ and } j$$

$$x_{ij}, z_{ij}, y_i \in \{0, 1\} \qquad \text{for all } i \text{ and } j$$

where the new symbols are

$$z_{ij} = \begin{cases} 1 & \text{if terminal at } j \text{ is connected to a concentrator at } i \text{ as backup} \\ 0 & \text{otherwise} \end{cases}$$

s_j = traffic generated per unit time by terminal j to a backup
concentrator.

It may be noted that in the original formulation, Pirkul et al. (1988) permit the case in which different amounts of concentrator capacity are needed if a concentrator is used as backup.

The parameter s_j will be only a fraction γ of t_j, where $\gamma < 1$ depends on the probability of line failure and other relevant factors. Moreover, if two or more backup lines are connected to a particular concentrator it is unlikely that more than one of these will be used at any one time. Narasimhan (1990) discusses the more general case in which the number of backup lines may vary from terminal to terminal.

A Lagrangean relaxation

Just as the constraints $\sum_i x_{ij} \geq 1$ were incorporated into the objective for CLP so it is natural to incorporate both sets of constraints $\sum_i x_{ij} \geq 1$ and $\sum_i z_{ij} = 1$ into the objective for BLP with, say, multipliers α_j and β_j respectively. This gives, after some manipulation,

$$P_{\alpha,\beta}: \quad \min \sum_i \sum_j (c_{ij} - \alpha_j) x_{ij} + \sum_i \sum_j (d_{ij} - \beta_j) z_{ij} + \sum_i g_i y_i + \sum_j (\alpha_j + \beta_j)$$

subject to

$$\sum_j (t_j x_{ij} + s_j z_{ij}) \leq cap_* \, y_i \qquad \text{for all } i$$

$$x_{ij} + z_{ij} \leq y_i \qquad \text{for all } i \text{ and } j$$

$$x_{ij}, \, z_{ij}, \, y_i \in \{0, 1\} \qquad \text{for all } i \text{ and } j.$$

This decomposes into subproblems, one for each value of i. In the ith subproblem, y_i is either 0 or 1. In the former case x_{ij} and z_{ij} are zero also and the value of the subproblem is zero. On the other hand if $y_i = 1$ the subproblem becomes a knapsack problem with the additional constraint $x_{ij} + z_{ij} \leq 1$ all j; this is called a *Multiple Choice Knapsack Problem* (or MCKP for short) (cf. Sinha and Zoltners, 1979). Suppose the optimal value is V_i, then the solution of $P_{\alpha,\beta}(i)$ is

$$x_{ij} = z_{ij} = y_i = 0 \text{ if } V_i < 0$$

$y_i = 1$ and x_{ij} and z_{ij} are as given by the solution to MCKP if $V_i \geq 0$.

Since a MCKP is by no means trivial to solve, Pirkul et al. (1988) relax the integrality constraint x_{ij}, $z_{ij} \in \{0, 1\}$ to $0 \le x_{ij}$, $z_{ij} \le 1$ for all i and j leading to a linear program with special structure for which special methods can be used (Johnson and Padberg, 1981).

4.8 EXERCISES

4.1   Terminals are distributed around a concentrator approximately as shown in figure 4.21; the distance matrix is shown on the right.

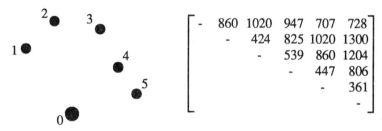

Figure 4.21

If traffic from all the terminals can be accommodated on a single line, find a set of multipoint lines of minimal total length connecting the terminals to the concentrator (ie. find an MST).

4.2   Suppose that the five terminals 1, ..., 5 of figure 4.21 have average traffic requirements of 210, 170, 180, 490 and 280 bps respectively. If, as in example 4.3, *cap* is set at 720 bps then at least

$$[(210 + 170 + 180 + 490 + 280)/720] = 2$$

lines from the concentrator are necessary. Accordingly add the constraint

$$\sum_{j=1}^{5} y_{ij} \ge 2$$

to the MST formulation, then relax and take into the objective with Lagrangean multiplier λ to obtain an MST problem with modified coefficients (cf. the discussion preceding example 4.6). Verify that the value obtained by solving this relaxation is

$248 + \lambda$ if $0 \le \lambda \le 32$,

280 if $32 \le \lambda \le 37$,

$317 - \lambda$ if $37 \le \lambda \le 50$.

Complete the description of this function as λ increases from 50 upwards. (Note that there is one further break point.)

4.3 (Question 4.2 continued) Terminals 4 and 5 cannot both be on the same line since their combined requirement is $490 + 280 = 770$ bps; consequently, 4 and 5 cannot be in the same cluster and so it is permissible to set $c_{ij} = \infty$.

Using the constraint $\sum_{i \notin R} \sum_{j \in R} y_{ij} \geq 2$ where $R = \{1, 2, 3, 5\}$, obtain a lower bound which improves upon that obtained in question 4.2.

By using B&B with the initial branching on the inclusion or exclusion of link 3-4 obtain an optimal solution.

4.4 With the data of table 4.1 and $\lambda = (7, 7, 4, 7, 8)$, $\mu = 0$, show that a solution of $SLP_{\lambda, \mu}$ is

$$\hat{x}_{11} = \hat{x}_{32} = \hat{x}_{23} = \hat{x}_{14} = \hat{x}_{45} = 1, \quad x_{ij} = 0 \text{ otherwise.}$$

$\hat{y}_1$, $\hat{y}_2$, $\hat{y}_3$ and $\hat{y}_4$ are zero,

and hence $v(SLP_{\lambda, \mu}) = 33$ (cf. 4.14).

4.5 For the problem of 4.4, the subgradient optimisation update formulae are

$$\lambda_j \leftarrow \max (0, \lambda_j + \theta^n (1 - \sum_j \hat{x}_{ij}))$$

$$\mu_{ij} \leftarrow \max (0, \mu_{ij} + \theta^n (\hat{x}_{ij} - \hat{y}_i)).$$

Starting from $\lambda = (7, 7, 4, 7, 8)$, $\mu = 0$, perform five subgradient optimisation iterations with step lengths

$$\theta^1 = 3, \quad \theta^2 = 1, \quad \theta^3 = 1/3, \quad \theta^4 = 1/5, \quad \theta^5 = 1/7.$$

4.6 Prove the result of theorem 4.9 with the condition on the uniqueness of the maximum being relaxed.

4.7 Prove that if all the constraints, other than discreteness (typically integrality) constraints, are relaxed then the Integrality Property holds and $v(LD) = v(D)$.

4.8 Investigate what happens for the problem of example 4.10 if the starting point is $x^0 = 3 - 1/\sqrt{3} \approx 2.42265$.

4.9 Find a zero subgradient at $\theta = (40/121, 40/169, 40/121, 40/169)$ for the problem of example 3.11. (Note: see exercise 3.8.)

Chapter 5

Communications Subnet Design

Chapters 2 and 3 looked at how packets of information may be routed when the network topology, link capacities and traffic demand matrix are given, while chapter 4 treated the design of local access networks. The scope will now be widened to include consideration of the design of the subnet itself. This is a difficult problem involving: the mutual dependence of optimal routing and optimal link capacity determination; the need to build in a certain amount of redundant capacity to guard against possible link or node failure; the tradeoffs between cost, delay and network robustness.

First, the topology of the subnet and the traffic demand matrix will be assumed given and the determination of optimal link capacities investigated for both fixed and variable routing. Section 5.1 considers the case when capacities are permitted to take any non-negative value. This is, of course, an approximation to the real situation in which capacities are available from a discrete range only, though LeBlanc and Simmons (1989) argue that '... it is possible to use parallel combinations of different capacity lines to greatly increase the number of possible capacities for a link. Furthermore, fractional equivalents of leased lines can be obtained by using public telephone lines with high speed modems to augment leased lines.' A corresponding discussion of the discrete case is taken up in section 5.2.

In section 5.3, bicriterion problems are considered for which it is desired to optimise simultaneously two conflicting objectives. The discussion shows how apparently different problems can effectively be equivalent. In the next section, there follows a discussion of the robustness of a network with regard to component (link or node) failure. It is shown how connectivity constraints (to ensure a certain amount of robustness) may be incorporated into a Lagrangean scheme.

The Optimal Network Problem (ONP) is introduced in section 5.5 and tackled using Lagrangean relaxation. Section 5.6 then uses ONP as a vehicle for discussing constructive heuristic methods. In the final section, a somewhat different class of heuristic method is described, namely the class of local search heuristics.

5.1 CAPACITY ASSIGNMENT (CONTINUOUS CASE)

First, the general relationship between link costs and average delay will be explored under conditions of fixed demand and network topology. Specifically, let $G_{ij}(c_{ij})$ be the cost of establishing a link between i and j with capacity c_{ij}. (In practice $G_{ij}(c_{ij})$ could be the cost of installing a link or of leasing an already existing line.) The functions G_{ij} may be of the same *form* for each link ij and may be expected to depend (possibly linearly) on the distance between i and j. Also it will be assumed that the functions G_{ij} are monotonic increasing and differentiable.

The capacities c_{ij} are to be chosen so that the network performs satisfactorily, and this is typically enforced by requiring the average delay over all links to be no greater than some prescribed value, T say. Thus, if the (M/M/1) approximation is used for packet queues,

$$\sum_i \sum_j \frac{x_{ij}}{c_{ij} - x_{ij}} \le \gamma T, \tag{5.1}$$

γ being the total arrival rate to the network as a whole (cf. section 3.1). The flows x_{ij} in (5.1) might be expected to depend on the capacity assignment; however, we shall assume for the moment that the flows are given (perhaps as the result of a fixed routing strategy based on a preliminary capacity assignment). The *Capacity Assignment Problem* (or CAP) may now be formulated as

CAP: minimise $\varphi = \sum_i \sum_j G_{ij}(c_{ij})$ (5.2)
       subject to

$$\sum_i \sum_j x_{ij}/(c_{ij} - x_{ij}) \le \gamma T \tag{5.3}$$

$$x_{ij} \le c_{ij} \tag{5.4}$$

the set $\{x_{ij}\}$ defines a prescribed conserved flow.   (5.5)

Derivation of the 'square root formula'

If it were not for the delay constraint (5.3), CAP could be solved straightforwardly, because of the monotonicity of G_{ij}, by setting $c_{ij} = x_{ij}$. On the other hand, it is intuitively clear that when (5.3) is enforced it will be satisfied with equality. The problem can hence be solved by the method of Lagrange multipliers (cf. Courant, 1934 for example). This depends on the result that for the *constrained* problem the minimum of φ corresponds to the minimum of $L = \varphi - \lambda[\gamma T - \Sigma_i \Sigma_j x_{ij}/(c_{ij} - x_{ij})]$ for the *unconstrained* problem (ie. without the delay constraint). The latter problem requires

$$\frac{\partial L}{\partial c_{ij}} = 0 \text{ for all arcs } ij, \text{ and } \frac{\partial L}{\partial \lambda} = 0.$$

Performing the differentiations gives the set of equations

$$\frac{\partial G_{ij}}{\partial c_{ij}} - \frac{\lambda x_{ij}}{(c_{ij} - x_{ij})^2} = 0 \tag{5.6}$$

and

$$\Sigma_i \Sigma_j \frac{x_{ij}}{c_{ij} - x_{ij}} = \gamma T. \tag{5.7}$$

No further progress can be made without a knowledge of the functions G_{ij}. A simple assumption to make is that each function G_{ij} is linear in the capacity c_{ij}; thus

$$G_{ij}(c_{ij}) = a_{ij} + p_{ij} c_{ij}. \tag{5.8}$$

Together with (5.6) this yields

$$p_{ij} = \lambda x_{ij}/(c_{ij} - x_{ij})^2 \tag{5.9}$$

or, solving for c_{ij} in terms of p_{ij} and x_{ij},

$$c_{ij} = x_{ij} + \sqrt{\frac{\lambda x_{ij}}{p_{ij}}}.$$

Substitution into (5.7) gives

$$\gamma T = S/\sqrt{\lambda} \text{ where } S = \Sigma_i \Sigma_j \sqrt{p_{ij}} x_{ij},$$

or $\sqrt{\lambda} = S/\gamma T$. Together with (5.9) this leads to the optimal solution

$$c_{ij} = x_{ij}\{1 + \frac{S}{\gamma T}/\sqrt{p_{ij} x_{ij}} \} \tag{5.10}$$

from which the total cost is

$$\varphi = \Sigma_i \Sigma_j \{a_{ij} + p_{ij} x_{ij}\} + \frac{S^2}{\gamma T}.$$

This will be called the *Linear Model*. As well as providing the optimal solution for the parameters given, it also yields a simple relationship between cost and average delay thus permitting the *cost v delay* tradeoff to be studied. Specifically

$$\frac{\partial \varphi}{\partial T} = S^2 / \gamma T^2.$$

Example 5.1 A network linking six cities in USA (cf. figure 5.1) is to be established to satisfy the given traffic demands and such that the average delay does not exceed $T = 0.3$ s. The values of p_{ij} are given in the diagram, the values of all a_{ij} are zero, and routing is along shortest routes relative to arc lengths given by p_{ij}. Use the Linear Model to obtain a first approximation for the link capacities. If now the constraint that the available link capacities are multiples of 9.6 kbps is added, what combination of capacities would you recommend?

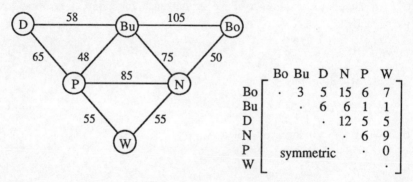

Figure 5.1 A network connecting the six cities of Bo≡Boston, Bu ≡ Buffalo, D≡Detroit, N≡New York, P≡Pittsburg, W≡Washington.   Each link cost p_{ij}, which is chosen to be approximately proportional to the distance between i and j, is shown beside each link. The traffic demand matrix is shown to the right, with entries given in terms of kbps.

Solution The total traffic entering the network is $2 \times 87 = 174$ kbps (the factor 2 occurring because $x_{ij} = x_{ji}$ for all i and j). With the specified routing, the link flows are as indicated in table 5.1 Note that as S does not depend on the units used we will work in terms of kbps. From table 5.1

$$S = 254.73 \times 2 \quad \text{and} \quad S/\gamma T = 254.73 \times 2/(87 \times 2 \times 0.3) = 9.76$$

giving

$$c_{ij} = x_{ij}(1 + 9.76/\sqrt{p_{ij}x_{ij}})$$

and

$$cost = \varphi = 2 \times \sum_i \sum_j p_{ij}c_{ij} = 20838.$$

Table 5.1

Link	p_{ij}	x_{ij}	$\sqrt{p_{ij}x_{ij}}$	c_{ij}	t_{ij}	$p_{ij}c_{ij}$	$t_{ij}x_{ij}$
Bo-Bu	105	8	28.98	10.55	0.394	1107	3.15
Bo-N	50	28	37.42	34.91	0.145	1746	4.06
Bu-D	58	23	36.52	28.81	0.172	1671	3.96
Bu-N	75	18	36.74	22.52	0.221	1689	3.98
Bu-P	48	2	9.80	3.88	0.532	186	1.06
D-P	65	10	25.50	13.62	0.276	885	2.76
N-P	85	12	31.94	15.47	0.288	1315	3.46
N-W	55	16	29.66	20.98	0.201	1154	3.22
P-W	55	6	18.17	9.05	0.328	498	1.97
Totals			254.73			10419	25.52

As a check, the average delay is

$$\sum_i \sum_j t_{ij}x_{ij}/\gamma = 25.52/87 = 0.30\,\text{s}$$

as required. With regard to the restricted range of capacities a feasible solution may be obtained by merely rounding up the values of c_{ij} to the next multiple of 9.6 kbps. This would give an average response appreciably less than 0.3 s and is likely to be more costly than necessary. The capacities for links Bu-D, Bo-Bu and N-W are respectively 1%, 11% and 14% above the next lower multiple of 9.6 kbps and are obvious candidates for rounding down. [The relatively large delay of 0.37 s on link Bo-Bu might be argued to rule out reducing the capacity of this link.] If these assignments are made, the data of table 5.2 is obtained, from which the average delay is calculated to be 23.02/87 = 0.26 s, this being well within the prescribed limit. □

Table 5.2

Link	p_{ij}	x_{ij}	c_{ij}	t_{ij}	$p_{ij}c_{ij}$	$t_{ij}x_{ij}$
Bo-Bu	105	8	9.6	0.625	1008	5.00
Bo-N	50	28	38.4	0.096	1920	2.69
Bu-D	58	23	28.8	0.172	1670	3.97
Bu-N	75	18	28.8	0.093	2160	1.67
Bu-P	48	2	9.6	0.132	461	0.26
D-P	65	10	19.2	0.109	1248	1.09
N-P	85	12	19.2	0.139	1632	1.67
N-W	55	16	19.2	0.313	1056	5.00
P-W	55	6	9.6	0.278	528	1.67
Totals					11683	23.02

Combined routing and capacity assignment

Though bifurcated routing is not favoured for operating networks, it does, in a sense, make optimal use of the communications equipment. Consequently, it provides a lower bound on communication capacity required and so it is natural to consider combined (bifurcated) routing and capacity assignment. The problem is to allocate capacities to the various links so that:

> *either*, total cost is minimised subject to delay constraints,
> *or*, performance (in terms of average delay) is optimised
> subject to a budget constraint.

These alternatives are closely related (cf. section 5.3) and we shall investigate the former only. It will be called the *Continuous Routing and Capacity Assignment Problem* (or CRCAP) and may be formulated as (cf. section 2.2):

CRCAP: minimise $\varphi = \sum_i \sum_j G_{ij}(c_{ij})$ (5.11)

subject to

$$x_{ij} = \sum_r \sum_t x_{ij}^{rt} \quad \text{for all } i \text{ and } j$$

$$\sum_i x_{ij}^{rt} - \sum_k x_{jk}^{rt} = \begin{cases} -D_{rt} & j = r \\ 0 & \text{all } j \neq r, t \\ D_{rt} & j = t \end{cases}$$

$$\sum_i \sum_j x_{ij}/(c_{ij} - x_{ij}) \leq \gamma T$$

$$x_{ij} \leq c_{ij} \quad \text{for all } i \text{ and } j$$

$$x_{ij}^{rt} \geq 0 \quad \text{for all } i, j, r \text{ and } t.$$

It should be noted that, unlike the case for CAP, both c_{ij} and x_{ij} are now variables. The method of Lagrange multipliers is again used with Lagrangian function

$$L = \varphi - \lambda[\gamma T - \Sigma_i \Sigma_j x_{ij}/(c_{ij} - x_{ij})].$$

When G_{ij} is linear with the form (5.8) then the optimal capacities corresponding to a particular set of links flows $\{x_{ij}\}$ are (cf. 5.10)

$$c_{ij} = x_{ij}\{1 + \frac{1}{\gamma T} \Sigma_m \Sigma_n \sqrt{P_{mn}x_{mn}}/\sqrt{P_{ij}x_{ij}}\}.$$

Hence CRCAP may be re-expressed as the following optimisation problem in terms of flow variables only

minimise $\varphi = \Sigma_i \Sigma_j (x_{ij}\{1 + \frac{1}{\gamma T} \Sigma_m \Sigma_n \sqrt{P_{mn}x_{mn}}/\sqrt{P_{ij}x_{ij}}\})$

subject to

$$x_{ij} = \Sigma_r x_{ij}^{rt} \qquad \text{for all } i \text{ and } j$$

$$\Sigma_i x_{ij}^{rt} - \Sigma_k x_{jk}^{rt} = \begin{cases} -D_{rt} & j = r \\ 0 & \text{all } j \neq r, t \\ D_{rt} & j = t \end{cases}$$

$$x_{ij}^{rt} \geq 0 \qquad \text{for all } i, j, r \text{ and } t.$$

This has the same structure as the bifurcated routing problem studied in sections 3.2 and 3.3, and the Frank-Wolfe algorithm is equally applicable here also. There is one snag though, namely that only a local optimum will be obtained as the objective function is no longer convex.

An algorithm for CRCAP becomes apparent. Generate several feasible solutions and apply the Frank-Wolfe algorithm (cf. section 3.3) to each one, finally accepting the best of the local optima generated. More formally:

Algorithm (G)
{Gerla's algorithm for finding a locally optimal solution for CRCAP.
 Input: values of *tol* and *n*.}
Set $\varphi^* = \infty$.
For $i = 1, ..., n$ **do**
begin
    Generate an initial feasible flow $x^{(i)}$ and apply algorithm (FW) to obtain a solution $x^{*(i)}$ which is optimal 'to with a tolerance *tol*'.
    If $\varphi(x^{*(i)}) < \varphi^*$ **then** set $\varphi^* \leftarrow \varphi(x^{*(i)})$ and $x^* \leftarrow x^{*(i)}$.
end
{Output: an approximate solution to CRCAP.}

The final solution x^* is, of course, still only guaranteed to be a local optimum, but clearly the larger the sample size n the more chance there is
that it will be globally optimal as well (cf. section 5.7). There is still
a difficulty though, and that is that with the lack of convexity many
links will be assigned a zero capacity yet still incur a cost of a_{ij}. This is
really bringing out the fact that the problem is combinatorial in nature
and such problems are considered in the following section. For the time
being this difficulty is side-stepped by letting $a_{ij} = 0$.

Example 5.2 Two nodes, r and t, could be connected by either or both
of two links as shown in figure 5.2. If the costs of establishing links 1
and 2 are 0.5 and 0.4 times their capacities respectively and the total
flow from r to t is 5 units, find a most economical assignment of capacities to the two links.

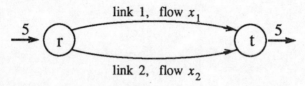

Figure 5.2 Capacities of links 1 and 2 are to be determined.

Solution Since $x_2 = 5 - x_1$ the cost is a function of a single variable
$u = x_1$, and so it is easy to study its behaviour. With the Linear Model

$$\varphi(u) = p_1 u + p_2(5-u) + \frac{1}{\gamma T}(\sqrt{p_1 u} + \sqrt{p_2(5-u)})^2$$

$$= 2.0 + 0.1u + 0.2(\sqrt{0.5u} + \sqrt{(2.0 - 0.4u)})^2.$$

If the initial $u(i)$ is chosen to be in the range $0 \le u(i) < 3.89$ then the
Frank-Wolfe algorithm generates $u = 0$ as a solution to the linearised
problem and upon performing the line search it is found that $\theta = 0$ and u
is updated to $u = 0$. At this point no further improvement would (or
indeed could) take place. Alternatively, the initial solution might be in
the range $3.89 < u(i) \le 5$ and the Frank-Wolfe algorithm leads to the
locally optimal solution $u = 5$. (cf. figure 5.3).   □

The difficulty with the above approach lies in the form of the
(M/M/1) total delay function $F(x_{ij}) = x_{ij}/(c_{ij} - x_{ij})$. For fixed x_{ij}, $F(x_{ij})$ and
hence $\sum_i \sum_j F(x_{ij})$ are convex, resulting in a unique solution for the ca-

pacities c_{ij} (cf. equation (5.10)). However, $\Sigma_i \Sigma_j F(x_{ij})$ is not convex as a function of c_{ij} and x_{ij} together as is evidenced by figure 5.3 and this leads to multiple local optima.

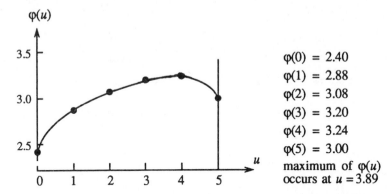

$\varphi(0) = 2.40$

$\varphi(1) = 2.88$

$\varphi(2) = 3.08$

$\varphi(3) = 3.20$

$\varphi(4) = 3.24$

$\varphi(5) = 3.00$

maximum of $\varphi(u)$
occurs at $u = 3.89$

Figure 5.3 Graph of $\varphi(u)$ as a function of u. Note the false zero.

LeBlanc and Simmons (1989) point out that the (M/M/1) total delay function is based on several unrealistic assumptions and suggest an alternative form, namely

$$F^*(x_{ij}) = \frac{a\, x_{ij}^{n+1}}{(\varepsilon + b c_{ij})^n} + k\, x_{ij} \qquad (5.12)$$

where $\varepsilon > 0$ is included so that the function is defined for $x_{ij} = c_{ij} = 0$. This function is simultaneously convex in x_{ij} and c_{ij}. Simulation experiments have shown that this and the (M/M/1) delay functions are of comparable accuracy: the form (5.12) is better for $x_{ij}/c_{ij} < 0.8$ but not so good for higher link loadings. Since networks are often designed so that $x_{ij}/c_{ij} < 0.8$ is normally satisfied it is reasonable to use (5.12). LeBlanc and Simmons have shown how this can be used to obtain a value for c_{ij} as a function of x_{ij} which is then used together with the Frank-Wolfe algorithm to obtain a globally optimal solution for x_{ij} and c_{ij}.

5.2 CAPACITY ASSIGNMENT (DISCRETE CASE)

Introducing the constraint that capacities must belong to a specified set of discrete values leads to a far from trivial extension of CAP. This, the *Discrete Capacity Assignment Problem* (DCAP) may be formulated:

DCAP: minimise $\sum_i \sum_j G_{ij}(c_{ij})$

   subject to

$$\sum_i \sum_j x_{ij}/(c_{ij} - x_{ij}) \leq \gamma T$$

$$x_{ij} \leq c_{ij} \qquad\qquad\qquad \text{for all } i \text{ and } j$$

$$c_{ij} \in \Delta = \{ c_1, c_2, ..., c_p \} \qquad \text{for all } i \text{ and } j$$

   the set $\{x_{ij}\}$ defines a prescribed conserved flow.

The delay constraint is now relaxed and incorporated into the objective with Lagrangean multiplier $\lambda \geq 0$ to give

DCAP$_\lambda$:   minimise $\sum_i \sum_j G_{ij}(c_{ij}) - \lambda [\gamma T - \sum_i \sum_j x_{ij}/(c_{ij} - x_{ij})]$

   subject to

$$x_{ij} \leq c_{ij} \qquad\qquad\qquad \text{for all } i \text{ and } j$$

$$c_{ij} \in \Delta = \{c_1, c_2, ..., c_p\} \ , \qquad \text{for all } i \text{ and } j$$

   the set $\{x_{ij}\}$ defines a prescribed conserved flow.

There is now no constraint connecting variables c_{ij} corresponding to different links i-j, and so the value of each c_{ij} may be calculated separately. If l_k denotes the value

$$l_k = G_{ij}(c_k) + \lambda x_{ij}/(c_k - x_{ij})$$

in which c_{ij} has been set equal to c_k, then it is only necessary to evaluate min ($l_1, l_2, ..., l_p$) where l_k is set equal to ∞ if $x_{ij} \leq c_{ij}$ is violated for $c_{ij} = c_k$.

Example 5.3 Using the data of example 5.1, find a good (ie. high) lower bound to $v(DCAP)$ if capacities are restricted to being multiples of 9.6 kbps.

Solution Start with $\lambda = 200$ say. Four values, l_1, l_2, l_3, l_4, of l_k corresponding to capacities of 9.6, 19.2, 28.8 and 38.4 kbps respectively, are given in table 5.3. For each arc the minimum l_k is starred; in the case of Bo-N it may be verified that $l_5 > l_4$ where l_5 corresponds to a capacity of 48 kbps.

Table 5.3

Link	p_{ij}	x_{ij}	l_1	l_2	l_3	l_4	c_{ij}	$\lambda_c(ij)$	$p_{ij}c_{ij}$	$t_{ij}x_{ij}$
Bo-Bu	105	8	2008*	2159	3101	4085	9.6	-	1008	5.00
Bo-N	50	28	-	-	8440	2458*	38.4	14.9	1920	2.69
Bu-D	58	23	-	-	2464*	2526	28.8	-	1670	3.97
Bu-N	75	18	-	4440	2493*	3056	28.8	54	2160	1.67
Bu-P	48	2	514*	945	1397	1854	9.6	-	461	0.26
D-P	65	10	-	1465*	1978	2566	19.2	-	1248	1.09
N-P	85	12	-	1965*	2591	3355	19.2	-	1632	1.67
N-W	55	16	-	2056	1834*	2255	28.8	140.8	1584	1.25
P-W	55	6	861*	1147	1637	2149	9.6	-	528	1.67
Totals									12211	19.27

The value $v(\text{DCAP}_{200})$ is obtained by subtracting $\lambda \gamma T$ from the sum of the starred entries in table 5.3 and multiplying the result by 2. Thus,

$$v(\text{DCAP}_{200}) = 2 \times [16068 - 5524] = 21088.$$

There is also the feasible solution of value $2 \times 12211 = 24422$.

The average delay is $19.27/87 = 0.22$ s which is well below the limit of 0.3s indicating that there may be scope for reducing capacities.

Should λ be increased or decreased? Since l_k is uniquely determined for each link it follows that $v(\text{DCAP}_\lambda)$ is linear at $\lambda = 200$ with gradient

$$\partial v(\text{DCAP}_\lambda)/\partial \lambda = (\Sigma_i \Sigma_j x_{ij}/(c_{ij} - x_{ij}) - \gamma T)$$

and this is, of course, the only subgradient at this point. By how much should λ be decreased? It is clearly profitable to reduce λ at least until there are two possibilities, c_k, c_{k-1} say, for the capacity c_{ij} of some link ij (that is, until a *break point* is reached). For link ij, the critical value $\lambda_c(ij)$ of λ occurs when

$$p_{ij} c_{k-1} + \lambda x_{ij}/(c_{k-1} - \lambda x_{ij}) = p_{ij}c_k + \lambda x_{ij}/(c_k - \lambda x_{ij})$$

which simplifies to

$$\lambda_c(ij) = p_{ij}(c_{k-1} - x_{ij})(c_{k-1} - x_{ij})/x_{ij}.$$

The values of $\lambda_c(ij)$ are listed in table 5.3 for those links for which a lower capacity is feasible. It is seen that when λ has been reduced to $max\{14.9, 54, 140.8\} = 140.8$, link N-W becomes critical. Taking the lower of the possibilities for the capacity of link N-W (that is 19.2 kbps) leads to a reduction of

$$v(DCAP_{140.8}) = 21088 + 2 \times [59.2][27.62 - 19.27] = 22077.$$

It is worthwhile reducing λ further and the next break point occurs at $\lambda = 54$. It may be verified from table 5.4 that $v(DCAP_{54}) = 22077 + 798 = 22875$.

If the capacity for Bu-N is chosen to be 28.8 kbps then there is a corresponding feasible solution of value 23366. On the other hand if the capacity for Bu-N is chosen to be 19.2 kbps then the corresponding solution for DCAP is *not* feasible. This also has the implication that there is a zero subgradient at $\lambda = 54$. At this point it can be asserted that

$$22872 \leq v(DCAP) \leq 23366.$$

Table 5.4

Link	p_{ij}	x_{ij}	l_1	l_2	l_3	l_4	c_{ij}	$p_{ij}c_{ij}$	$t_{ij}x_{ij}$
Bo-Bu	105	8	1278*	2055	3045	4085	9.6	1008	5.00
Bo-N	50	28	-	-	3330	2065*	38.4	1920	2.69
Bu-D	58	23	-	-	1885*	2526	28.8	1670	3.97
Bu-N	75	18	-	2250*	2250	3056	28.8	2160	1.67
Bu-P	48	2	475*	928	1386	1854	9.6	461	0.26
D-P	65	10	-	1307*	1891	2566	19.2	1248	1.09
N-P	85	12	-	1722*	2487	3355	19.2	1632	1.67
N-W	55	16	-	1326*	1652	2255	19.2	1056	5.00
P-W	55	6	618*	1081	1598	2149	9.6	528	1.67
Totals								11683	23.02

In order to check whether the incumbent is optimal it is convenient to use B&B, branching according as link Bu-N has capacity 19.2 kbps or at least 28.8 kbps. This is followed up in exercise 5.3. $\square$

Discrete routing and capacity assignment

For example 5.3, the routes (and hence flow variables x_{ij}) were chosen without reference to link capacities. After the capacities have been calculated it is likely that there will be an improved routing; indeed the reader may verify that one such improvement is to reroute flow for the OD pairs (Bo, Bu) and (Bu, Bo) via node N. A new set of routes may in turn permit a better set of capacities to be chosen, and so on. Thus one approach to combined routing and capacity determination is alternatively to solve a routing problem and a capacity determination problem until convergence takes place. This is a heuristic procedure and a more attractive approach will now be outlined.

DCAP may be modified in a natural way to give a *Discrete Routing and Capacity Assignment Problem* (or DRCAP for short) by introducing path flow variables y_π where

DRCAP: minimise $\sum_i \sum_j G_{ij}(c_{ij})$
      subject to

$$x_{ij} = \sum_r \sum_t \sum_{\pi \in P_{rt}} \delta_{ij}^\pi D_{rt} y_\pi \quad \text{for all } i \text{ and } j$$

$$\sum_i \sum_j x_{ij}/(c_{ij} - x_{ij}) \le \gamma T$$

$$\sum_{\pi \in P_{rt}} y_\pi = 1 \qquad \text{for all } r \text{ and } t \qquad (5.13)$$

$$0 \le x_{ij} \le c_{ij} \qquad \text{for all } i \text{ and } j$$

$$c_{ij} \in \Delta = \{c_0, c_1, c_2, ..., c_p\} \qquad \text{for all } i \text{ and } j$$

$$y_\pi \in \{0, 1\} \qquad \text{for all } \pi$$

where P_{rt} is a specified set of permissible routes for the OD pair (r, t), only one of which may be used (cf. (5.13)). (To allow for the absence of a link $c_0 = 0$ and $G_{ij}(0) = 0$.) Treating the delay constraint as the complexifying constraint and incorporating it into the objective with multiplier λ gives

DRCAP$_\lambda$: minimise $\sum_i \sum_j \lambda x_{ij}/(c_{ij} - x_{ij}) + \{\sum_i \sum_j G_{ij}(c_{ij}) - \lambda \gamma T\}$
      subject to

$$x_{ij} = \sum_r \sum_t \sum_{\pi \in P_{rt}} \delta_{ij}^\pi D_{rt} y_\pi \quad \text{for all } i \text{ and } j \quad (5.14)$$

$$\sum_{\pi \in P_{rt}} y_\pi = 1 \qquad \text{for all } r \text{ and } t$$

$$0 \le x_{ij} \le c_{ij} \qquad \text{for all } i \text{ and } j$$

$$c_{ij} \in \Delta = \{c_0, c_1, c_2, ..., c_p\} \qquad \text{for all } i \text{ and } j$$

$$y_\pi \in \{0, 1\} \qquad \text{for all } \pi.$$

This is still a difficult problem but for a given set of capacities, $\{c_{ij}\}$, reduces to the Discrete Routing Problem, DRP, of section 3.6. As was done there, the flow definition constraints (5.14) are incorporated into the objective with multipliers θ_{ij} and the resulting problem decomposes into:

$\text{DRCAP}_{\lambda\theta x}$: minimise $\sum_i \sum_j \lambda x_{ij}/(c_{ij} - x_{ij}) + \{\sum_i \sum_j G_{ij}(c_{ij}) - \lambda\gamma T\}$

$$- \sum_i \sum_j \theta_{ij} x_{ij}$$

subject to

$$0 \le x_{ij} \le c_{ij} \qquad\qquad \text{for all } i \text{ and } j$$

$$c_{ij} \in \Delta = \{c_1, c_2, ..., c_p\} \qquad \text{for all } i \text{ and } j$$

and

$\text{DRCAP}_{\lambda\theta y}$: minimise $\varphi_2 = \sum_r \sum_t \sum_{\pi \in P_{rt}} \sum_i \sum_j \theta_{ij} \delta_{ij}^{\pi} D_{rt} y_{\pi}$

subject to

$$\sum_{\pi \in P_{rt}} y_{\pi} = 1 \qquad\qquad \text{for all } r \text{ and } t$$

$$y_{\pi} = \{0, 1\}, \qquad\qquad \text{for all } \pi.$$

$\text{DRCAP}_{\lambda\theta x}$ has no constraints relating variables corresponding to different arcs ij, and the problem decomposes into independent subproblems $Q_{ij} = \text{DRCAP}_{\lambda\theta xij}$ connecting x_{ij} and c_{ij}:

Q_{ij}: minimise $\lambda x_{ij}/(c_{ij} - x_{ij}) + \sum_i \sum_j G_{ij}(c_{ij}) - \theta_{ij} x_{ij}$

subject to

$$0 \le x_{ij} \le c_{ij}$$

$$c_{ij} \in \Delta = \{c_0, c_1, c_2, ..., c_p\},$$

$\text{DRCAP}_{\lambda\theta y}$ decomposes into a set of independent subproblems, $\{Q_{rt}\}$, connecting the y_{π} variables where $Q_{rt} = \text{DRCAP}_{\lambda\theta yrs}$ is

Q_{rt}: minimise $\sum_i \sum_j \sum_{\pi \in P_{rt}} \lambda_{ij} \delta_{ij}^{\pi} D_{rt} y_{\pi}$

subject to

$$\sum_{\pi \in P_{rt}} y_{\pi} = 1, \qquad\qquad \text{for all } r \text{ and}$$

$$y_{\pi} \in \{0, 1\}, \qquad\qquad \text{for all } \pi.$$

The latter is a shortest distance problem in which arc ij is assigned a length $a_{ij} = \sum_{\pi \in P_{rt}} \lambda_{ij} \delta_{ij}^\pi D_{rt}$ and solves easily.

Note that with this decomposition there remains no constraint requiring the $\{c_{ij}\}$ to yield a connected network. A solution strategy for DRCAP now becomes apparent. At a high level, an optimal value for λ is sought assuming that a subroutine is available for the solution of DRCAP$_\lambda$. An outline for this is:

Optimising λ

{Input: set of cost coefficients $\{c_{ij}\}$, an initial value for λ and *tolerance*.}

    Set $\varepsilon = \infty$.

    while $|\varepsilon| > tolerance$ **do**

    begin

        Solve DRCAP$_\lambda$ (to prescribed *tolerance*).

        Check $\varepsilon = \gamma T - \sum_i \sum_j \lambda x_{ij} / (c_{ij} - x_{ij})$.

        if $\varepsilon > 0$ **then** decrease λ **else** increase λ

    end

{Output: a value of λ for which $v(\text{DRCAP}_\lambda)$ is approximately minimal.}

Other termination criteria could be used instead of requiring $|\varepsilon|$ to be small. Also, if the gap between the value of the incumbent solution and the best bound $v(\text{DRCAP}_\lambda)$ obtained is not sufficiently small, then the solution process could be continued using B&B.

DRCAP$_\lambda$ is very similar to the Discrete Routing Problem DRP studied in section 3.6 and may be solved by a similar algorithm. An outline for this will now be given:

Solving DRCAP$_\lambda$

    Choose initial values for θ_{ij} (eg. $\theta_{ij} = c_p$) for all i, j.

    Set $LB = -\infty$, $UB = \infty$, $k = 1$, *incvalue* $= \infty$.

    while the termination criterion is **not** satisfied **do**

    begin

    a. **for all** i, j set $v(Q_{ij}) = \min_k v(Q_{ij} \mid c_{ij} = c_k)$.

        for all r, t solve Q_{rt}.

b. $lb \leftarrow \sum_i \sum_j v(Q_{ij}) + \sum_r \sum_t v(Q_{rt}) - \lambda \gamma T.$

   if $lb > LB$

   then $LB \leftarrow lb.$

c. Check the feasibility of the solution (x, c, y) to DRCAP obtained from 2a.

   if feasible and its value is lower than *incvalue*

   then update the incumbent solution and *incvalue*.

d. Use subgradient optimisation to obtain updated values for θ_{ij}.

end

{Output: a set $\{\theta_{ij}\}$ which approximately solves DRCAP$_\lambda$.}

The above algorithm is abstractly almost identical to that of Gavish and Neumann (1989). Instead of determining λ they prescribe a value based on the perceived worth of response time. Their cost function, G_{ij}, is based on hire of lines, and is composed of:

(1) a fixed set up cost a_{ijk} for setting up a link of size k (including base monthly charge and a term proportional to the distance between i and j);

(2) a variable cost $p_{ijk}x_{ij}$ for a link of size k depending on the traffic intensity x_{ij}.

Although G_{ij} is given in terms of c_{ij} and x_{ij}, explicit dependence on the latter can be removed since there is an analytic relation between c_{ij} and x_{ij}. Gavish and Neumann (1989) report considerable numerical experience suggesting that the method yields optimal solutions in a reasonable amount of time for realistically sized problems.

5.3 MULTIOBJECTIVE PROBLEMS

Optimisation problems are usually posed and solved in terms of a single criterion, or objective. In real life, however, there is often more than one feature which it is desired to optimise. For example, in relation to computer networks likely design aims are that the network should be as cheap as possible to establish, have as short an average response time as

possible, be as reliable as possible, etc. These criteria cannot all be optimised simultaneously; cheaper networks are likely to be less reliable and
lead to slower response times, whereas more reliable and 'faster' networks will be more expensive. Thus there are tradeoffs between cost
and reliability, and between cost and average response time. There is also
a less obvious tradeoff between reliability and average response time.

Often a criterion of interest is not included in the objective but
rather is taken into account by imposing a performance constraint. For
example, with regard to the cost v reponse time tradeoff there are three
possibilities.

(1) Minimise cost subject to a maximum average delay constraint.
This approach is adopted for the Capacity Assignment Problem,
CAP, of section 5.1 by imposing the constraint

$$\Sigma_i \Sigma_j x_{ij}/(c_{ij} - x_{ij}) \leq \gamma T.$$

This constraint also appears in the discrete analogue, DCAP of
CAP (cf. section 5.2).

(2) Minimise average delay subject to a budget constraint. This
effectively is the approach implicit in the formulation of the
Optimal Network Problem in section 5.5 (with total path
length being used in place of average delay); see also exercise 5.1.

(3) Minimise a combination of cost and average delay.

Interestingly, CAP was solved by incorporating the delay constraint into
the Lagrangian function and DCAP was solved by relaxing the delay constraint and incorporating into the objective to obtain the Lagrangean relaxation DCAP$_\lambda$; that is, CAP and DCAP were solved by considering
related problems of type (3). Thus, there is seen to be close relationships between problems (1), (2) and (3); such relationships will be investigated in this section.

The tradeoff between cost and network reliability is complicated by
the difficulty of accurately calculating the reliability. Consequently it
is appropriate to treat reliability via a surrogate constraint in terms of
network connectivity (cf. section 5.4).

From now on we shall concentrate on *bicriterion* problems in which
there are just two objectives to be optimised; the extension to the case of
three or more objectives is straightforward in principle but more complicated because of the higher dimensionality involved. For definiteness,
and without loss of generality, it will be assumed that both objectives
are to be minimised. The general bicriterion problem may now be written

minimise $\{Z_1(x), Z_2(x)\}$

subject to

$$g_i(x) \le b_i \quad i = 1, ..., m \quad (m > 0)$$

$$x \in \Omega,$$

where $Z_1(x)$, $Z_2(x)$ are the two single criteria, or objective functions, and the vector of *decision* variables x is constrained to belong to some specified set, Ω. This specification may be via constraint equations or inequalities, or it might, for example, restrict (some of) the components of x to be integers. For a solution to be *feasible* it must also satisfy the *explicit* constraints $g_i(x) \le b_i$.

Although the two objectives of a bicriterion problem are usually 'in conflict' there are often pairs of solutions x, y such that x is 'better than' y with respect to *at least one* objective and 'as good as' y with respect to the other objective. In this case y is said to be *inferior* to x or x *dominates* y. Clearly, in such cases y may be removed from consideration; in terms of the above example, there is not a market for a dear, slow and unreliable network! The set of all solutions which are **not** inferior to any other solution is called the *non inferior set* (or NIS). An important problem in the analysis of a multiobjective problem is to identify, or at least approximate, the NIS.

Example 5.4 Find the NIS for the problem

minimise $\{x - 2y, 5 - x - y\}$

subject to

$$-x + y \le 2$$
$$y \le 3$$
$$x \quad \le 5$$
$$4x + 5y \le 25$$
$$x, y \ge 0.$$

Solution The feasible region for this problem is shown in figure 5.4. There is clearly a choice as to which constraints to subsume into the definition of Ω and which to give explicitly. Here we might for example choose $\Omega = \{x, y \mid x \ge 0, y \ge 0\}$.

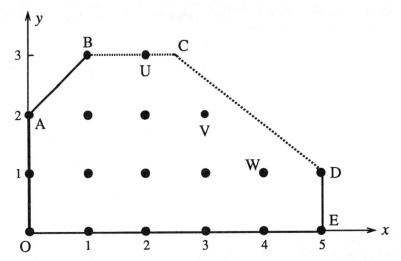

Figure 5.4 The feasible region for the problem of example 5.4 is the polygonal area $OABCDEO$, and the NIS is the set of points on the edges BC and CD. The large blobs are integer feasible solutions (cf. example 5.7).

The values of the two objectives are given in table 5.5 for each of the points of the feasible region.

Since the problem is *linear* it is known from linear programming theory that optimal points for both Z_1 and Z_2 occur on the boundary of the feasible region. From the data of table 5.5 it is seen that the sole optimal solutions for Z_1 and Z_2 occur at $B(1, 3)$ and $D(5, 1)$ respectively.

Table 5.5 Objective values for each of the extreme points of the problem of example 5.4.

Point	Coordinates	Z_1	Z_2
O	$(0, 0)$	0	5
A	$(0, 2)$	-4	3
B	$(1, 3)$	-5	1
C	$(2.5, 3)$	-3.5	-0.5
D	$(5, 1)$	3	-1
E	$(5, 0)$	5	0

Notice that solution A is *inferior to* (or *dominated by*) B since the values assumed by both Z_1 and Z_2 are better for B than for A. Similarly, O is inferior to B and E is inferior to D. Also, every point strictly interior to the feasible region is easily seen to be inferior to a point on the boundary. Finally, all points on *OA*, *OE*, *AB* and *ED* except *B* and *D* are also seen to be inferior. This leaves the set of points on *BC* and *CD* as constituting the NIS for this problem. □

The weighting method

Nothing further can be said about the solutions in the NIS unless there is some information on the 'relative worths' of Z_1 and Z_2. If the objectives can be explicitly reduced to some common unit (perhaps dollar value) then progress can be made. For example if one unit of Z_1 is worth two units of Z_2 then it would be appropriate to minimise $2Z_1 + Z_2$. [It would have been sensible of course to have formulated the problem in terms of this single objective at the outset.]

Generally, the tradeoff between criteria is at best only likely to be known approximately. One approach (the *weighting method*) that can be used in this situation is for

(1) the analyst to determine, as a function of *w*, the optimal solution relative to the objective $(1-w)Z_1 + wZ_2$, where $0 \le w \le 1$,

(2) the analyst to present this information to the *decision maker*,

(3) the decision maker to make the final choice in the light of 'experience' and non-modelled features of the problem.

Example 5.5 Apply (part (1) of) the weighting method using the data of example 5.4.

Solution *B* is the optimal point for $w = 0$, and will continue to be optimal as *w* increases until such point as the objective values at *B* and *C* are the same, that is

$$(1-w)Z_1(B) + wZ_2(B) = (1-w)Z_1(C) + wZ_2(C)$$

or

$$(1-w)(-5) + w(1) = (1-w)(-3.5) + w(-0.5)$$

leading to $w = 1/2$. After further similar calculations the solution as a function of *w* is found to be:

B is the sole optimal point for $0 \le w < 1/2$,

All points on *BC* are optimal for $w = 1/2$,

C is the sole optimal point for $1/2 < w < 13/14$,

All points on *CD* are optimal for $w = 13/14$,

D is the sole optimal point for $13/14 < w \le 1$. □

The above problem was solved easily because it had only two variables; in general many more variables might be expected. How then might the NIS be displayed? One possibility that is sometimes useful is to transfer attention to *objective space*, in which all points are plotted as functions of Z_1 and Z_2; that is, the problem is effectively converted to

minimise $[Z_1, Z_2]$
subject to
$$G_i(Z_1, Z_2) \le b_i$$
$$Z_1, Z_2 \in \Omega^*$$

where G_i are appropriate functions and Ω^* is an appropriate set of points.

Example 5.6 Display in objective space the feasible region of the problem of example 5.4.

Solution The coordinates of the points O', ..., E', which correspond to the points O, ..., E of figure 5.4, are obtained immediately from table 5.5. Joining these points yields the feasible region in objective space shown in figure 5.5. Notice that it is obvious from this representation which are the solutions optimising the separate objectives. □

Example 5.7 Consider again the problem of example 5.4 but with the added constraint that x and y must be integers. Find the NIS.

Solution Since the NIS contains only feasible solutions it must be a subset of the 'integer points' shown by large blobs in figure 5.4. It may readily be verified that every point except B, U, V, W and D is inferior to some other solution. Consequently, NIS = { B, U, V, W, D }. Note the 'indent' in NIS between U and D; this has the consequence that if the weighting method is used then V and W are not generated. Specifically,

B is the sole optimal point for $0 \le w < 1/2$,
B and U are optimal for $w = 1/2$,
U is the sole optimal point for $1/2 < w < 7/8$,
U and D are optimal for $w = 7/8$,
D is the sole optimal point for $7/8 < w \le 1$.

The non inferior solutions V and W are not generated because it was *assumed* that the tradeoff between the objectives was linear; if this tradeoff were permitted to be nonlinear then it is possible for V and/or W to be obtained. □

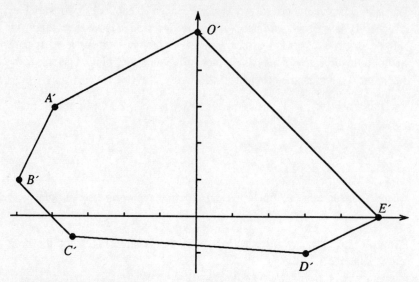

Figure 5.5 The feasible region defined by the constraints of example 5.4 plotted in *objective space*.

Problem interrelationships

An alternative approach to solving the bicriterion problem

P: minimise $[f(x), g(x)]$
        subject to $x \in \Omega$

is to solve the problem

P(b):   minimise $f(x)$
         subject to
$$g(x) \leq b$$
$$x \in \Omega$$

for a range of values of b. If $g_m = \min_{x \in \Omega} g(x)$, $f_m = \min_{x \in \Omega} f(x)$ and $g_M = \max_{x \in \Omega^*} g(x)$, where $\Omega^* = \Omega \cap \{x \mid f(x) = f_m\}$ (cf. figure 5.6), it may be seen that solving P(b) for all b in the range $g_m \leq b \leq g_M$ yields the NIS. An approximation scheme (cf. Cohon, 1978) solves P(b) for a prescribed number, $K+1$, of values b_i of b where

$$b_i = g_m + \left(\frac{i}{K}\right)(g_M - g_m) \quad i = 0, 1, ..., K.$$

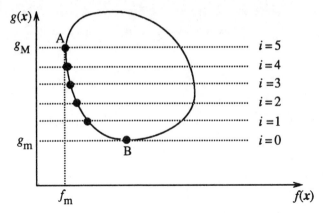

Figure 5.6 The curve *AB* is the NIS for problem P; the set of six solid circles is a (discrete) approximation to NIS corresponding to choosing *K* = 5 in the constraint method.

Of course some members of NIS might not be generated, even approximately, unless *K* is sufficiently large.

It will be helpful in what follows to imagine that P is a design problem with

$g(x)$ the cost of the system x,

b the budget available,

$f(x)$ a measure of performance, such as response time,

$1/\lambda$ the *worth* of one unit of criterion f in terms of one unit of g (ie. unit expenditure).

Now, for $\lambda \geq 0$, define the associated problem:

Q(λ): minimise $f(x) + \lambda g(x)$
    subject to $x \in \Omega$

which is, in fact, a Lagrangean relaxation of P(*b*) with the constant term $-\lambda b$ omitted from the objective. We shall now show that certain values of worth correspond to particular budget values. More precisely, for specified λ let $W(\lambda)$ be the set of optimal solutions of Q(λ) and let $b = g(\hat{x})$ for some $\hat{x} \in W(\lambda)$, then:

Theorem 5.1 If x_P is an optimal solution of P(*b*) it is also an optimal solution of Q(λ).

Proof First, $x_p \in \Omega$ since x_p is feasible for P(b), and so it must be feasible for Q(λ) also. Next, the optimality of x_p with regard to P(b) means that

$$f(x_p) \leq f(\hat{x}), \tag{5.15}$$

and the feasibility of x_p implies that

$$g(x_p) \leq b = g(\hat{x}). \tag{5.16}$$

Hence, by (5.15) and (5.16) and since $\lambda \geq 0$,

$$f(x_p) + \lambda g(x_p) \leq f(\hat{x}) + \lambda g(\hat{x}). \tag{5.17}$$

Also, as $\hat{x}$ is an optimal solution of Q(λ)

$$f(x_p) + \lambda g(x_p) \geq f(\hat{x}) + \lambda g(\hat{x}). \tag{5.18}$$

This together with (5.17) implies that (5.17) is satisfied with equality and consequently x_p is an optimal solution of Q(λ). $\qquad\square$

In summary, to a particular λ there corresponds a set

$$\{\, b \mid b = f(\hat{x}) \text{ and } \hat{x} \text{ is an optimal solution of } Q(\lambda) \,\}$$

such that an optimal solution of P(b) is also an optimal solution of Q(λ); that is, Q(λ) may be solved by solving P(b).

Theorem 5.1 has a partial converse. Let b be a specified budget in the range $g_m \leq b \leq g_M$ and suppose that there exists a $\hat{\lambda}$ such that $\hat{x} \in W(\hat{\lambda})$ where $g(\hat{x}) = \max \{g(x) \mid x \in \Omega \text{ and } g(x) \leq b\}$. Then:

Theorem 5.2   If x_Q is an optimal solution of Q($\hat{\lambda}$) and $g(x_Q) = g(\hat{x})$ then it is also an optimal solution of P(b).
Proof

$$f(x_Q) + \hat{\lambda} g(x_Q) = f(\hat{x}) + \hat{\lambda} g(\hat{x}) \quad \text{(definition of } \hat{x} \text{ and } x_Q\text{)}$$
$$= f(x_p) + \hat{\lambda} g(x_p).$$

But,

$$g(x_p) \leq b \quad \text{(since } x_p \text{ is feasible for P(b)),}$$

hence $g(x_p) \leq g(x_Q)$, and by (5.17) and (5.18), $f(x_Q) \leq f(x_p)$. The desired result follows by noting that x_Q is feasible for P(b). $\qquad\square$

Thus, if for a particular budget b there is a corresponding $\hat{\lambda}$, then

P(*b*) may be solved by solving Q($\hat{\lambda}$).

Example 5.8 Let $f(x) = \xi - 2\eta$, $g(x) = 5 - \xi - \eta$ and

$$\Omega = \{ (\xi, \eta) \mid -\xi + \eta \leq 2, \eta \leq 3, \xi \leq 5, 4\xi + 5\eta \leq 25, \xi \geq 0, \eta \geq 0 \}$$

$$\Omega* = \{ (\xi, \eta) \mid (\xi, \eta) \in \Omega, \xi \text{ \& } \eta \text{ are integers } \},$$

(cf. example 5.4). Illustrate theorems 5.1 and 5.2.

Solution The feasible region in objective space is shown in figure 5.7, from which it is seen that $g_m = -1$, $f_m = -5$, $g_M = 1$.

For $\lambda = 0.5$, lines of constant $f(x) + \lambda g(x)$ are parallel to $B'C'$ in figure 5.7. The set $W(0.5)$ of optimal solutions of $Q(0.5)$ is the set of points $1 \leq \xi \leq 2.5$, $\eta = 3$ (cf. segment BC in figure 5.4). As an example $\hat{x} = (2, 3) \in W(\lambda)$ giving $b = g(\hat{x}) = 0$. $x_p = (2, 3)$ is the sole optimal solution of $P(0)$. Solving $Q(0.5)$ solves $P(b)$ for $-0.5 \leq b \leq 1$.

When $\lambda = 0.6$ the unique solution to $Q(0.6)$ is $x = (2.5, 3)$ corresponding to budget $b = -0.5$.

If Ω is augmented (to $\Omega*$) by adding integrality constraints then the theorem still holds but, for $\lambda = 0.5$, the set of corresponding budgets is $\{0, 1\}$. For $\lambda = 0.6$ the sole corresponding budget is 0.

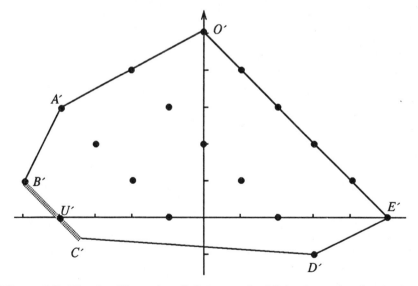

Figure 5.7 The feasible region Ω for example 5.8 is shown by the shaded line B'C'. The regions $\Omega*$ comprises the set of solid circles.

Now consider theorem 5.2; for b in the range $-0.5 \le b \le 1$ the corresponding λ is 0.5. For $b = 0.5$ each λ in the range $0.5 \le \lambda \le 13/14$ corresponds to b. In the discrete case the budget $b = 0$ corresponds to λ in the range $0.5 \le \lambda \le 7/8$. For $0 < b < 1$ the corresponding λ is 0.5. $\quad\quad\quad\Box$

5.4 NETWORK ROBUSTNESS

An MST provides a network of minimal cost, but also a *vulnerable* one (cf. figure 5.8). The failure of a critical link in a vulnerable network can be very serious and costly. Such situations have been experienced, as when much of the telephone system on the US East Coast was disabled through an excavation induced cable break. Because of the possible consequences, it is worth investing somewhat more than the absolute minimum in a network in order to increase its *robustness* to disruption through component failure. Of course extra investment to get more reliable components will help to reduce intrinsic failures, but investment to obtain a more suitable network topology is also important and it is this latter aspect that will be considered here.

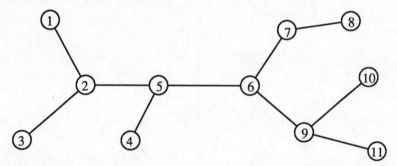

Figure 5.8 If every pair (r, t), $r, t = 1, ..., 11$ and $r \ne t$, is an OD pair then the failure of link 5-6 results in over a half of the OD pairs becoming disconnected (60 out of a possible 110).

When networks are evolving over a period of time and future requirements are imprecisely known, then a sensible strategy is to design for the current needs a network that is robust in the following sense:

> links appearing in the network should be ones appearing
> in many scenarios for designs related to the time horizon.

Reliability concepts

Let $G = (X, E)$ be a network with link weights p_{ij} and node weights p_k where

p_{ij} = probability that link $ij \in E$ fails

p_k = probability that node $k \in X$ fails.

It will be assumed that all p_{ij} and p_k are statistically independent. Then for any simple (ie. without repeated nodes) route π fiom r to t the probability that it is working (ie. no node or link on π has failed) is

$$p_\pi = \Sigma_{ij \in \pi} (1 - p_{ij}) \Sigma_{k \in \pi} (1 - p_k).$$

The probability, P_{rt}, that there is a working route between r and t (called the *availability of t* from r) satisfies

$$P_{rt} \le 1 - \Pi_\pi (1 - p_\pi) \tag{5.19}$$

the product being over all simple routes from r to t. [Equality holds when the simple routes are pairwise edge disjoint and $p_k = 1$ for all nodes k.] This is readily extended to the availability of a node t from a subset of nodes V:

$$P_{Vt} \le \Sigma_{i \in V} P_{it}. \tag{5.20}$$

Finally, the *reliability*, r_G, of the network G is the probability that there is a working route between every pair of nodes. A little thought shows that

$$r_G = P_{X-\{t\},t} \tag{5.21}$$

for any node t.

It is not surprising, since links are shared among paths (leading to the inequalities in (5.19), (5.20)) that the calculation of network reliability is a computationally difficult task. To incorporate reliability considerations into network design directly from (5.21) is not viable even for small networks; in view of uncertainties in the model it would not be justifiable anyway.

Connectivity

From the above discussion it is seen that, generally speaking, it is desirable to have two or more routes between each pair of nodes r and t, and that such routes should preferably have no common links since the fail-

ure of a common link would put both routes out of action. Put otherwise, the greater the 'connectivity' the more *robust* a network is likely
to be. In order to proceed further it is necessary to be more precise as to
the meaning of 'connectivity' in this context.

Node $r \neq t$ is said to be *k edge-connected* to *t* if *k* is the maximal
number of *edge-disjoint* simple chains (that is, having no links in common and without repeated nodes) between *r* and *t*. Node *r* is *k node-connected* to *t* if *k* is the maximum number of *node-disjoint* simple chains
between *r* and *t*. A network is *k edge-connected* (respectively *k node-
connected*) if every pair of nodes is *k* edge-connected (*k* node-connected)
but there is at least one pair of nodes which is not $(k+1)$ edge-connected
$((k+1)$ node-connected).

The concepts of edge- and node-connectivity coincide when $k=1$ and
become just the familiar concept of connectivity introduced in section
2.1. For $k>1$, node-connectivity is a stronger concept than edge-connectivity as may be seen from figure 5.9.

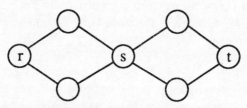

Figure 5.9   This network is 2 edge-connected but not 2 node-connected
since there are not two node-disjoint routes between *r* and *t*.

Returning to the question of network robustness, it may be noted
that the probabilities p_{ij}, p_k are likely to be small (the node failure probabilities particularly so). As statistical independence has been assumed,
the probability of two (or more) simultaneous failures will be *very*
small and so a reasonable requirement to impose is that a network should
be designed to withstand any single failure without any OD pair becoming disconnected. This would be the case if the network is 2 node-
connected (or 2 edge-connected if nodes are regarded as being perfectly
reliable).

Whether or not two nodes *a* and *b* are two edge-connected can be verified by finding a maximal conserved flow from *a* to *b* assuming all
links have capacity 1. The details of maximal flow techniques would
take us too far afield but may be found in many texts (eg. Ford and Fulkerson, 1962; Christofides, 1975; Boffey, 1982).

It can be checked very easily whether a network is 2 node-connected by using an algorithm based on the following result (Kleitman (1969)). $v(x, y)$ will denote the maximum number of node-disjoint chains between x and y; $v(G)$ will denote $\min_{x \neq y} v(x, y)$.

Theorem 5.3 Let $G = (X, E)$ be a graph and $s \in X$ a node such that $v(s, x) \geq 2$ for all $x \in X\text{-}\{s\}$. Define the graph G^* to be the graph obtained from G by removing node s and all adjacent edges. If $v^*(a, b)$ denotes the number of node-disjoint chains between arbitrary distinct nodes a and b in $X\text{-}\{s\}$ then

$v^*(a, b) \geq 1$ if and only if $v(G) \geq 2$.

Proof (1) If $v^*(a, b) < 1$ then any chain between a and b must pass through s implying $v(G) = 1 < 2$.

(2) If $v(G) < 2$ then there is a pair of distinct nodes such that $v(a, b) < 2$. That is, the removal of (at most) one node disconnects a and b. However, the removal of any node $e \in X\text{-}\{a, b, s\}$ cannot disconnect a and s or b and s (since $v(s, x) \geq 2$ for all $x \in X\text{-}\{s\}$) implying a and b are still connected. Consequently, the only node whose removal can disconnect a and b must be s itself and so $v^*(a, b) < 1$.

It has been shown that $v^*(a, b) < 1$ if and only if $v(G) < 2$ which is equivalent to the desired result. $\qquad\square$

The above result leads to the following algorithm.

Algorithm (KI)
{To determine whether a network $G = (X, E)$ is 2 node-connected.}

STEP 1 Select any $s \in X$. For every node $x \in X\text{-}\{s\}$ check whether s and x are 2 node-connected. **If** not **then** terminate: the graph is *not* 2 node-connected.

STEP 2 Check whether the remaining network is connected.
If yes **then** G is 2 node-connected, otherwise it is not.

This still leaves the question (step 1) of checking that s and x are 2 node-connected. This may be achieved as follows. Suppose there is not a link sx and replace each node $j \neq s, x$ by a pair of nodes j_{in} and j_{out} and replace every arc ij by an arc ij_{in} and every arc jk by an arc $j_{out} k$. This is repeated for all $j \in X\text{-}\{s, x\}$. Finally arcs $j_{in} j_{out}$ are added. The capacity of each arc $j_{in} j_{out}$ is set to 1 and that of every other arc to ∞. Then two node-disjoint chains between s and x exist if and only if there is a conserved flow from s to x of value at least 2. (For the case when there is an arc sx see exercise 5.5.)

Algorithm (Kl) can be extended to test for k node-connectedness when $k \geq 3$ (cf. Kleitman, 1969). An alternative and computationally more efficient algorithmn when $k > 2$ is due to Even (1975).

Heuristic approach

In practice, link costs will be roughly proportional to link lengths so that if a uniform type of link is being used (eg. fibre optic cable of a given capacity) then the *triangle property*

$$c_{ik} \leq c_{ij} + c_{jk} \quad \text{for all } i \neq j \neq k \neq i$$

and often the *strict* triangle property

$$c_{ik} < c_{ij} + c_{jk} \quad \text{for all } i \neq j \neq k \neq i$$

will hold.

Theorem 5.4 Let G be a minimal cost 2 edge-connected network, with a set of non-negative edge costs, $\{c_{ik}\}$, satisfying the strict triangle property. Then the degree of every node of G is 2 or 3.

Proof For 2 edge-connectivity the degree of every node must be at least 2. Suppose now that there is a node, s say, whose degree exceeds 3. Then there are links su, sv, sw and sx for distinct nodes u, v, w, $x \in X - \{s\}$. Since the network is 2 edge-connected, there must be a chain π_{ux} between u and x which does not use link us, and also a chain π_{vw} between v and w which does not use link sv. It may be assumed without loss of generality that π_{ux} and π_{vw} have no links in common. [If this were not so, then it is readily seen that from links in π_{ux} and π_{vw} there is a pair π_{uv} and π_{wx} of chains between u and v and between w and x respectively which have no common edge. Renaming u, v, w, x by v, w, x, u respectively leads to the required property holding.]

Now form a network G^* by removing su and sv and including uv if not already present. By the strict triangle property the cost of G^* is less than the cost of G. Since G is a minimum cost 2 edge-connected network it follows that G^* cannot be 2 edge-connected. However, it will be shown that this is not the case and so the supposition that node *s* had degree 4 (or more) was false and the desired result follows.

To show that *G** is 2 edge-connected requires an extra result (theorem 5.6), and so the rest of the proof is established as a corollary to theorem 5.6.   □

From theorem 5.4 it follows that a minimum cost 2 edge-connected network may be described as a *cycle with 'ears'* and possibly ears on ears, etc. Given a set of nodes and edges, an *ear* may be described as a chain between two nodes already present and containing no other nodes or edges already present. An example is shown in figure 5.10. (Note that there are alternative descriptions with other starting cycles, for example the network could start with the cycle formed by the shaded nodes together with two open circles and the edges connecting them.)

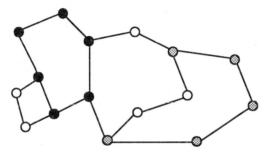

Figure 5.10 A 2 edge-connected network of the form of a cycle (solid circles) with two ears and an ear (shaded circles) on one of these ears.

This characterisation has been used by Monma and Shallcross (1989) to devise heuristic methods for finding a minimum cost, or near minimum cost, 2 edge-connected network. One of these methods is given below.

Algorithm (MS)
{Monma & Shallcross 'Greedy-Ears Sparse' method.
  Input: a set of nodes and internode distances.}
    (Find cycle)
    Randomly select a node *v*. Select a node *w* whose shortest chain π_{wv} to *v* is the longest. Let *u* be the node next to *w* on π_{wv}. A cycle is constructed from edge *uw* and a shortest chain from *u* to *w* not using *uw*.

while not all nodes connected **do**
begin

Select a node z not already in the solution whose shortest chain π_1 to a node on the solution is longest among all nodes not already on the solution. Find a chain π_2 from z to a node on the partial solution graph which does not use any of the edges or nodes on π_1. The combination of π_1 and π_2 forms an ear which is added to the solution.

end

{Output: a 'low cost' 2 edge-connected network.}

For various other heuristic methods the reader is referred to Monma and Shallcross (1989).

A Lagrangean approach to connectivity

A Lagrangean approach to connectivity was developed in section 4.3. In order to extend this, alternative characterisations of 2 edge-connectivity and 2 node-connectivity are required.

For any graph $G = (X, E)$ an *s-bipartition*, $<R, s, T>$, of G comprises an element $s \in X$ and a pair of sets R and T which form a partition of X. That is,

$$R \cup \{s\} \cup T = X$$
$$R \cap T = \varnothing$$
$$s \notin R \cup T.$$

$<R, s, T>$ is a *proper s-bipartition* if neither R nor T is the empty set.

The *capacity* $c(R, T)$ of a proper bipartition $<R, T>$ of graph G is the number of links with one end node in R and the other in T. The *capacity* $c(R, s, T)$ of a proper s-bipartition $<R, s, T>$ is the number of links with one end node in R and the other in T. If G is connected and $c(R, s, T) = 0$ then s is called an *articulation point*, and if $c(R, T) = 0$ then the single link between R and T is called a *bridge*. These concepts are illustrated in figure 5.11.

The following result is immediate.

Theorem 5.5 If $G = (V, E)$ is 2 edge-connected then it is connected and has no bridges. If further, G is 2 node-connected then it has no articulation point either.

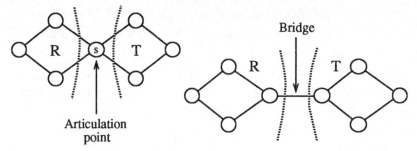

Figure 5.11 On the left is shown an example of a proper s-bipartition $<R, s, T>$ and an articulation point; on the right is shown a proper bipartition $<R, T>$ and a bridge.

The converse of theorem 5.5 will now be established in theorems 5.6 and 5.7.

Theorem 5.6 If G is connected and has no bridges then it is 2 edge-connected.

Proof Let r and t be arbitrary distinct nodes of G and

$$\pi = u_0 u_1 \ldots u_{m+1} \text{ (where } u_0 \equiv r \text{ and } u_{m+1} \equiv t)$$

be a chain from r to t - there must be at least one since G is connected. The desired result holds if r and t can be shown to be 2 edge-connected. Suppose they are not, then there is a node u_p, $p \leq m$ say, such that u_0 is 2 edge-connected to $u_1 \ldots u_p$ but not to u_{p+1}. [Since there is no bridge, $p \geq 1$.] Then for each $j \leq p$ there is a chain π_{alt}^j between r and u_j which does not include any edge $u_i u_{i+1}$, $0 \leq i < j$. Now denote by D the set

$$D = \{ x \mid x \text{ is on } \pi_{alt}^j \text{ for some } j \text{ with } 1 \leq j \leq p \}.$$

and consider the graph G^* that is obtained from G by removing the edge $u_p u_{p+1}$. G^* must be connected (otherwise $u_p u_{p+1}$ is a bridge) and so

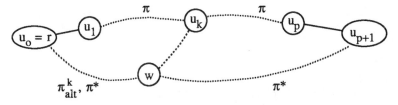

Figure 5.12 Illustration of the chain π^* of theorem 5.6.

there is a chain π^* between u_{p+1} and u_o. Let w be the first node in D encountered by π^* (travelling from u_{p+1}) and suppose that w lies on π_{alt}^k (that is, $j = k$) (cf. figure 5.12). [Note that w may coincide with u_o or u_k but this does not matter.] A new chain π_{alt}^{p+1} between u_o and u_{p+1} can now been found by following π_{alt}^k as far as w then following π^* from w to u_{p+1}. By construction, π_{alt}^{p+1} does not contain any edge $u_i u_{i+1}$, $0 \le i \le p$ and so $r = u_o$ is 2 edge-connected to u_{p+1}; but this is a contradiction and so the desired result follows.   □

Corollary The graph G^* of theorem 5.4 is 2 edge-connected.

Proof It is sufficient to show that the capacity $c^*<R, T>$ in G^* of every proper bipartition $<R, T>$ is at least 2. Let $<R, T>$ be such a proper bipartition. If $\{s, u, v\} \subset R$ or $\{s, u, v\} \subset T$ then $c^*<R, T> = c<R, T> \ge 2$. If $u \in R$, $\{s, v\} \subset T$ or vice versa then link uv and a link on π_{ux} 'cross the gap' between R and T and so $c^*<R, T> \ge 2$. Similarly if $v \in R$, $\{s, u\} \subset T$ or vice versa. The only remaining possibility is that $s \in R$, $\{v, w\} \subset T$ (or vice versa), but in this case there must be links from both (π_{ux} or sx) and (π_{vw} or sw) 'crossing the gap' and as these links distinct, $c^*<R, T> \ge 2$.

2 edge-connectivity can now be incorporated into a Lagrangean scheme by imposing the constraints (cf. section 4.1)

$$\Sigma_{i \in R} \Sigma_{j \in T} y_{ij} \ge 2 \text{ for all proper bipartitions } <R, T>. \qquad (5.22)$$

Theorem 5.7 If a graph G is 2 edge-connected and has no articulation point then it is also 2 node-connected.

Proof The proof is very similar to that of theorem 5.5 and hence is only given in outline.

A chain

$$\pi = u_o u_1 \ldots u_{m+1} \text{ (where } u_o \equiv r \text{ and } u_{m+1} \equiv t)$$

from $r = u_o$ to $t = u_{m+1}$ is considered as before, but this time u_o is 2 node-connected to $u_1 \ldots u_p$ but not to u_{p+1}. π_{alt}^j is a chain between u_o and u_j which does not include any edge $u_i u_{i+1}$, $0 \le i < j$. Let

$$D = \{ x \mid x \text{ is on } \pi_{alt}^j \text{ for some } j \text{ with } 1 \le j < p \}$$

and G^* the graph G with u_p and incident edges removed. Let π^* be a chain between u_{p+1} and u_o in G^* and w the first node in D encountered by π^* (travelling from u_{p+1}). If w lies on π_{alt}^k then two node disjoint chains between u_0 and u_{p+1} may be obtained from $\{ \pi, \pi^*, \pi_{alt}^k \pi_{alt}^{k+1} \}$. $\square$

2 node-connectivity can thus be incorporated into a Lagrangean scheme by imposing the constraints (cf. section 4.1)

$$\Sigma_{i \in R} \Sigma_{j \in T} y_{ij} \geq 2 \text{ for all proper } s\text{-bipartitions} <R, s, T>. \qquad (5.23)$$

The complete sets of constraints (5.22), (5.23) would not normally be used explicitly. Rather, a convenient subset would be used initially, then other constraints that are found to be violated would be added as necessary. This is a case of *constraint generation* and is illustrated by the next example.

Example 5.9 Find a minimal cost 2 edge-connected network connecting the nodes 1, ..., 7 of figure 5.13 for the given cost matrix (p_{ij}).

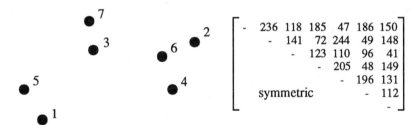

Figure 5.13 The matrix (p_{ij}) of costs to establish links between nodes 1, ..., 7 is shown on the right.

Solution Bipartitions $<R, T>$ will first be considered in which R is a singleton set and $T = \{1, ..., 7\} - R$. From figure 5.13 it is apparent that the nodes form three natural clusters: $\{1, 5\}$, $\{2, 4, 6\}$ and $\{3, 7\}$. For cluster $\{2, 4, 6\}$ it is easily verified that a set of multipliers maximising $\Sigma_R \lambda_R$ is $\lambda_{\{2\}} = 36.5$, $\lambda_{\{4\}} = 35.5$ and $\lambda_{\{6\}} = 12.5$. For $\{1, 5\}$ giving approximately equal attention to the two nodes is satisfactory and it is optimal to set $\lambda_{\{1\}} = 23$ and $\lambda_{\{5\}} = 24$. It is less clear why $\lambda_{\{3\}} = 10$ and $\lambda_{\{7\}} = 31$ are the right choices; it is in fact so that $p_{35} - \lambda_{\{3\}} - \lambda_{\{5\}} = p_{57} - \lambda_{\{5\}} - \lambda_{\{7\}}$. Figure 5.14 illustrates the reductions so far; the interpretation is that the parts of potential links that fall within any circle have been 'used up' in building the bound $\Sigma_R \lambda_R$. Notice that the circles for each cluster just touch and nothing is to be gained by increasing the multipliers (radii).

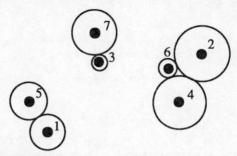

Figure 5.14 The radius of the circle about node i is proportional to the corresponding multiplier λ_i, for $i = 1, ..., 7$.

Let $q_{ij} = p_{ij} - \sum_{R \mid i \in R, j \notin R} \lambda_R - \sum_{R \mid i \notin R, j \in R} \lambda_R$ for all i and j, $i \neq j$. Since all sets R that have been chosen are singleton sets this reduces to $q_{ij} = p_{ij} - \lambda_{\{i\}} - \lambda_{\{j\}}$ and for the given set of multipliers the *reduced* matrix (q_{ij}) is

$$(q_{ij}) = \begin{bmatrix} - & 176.5 & 85 & 126.5 & 0 & 150.5 & 96 \\ & - & 94.5 & 0 & 183.5 & 0 & 80.5 \\ & & - & 77.5 & 76 & 73.5 & 0 \\ & & & - & 145.5 & 0 & 82.5 \\ & \text{symmetric} & & & - & 159.5 & 76 \\ & & & & & - & 68.5 \\ & & & & & & - \end{bmatrix}$$

and $\Lambda = \sum_R \lambda_R = 345$. The reduced matrix has a zero in each row and one in each column. At this point we could continue with the full matrix considering $\{1, 5\}$, $\{2, 4, 6\}$ and $\{3, 7\}$ as candidates for the set R. Since our interest is in zero (or negative) matrix elements it is sufficient for our purposes to continue with the problem in which clusters are regarded as though they were single nodes. For this, p_{RS}, the cost of establishing a link between *cluster R* and *cluster S* is defined to be

$$p_{RS} = \min_{i \in R, j \in S} q_{ij}.$$

The set of cluster nodes and the matrix are given in figure 5.15. The optimal allocation of multipliers is $\lambda_{\{1, 5\}} = 67$, $\lambda_{\{2, 4, 6\}} = 59.5$ and $\lambda_{\{3, 7\}} = 9$. The revised lower bound is

$$\Lambda = \sum_R \lambda_R = 345 + 2(67 + 59.5 + 9) = 616.$$

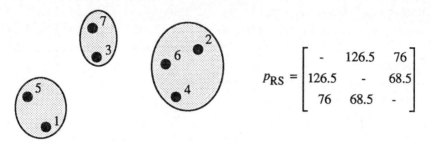

$$P_{RS} = \begin{bmatrix} - & 126.5 & 76 \\ 126.5 & - & 68.5 \\ 76 & 68.5 & - \end{bmatrix}$$

Figure 5.15 The matrix of link establishment costs between cluster nodes $\{1, 5\}$, $\{2, 4, 6\}$ and $\{3, 7\}$ is shown on the right.

Tracing back through the calculations it is found that no p_{ij} has been reduced below zero and that the zeros correspond to the links of the network in figure 5.16.

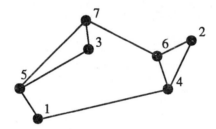

Figure 5.16 Links with zero reduced cost.

Discarding links 5-7 and 4-6 leaves a feasible network (cf. figure 5.17) with zero cost relative to the reduced matrix, the one with cost 616 relative to the original matrix (p_{ij}). Thus an upper bound of 616 has been found as well as a lower bound of 616. Consequently, the network of figure 5.16 is the required optimal solution. □

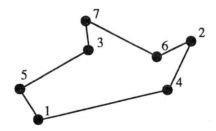

Figure 5.17 The optimal solution for example 5.9.

Note that the network of figure 5.17 is 2 node-connected as well as being 2 edge-connected. Also, the reader familiar with the travelling salesman problem will notice the similarity of that problem to the present one. However, the solution to the present problem is not guaranteed to yield a salesman tour (cf. exercise 5.6).

Another restriction that is sometimes imposed is that there should be no long 'strings of nodes' of degree 2. More precisely, on any chain π containing m nodes at least one must have degree 3 or greater; that is

$$\Sigma_{i \in R} \Sigma_{j \in T} y_{ij} \geq 3 \quad \text{if } |R| = m. \tag{5.24}$$

5.5 LINEAR NETWORK DESIGN

The minimum number of links necessary to obtain a connected network on n nodes is n-1, and this number is realised by spanning trees and spanning trees only. Thus it is clear that an MST must provide a minimal cost connected network when $d_{ij} > 0$ for all i and j. In this section it will be assumed that the budget available will permit more than the bare minimum number of links to be established. How then can these extra resources be used to best advantage? As a first step the problem of minimising the average path length will be considered when the linear flow approximation is made; this problem is called the *Optimal Network Problem* (or ONP for short).

ONP will now be formulated as a mathematical program. First, note that in the formulation of the minimal cost multicommodity flow problem of section 2.2, the summations were implicitly limited to links actually present. The presence or absence of a link will now be part of the optimisation process and for this variables y_{ij} are introduced where

$$y_{ij} = \begin{cases} 1 & \text{if link } ij \text{ is in the network} \\ 0 & \text{otherwise} \end{cases}$$

together with constraints

$$x_{ij}^{rt} \leq D_{rt} y_{ij}.$$

When $y_{ij} = 0$ the flow x_{ij}^{rt} for each OD pair (r, t) must be zero. If $y_{ij} = 1$

then x_{ij}^{rt} may have value up to the total flow (D_{rt}) to be sent from r to t. The optimal network problem now becomes:

ONP: minimise $\sum_i \sum_j c_{ij} \left(\sum_r \sum_t x_{ij}^{rt} \right)$

      subject to

$$\sum_i x_{ij}^{rt} - \sum_k x_{jk}^{rt} = \begin{cases} -D_{rt} & j=r \\ 0 & j \neq r, t \\ D_{rt} & j=t \end{cases}$$

$$x_{ij}^{rt} \leq D_{rt} y_{ij} \qquad \text{for all } i, j, r \text{ and } t \qquad (5.25)$$

$$\sum_i \sum_j p_{ij} y_{ij} \leq B$$

$$x_{ij}^{rt} \geq 0 \qquad \text{for all } i, j, r \text{ and } t$$

$$y_{ij} \in \{0, 1\} \qquad \text{for all } i \text{ and } j.$$

This is the Optimal Network Problem, in *disaggregate form*. As noted in section 2.1 the flows could be aggregated to a set $\{ x_{ij}^r \}$ where x_{ij}^r is the total flow from origin node r flowing along link ij. It has been found, however, that it is often better when using dual-based methods to work with the disaggregate form even though many more variables are involved (Magnanti et al, 1986). The reason for this is that though the aggregate and disaggregated formulations are equivalent for the integer - constrained problem, they are not equivalent for the linear programming relaxations with the relaxation of the disaggregate version tending to be 'stronger' (that is, it has a smaller feasible region).

A Lagrangean relaxation

The constraints of (5.25), which relate the x and y variables, cause the problem to be difficult and so these are incorporated into the objective with multipliers λ_{ij}^{rt} to get

ONP: minimise $\sum_i \sum_j \sum_r \sum_t (c_{ij} + \lambda_{ij}^{rt}) x_{ij}^{rt} - \sum_i \sum_j \sum_r \sum_t \lambda_{ij}^{rt} D_{rt} y_{ij}$

      subject to

$$\sum_i x_{ij}^{rt} - \sum_k x_{jk}^{rt} = \begin{cases} -D_{rt} & j=r \\ 0 & j \neq r, t \\ D_{rt} & j=t \end{cases}$$

$$\Sigma_i \Sigma_j p_{ij} y_{ij} \le B$$

$$x_{ij}^{rt} \ge 0 \qquad\qquad \text{for all } i, j, r \text{ and } t$$

$$y_{ij} \in \{0, 1\} \qquad\qquad \text{for all } i \text{ and } j.$$

This decomposes readily into two independent subproblems.

$P_{x\lambda}$:   minimise $\Sigma_i \Sigma_j \Sigma_r \Sigma_t (c_{ij} + \lambda_{ij}^{rt}) x_{ij}^{rt}$
     subject to

$$\Sigma_i x_{ij}^{rt} - \Sigma_k x_{jk}^{rt} = \begin{cases} -D_{rt} & j = r \\ 0 & j \ne r, t \\ D_{rt} & j = t \end{cases}$$

$$x_{ij}^{rt} \ge 0 \quad \text{for all } i, j, r \text{ and } t.$$

and

$P_{y\lambda}$:   maximise $\Sigma_i \Sigma_j \Sigma_r \Sigma_t \lambda_{ij}^{rt} D_{rt} y_{ij}$
     subject to

$$\Sigma_i \Sigma_j p_{ij} y_{ij} \le B$$

$$y_{ij} \in \{0, 1\} \qquad\qquad \text{for all } i \text{ and } j.$$

$P_{x\lambda}$ solves straightforwardly using a shortest distance algorithm (cf. section 2.2). The subproblem $P_{y\lambda}$ (converted to a maximisation problem because of the negative sign) is just a 0-1 knapsack problem. While this is computationally complex (to be more precise it is NP-hard: cf. Garey and Johnson, 1979) there is a very simple bound obtained by relaxing the constraint $y_{ij} \in \{0, 1\}$ to $0 \le y_{ij} \le 1$. Thus a lower bound to $v(\text{ONP})$ is

$$\text{LB(ONP)} = v(P_{x\lambda}) - v(\bar{P}_{y\lambda})$$

where $\bar{P}_{y\lambda}$ is obtained from $P_{y\lambda}$ by relaxing the integrality constraint. Suppose, for a prespecified $\varepsilon \ge 0$, that a value $\lambda = \lambda^*$ and a feasible solution (x^*, y^*) can be found such that

$$v(\text{ONP} \mid (x, y) = (x^*, y^*)) - \text{LB}(\lambda^*) < \varepsilon.$$

Then (x^*, y^*) may be accepted as being 'optimal to within a tolerance of ε' and is said to be ε-*optimal*. If ε is chosen to be zero then 'ε-optimality' is just the normal concept of optimality. When, for the chosen value of ε, an ε-optimal solution cannot be found then the solution of the problem may completed using B&B.

Initial lower bounds

To start with consider the simplest case in which $\lambda = 0$. $v(P_{x0})$ is just the total communication cost relative to the link lengths a_{ij}, and if the triangle property holds then

$$v(P_{x0}) = \Sigma_r \Sigma_t a_{rt} D_{rt} \tag{5.26}$$

$v(P_{y0})$ is clearly zero and the value of LB(ONP), denoted by LB(0), is just $v(P_{x0})$ as expressed in (5.26). It should be noted that since $\lambda = 0$ no account is being taken of the constraint connecting x and y variables.

Example 5.10 Seven nodes are situated as shown in figure 5.18 (cf. example 5.9). The matrix of link establishment costs, $\{p_{ij}\}$, and the traffic demand matrix are given below. Path lengths are measured in hops.

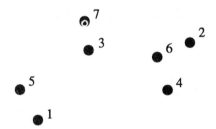

Figure 5.18 The seven nodes 1, ..., 7 are to be connected together so as to minimise total communication cost subject to a budget of $B = 836$.

$$(p_{ij}) = \begin{bmatrix} - & 236 & 118 & 185 & 47 & 186 & 150 \\ & - & 141 & 72 & 244 & 49 & 148 \\ & & - & 123 & 110 & 96 & 41 \\ & & & - & 205 & 48 & 149 \\ \text{symmetric} & & & & - & 196 & 131 \\ & & & & & - & 112 \\ & & & & & & - \end{bmatrix}$$

$$(D_{ij}) = \begin{bmatrix} - & 17 & 7 & 13 & 10 & 7 & 16 \\ & - & 8 & 11 & 13 & 9 & 18 \\ & & - & 6 & 5 & 4 & 6 \\ & & & - & 9 & 4 & 11 \\ & \text{symmetric} & & & - & 8 & 15 \\ & & & & & - & 5 \\ & & & & & & - \end{bmatrix}$$

Find a low cost communication network and a lower bound to the minimal cost if the available budget is 836 (ie. 30% of the cost of establishing all possible links).

Solution Here, only the lower bound LB(0) will be calculated with feasible solutions and better lower bounds being derived in examples 5.11 and 5.12.

Recalling that to each OD pair (r, t) there is an OD pair (t, r) with the same level of traffic demand,

$$\text{LB}(0) = v(P_{x0}) = \Sigma_r \, \Sigma_t \, c_{rt} D_{rt} = 404 \text{ hops.}$$

Note that as $\lambda = 0$ there is no restriction on the links chosen other than that their total cost does not exceed B; consequently there is no easy way of deriving a feasible solution from the calculation of LB(0). ☐

As λ_{ij}^{rt} is increased so account can be taken of the interdependence of the x and y variables. Suppose that a particular link ij is not included in the network then traffic between i and j has to travel an extra 'distance', δ_{ij} say. When the triangle property is satisfied

$$\delta_{ij} = \min_{k \neq i, j} (c_{ik} + c_{kj}) - c_{ij}.$$

When calculating $v(P_{x\lambda})$ the contribution per unit flow corresponding to OD pair (i, j) is

$$c_{ij} + \lambda_{ij}^{ij} \quad \text{if } \lambda_{ij}^{ij} \leq \delta_{ij}$$
$$c_{ij} + \delta_{ij} \quad \text{if } \lambda_{ij}^{ij} \geq \delta_{ij}$$

assuming $\lambda_{ij}^{rt} = 0$ for all $(r, t) \neq (i, j)$. Thus setting

$$\lambda_{ij}^{rt} = \begin{cases} \delta_{ij} & \text{if } (r, t) = (i, j) \\ 0 & \text{otherwise} \end{cases} \tag{5.27}$$

for all i and j $(i \neq j)$ leads to

$$v(P_{x\lambda}) = \Sigma_r \Sigma_t (c_{rt} + \delta_{rt})D_{rt}.$$

Moreover, there is a non-trivial knapsack problem to solve resulting in a non-zero value for $v(\overline{P}_{y\lambda})$. The lower bound $v(P_{x\lambda}) - v(\overline{P}_{y\lambda})$ obtained from this prescription for λ will be denoted by LB(1).

Example 5.11 Continue the solution of example 5.10.

Solution Since $c_{ij} = 1$ for all links ij (hops are being counted) it follows that $\delta_{ij} = 1$ for all i, j also. Hence $v(P_{x\lambda}) = \Sigma_r \Sigma_t (c_{rt} + \delta_{rt})D_{rt} = 808$ hops. To compute $v(\overline{P}_{y\lambda})$ the links are arranged in order of decreasing $(\Sigma_r \Sigma_t \lambda_{ij}^{rt} D_{rt})/p_{ij}$ which for the given values of λ_{ij}^{rt} reduces to D_{ij}/p_{ij}.

Table 5.6

Link	D_{ij}	p_{ij}	D_{ij}/p_{ij}	$\Sigma_{\text{cumulative}}\, p_{ij}$
1-5	10	47	0.213	47
2-6	9	49	0.184	96
2-4	11	72	0.153	168
3-7	6	41	0.146	209
2-7	18	148	0.122	357
5-7	15	131	0.115	488
1-7	16	150	0.107	638
4-6	4	48	0.083	686
4-7	11	149	0.074	835
1-2	17	236	0.072	1071
1-4	13	185	0.070	1256
1-3	7	118	0.059	1374
2-3	8	141	0.057	1515
2-5	13	244	0.053	1759
3-4	6	123	0.049	1882
3-5	5	110	0.045	1992
6-7	5	112	0.045	2104
4-5	9	205	0.044	2309
3-6	4	96	0.042	2405
5-6	8	196	0.041	2601
1-6	7	186	0.038	2787

The budget available is 836 and this is expended when y_{ij} has been set to 1 for $i\text{-}j$ = 1-5, 2-6, 2-4, ..., 4-7 and y_{12} = $(836 - 835)/236$ = 0.004; all other y_{ij} are set to zero. The value of the knapsack problem is then

$$v(\overline{P}_{y\lambda}) = 2 \times \{100 + 0.004 \times 17\} \approx 200$$

from which $LB(1) = 808 - 200 = 608$, a substantial improvement on $LB(0)$. From this calculation there is a corresponding feasible solution, namely the one given by the links for which $y_{ij} = 1$; this solution is shown in figure 5.19. The associated cost is readily computed to be 646. Hence the minimal cost of a feasible network is limited by

$$608 \le v(ONP) \le 646; \tag{5.28}$$

that is, the feasible solution found (the *incumbent*) is within 6% of optimality at worst.   □

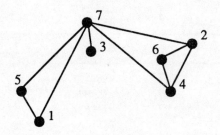

Figure 5.19 A feasible solution to the problem of example 5.11.

The weakness of the bound $LB(1)$ is that it is based on the extra cost resulting when link $i\text{-}j$ is prohibited, calculated relative to *one OD pair only* (namely, $(i,\ j)$). However, for relatively sparse networks, traffic for several OD pairs may well need to be re-routed if $i\text{-}j$ is not permitted. To take (some) account of this, increasing λ_{ij}^{rt} for $(r,\ t) \ne (i,\ j)$ will now be considered.

Exercise 5.12 For the problem of examples 5.10, 5.11, obtain a better lower bound, $LB(2)$, using the strategy indicated above.

Solution There are three (pairs of) OD pairs, viz $(1,\ 6)$ and $(6,\ 1)$, $(3,\ 6)$ and $(6,\ 3)$, and $(5,\ 6)$ and $(6,\ 5)$ for which the origin and destination are three links apart in the solution of figure 5.19. Consider OD pair $(3,\ 6)$ and set

$\lambda_{36}^{36} \leftarrow 1 + \varepsilon$

$\lambda_{16}^{36} \leftarrow \varepsilon$ (alternative is $\lambda_{13}^{36} \leftarrow \varepsilon$)

$\lambda_{23}^{36} \leftarrow \varepsilon$

$\lambda_{34}^{36} \leftarrow \varepsilon$

$\lambda_{56}^{36} \leftarrow \varepsilon$ (alternative is $\lambda_{35}^{36} \leftarrow \varepsilon$)

$\lambda_{67}^{36} \leftarrow \varepsilon.$

With ε set to 2.4 the analogue of the data of table 5.6 is given in table 5.7, from which the lower bound LB(2) may now be calculated. The distance between nodes 3 and 6 has been increased by 2.4 and so $v(P_{x\lambda})$ is increased by $2\times(4\times2.4) = 19.2$. $v(\bar{P}_{y\lambda})$ is unchanged at 200 so that

$$LB(2) = 808 + 19.2 - 200 = 627.2.$$

Table 5.7

Link	$\sum_r \sum_t \lambda_{ij}^{36} D_{ij}$	P_{ij}	$\sum_r \sum_t \lambda_{ij}^{36} D_{rt} / P_{ij}$	$\sum_{\text{cumulative}} P_{ij}$
1-5	10	47	0.213	47
2-6	9	49	0.184	96
2-4	11	72	0.153	168
3-7	6	41	0.146	209
2-7	18	148	0.122	357
5-7	15	131	0.115	488
1-7	16	150	0.107	1340
4-6	4	48	0.083	2584
4-7	11	149	0.074	749
2-3	8+2.4	141	0.074	2440
1-2	17	236	0.072	1190
1-4	13	185	0.070	1689
3-4	6+2.4	123	0.068	2707
3-6	4+2.4	96	0.067	2536
6-7	5+2.4	112	0.066	600
1-3	7	118	0.059	2299
5-6	8+2.4	196	0.053	1885
2-5	13	244	0.053	1584
1-6	7+2.4	186	0.051	2071
3-5	5	110	0.045	2181
4-5	9	205	0.044	954

Since the solution of the ONP must be an integer the bound may be rounded up to 628. At this point it may be asserted that

$$628 \leq v(\text{ONP}) \leq 646,$$

an appreciable improvement on (5.19). Indeed the improvement is very much better than it appears since there is a superior feasible solution with value 628 as shown in figure 5.20. Thus

$$628 \leq v(\text{ONP}) \leq 628$$

and an optimal solution has been obtained.   □

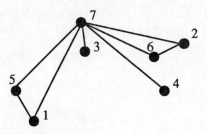

Figure 5.20 A solution of value 628.

5.6 CONSTRUCTIVE HEURISTIC METHODS

For many problems use of exact methods is neither feasible nor sensible, and heuristic methods are appropriate. A *heuristic* method is one which does not guarantee an optimal solution (and so is 'approximate') but should yield a 'good' solution for 'relatively little effort'. In tsis section *constructive* and *improvement* heuristic methods will be described with reference to the Optimal Network Problem.

By a *constructive* method will be meant one which starts from some initial *infeasible* state and 'works towards feasibility' by, in some sense, 'constructing' a feasible solution. Kruskal's algorithm (cf. section 4.1) is a good example of a constructive method, the initial state being that in which no links have been assigned, then links are added one at a time until *n*-1 links have been added and a tree has resulted. Since an optimal solution (MST) results, Kruskal's algorithm is a constructive *exact* method, but in this section the interest will be in constructive heuristic methods.

The term 'construct' will be used in a wide sense. In example 5.13 below, construction corresponds to the *removal* of links; however, the idea of working towards feasibility is still present.

Heuristic methods are generally flexible and can be adapted fairly easily to 'small' changes in problem structure. This will be taken advantage of with ideas concerning heuristics being introduced via the Optimal Network Problem (cf. section 5.5), then similar methods for non-linear design problems are indicated by analogy.

A greedy algorithm

Consider what happens as links are successively removed from an undirected network in which initially all $n(n-1)/2$ possible (undirected) links are present. (Such a network is called *complete*.) If these removals are performed for as long as possible while maintaining connectivity then after $t = n(n-1)/2 - (n-1) = (n-1)(n-2)/2$ links have been removed a spanning tree will be obtained. When the p-th link, $i_p j_p$ say, is removed then some OD pairs are unaffected, but for others new shortest paths will be required and these will be at least as long as the previously shortest paths. This observation leads immediately to the following result.

Theorem 5.8 Let (X, A) and (X, B) be two connected undirected graphs on node set X with $B \subset A$. Then, with respect to link lengths d_{ij}

$$d^A(x, y) \le d^B(x, y) \text{ for all nodes } x, y$$

where $d^A(x, y)$ and $d^B(x, y)$ denote the shortest distances between x and y using only links in A and B respectively. Moreover, if traffic is fixed for each OD pair, the average path length is less for (X, A) than for (X, B). $\qquad\square$

Theorem 5.8 shows that, budget aside, it is not possible to better the complete network (or more generally the network in which all permitted links are included). Of course the budget available is unlikely to be sufficient for this to be a feasible solution. Consequently, in order to obtain a feasible solution at least one of the links must be 'discarded'; it seems sensible to discard the one which leads to the least increase in average path length - hence the use of the term 'greedy'. If the budget constraint is still not met then the link which gives rise to the least further increase in path length is discarded, and so on until a feasible solution is obtained. More formally, if $e(ij)$ is the increase in average path length when link ij is removed from the graph $G^{(t)} = (X, A^{(t)})$, the algorithm may be formulated as

Algorithm (ONP-G)
{A greedy method for obtaining an approximate solution to ONP.
  Input: a network (X, A) and a set of link weights $\{d_{ij}\}$. }
    Calculate the set of increases $\{e(ij)\}$. Set $t = 0$.
    Let $G^{(0)} = (X, A)$ be the network on node set A which contains all permissible links.
    while the budget constraint is **not** satisfied **do**
    begin
      if $e(pq) = \min_{ij \in A^{(t)}} [e(ij)]$
      then set $G^{(t+1)} = (X, A^{(t+1)})$ where $A^{(t+1)} = A^{(t)} - \{pq\}$, and $t \leftarrow t+1$.
      Update the set of increases $\{e(ij)\}$.
    end
{Output: $G^{(t)}$ is an approximate solution to ONP.}

Note that it is implicitly assumed that a feasible solution exists.

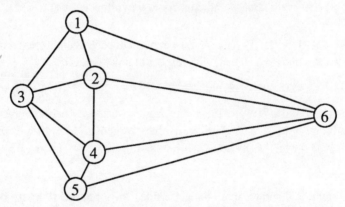

Figure 5.21 The six nodes are to be connected using no more than 650 miles of cable so that the average number of hops made by packets is minimised. Only links from among those shown may be established.

Example 5.13 Six nodes, distributed approximately as indicated in figure 5.21 are to be connected subject to a budget constraint B sufficient to install 650 miles of cable; the only links that may be considered are the ones shown in the figure. The traffic generated is the same for all possible OD pairs (30 in number) and the internode distances, in miles, are given by the matrix that follows.

$$
(a_{ij}) = \begin{bmatrix}
- & 32 & 50 & \infty & \infty & 149 \\
 & - & 41 & 40 & \infty & 132 \\
 & & - & 50 & 58 & \infty \\
 & & & - & 22 & 132 \\
 & & & & - & 146 \\
 & & & & & -
\end{bmatrix}
$$

If routing is by shortest path with respect to hop length, use algorithm (ONP-G) to find a feasible network with a low (preferably least) average number of hops per packet.

Solution Denote by $c(G)$ the cost $\sum_{i<j,\ ij\in A} a_{ij}$ of $G = (X, A)$, in terms of miles of cable installed. Also since the traffic is the same for each OD pair we may solve the problem by minimising $v(G) = \sum_r \sum_t d(r, t)$ where $d(r, t)$ is the number of hops travelled by each packet from origin r to destination t. For the initial network $G^{(0)}$

$$
(d(r, t)) = \begin{bmatrix}
- & 1 & 1 & 2 & 2 & 1 \\
 & - & 1 & 1 & 2 & 1 \\
 & & - & 1 & 1 & 2 \\
 & & & - & 1 & 1 \\
 & & & & - & 1 \\
 & & & & & -
\end{bmatrix}
$$

$c(G^{(0)}) = 852$ miles of cable,

$v(G^{(0)}) = 2 \times 19 = 38$ hops.

On the other hand there are two MSTs, T_1 and T_2 with

$c(T_1) = c(T_2) = 267$ miles of cable,

$v(T_1) = 56$ hops, $v(T_2) = 58$ hops.

With a budget of 650 miles of cable, $650 - 267 = 383$ miles are available over and above that used by an MST and it is required to use this in the best way.

It is readily verified that removal of any of links 1-2, 1-3, ... leads to an increase of 2 hops in $v(G)$. Choose the first of these links, that is link 1-2, and remove it to get $G^{(1)}$ and the updated shortest distance matrix below (the only changed element being circled). After this the cost of the network has been reduced by 32 miles to 820 miles of cable.

$$\begin{bmatrix} - & ② & 1 & 2 & 2 & 1 \\ & - & 1 & 1 & 2 & 1 \\ & & - & 1 & 1 & 2 \\ & & & - & 1 & 1 \\ & & & & - & 1 \\ & & & & & - \end{bmatrix}$$

Now removal of 2-3, 2-4, ..., 5-6 each leads to an increase of 2 in total path length whereas removal of 1-3 or 1-6 leads to an increase of 4. Link 2-3 is chosen for removal thus decreasing the cost of the network by 41 miles to 779 miles of cable. Path lengths are increased (by 1 hop) for OD pairs (2,3) and (3,2) only.

At the third iteration, removal of 3-5, 4-5, 4-6 or 5-6 leads to an increase of 2 hops in total path length. Link 3-5 is removed, the cost being reduced by 58 miles to 721 miles of cable, and the total path length becomes 44 hops.

At the fourth iteration, 4-6 is the only link whose removal leads to an increase of but 2 hops in total path length. It is removed reducing the network cost to 589 miles of cable. This is thus a feasible solution, details of which are shown in figure 5.22.   □

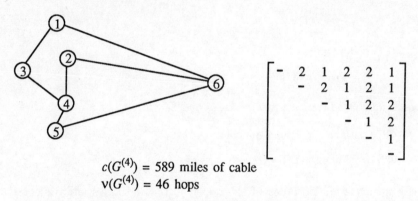

$$\begin{bmatrix} - & 2 & 1 & 2 & 2 & 1 \\ & - & 2 & 1 & 2 & 1 \\ & & - & 1 & 2 & 2 \\ & & & - & 1 & 2 \\ & & & & - & 1 \\ & & & & & - \end{bmatrix}$$

$c(G^{(4)}) = 589$ miles of cable
$v(G^{(4)}) = 46$ hops

Figure 5.22 The solution to example 5.13 showing the final network, the updated distance matrix and the values of cost and total path length.

An improved algorithm

In reducing the cost by 221 miles of cable the total path length has been increased by 8 hops. Could this be improved upon? A deficiency of algorithm (ONP-G) is that no account is taken of the cost of the links being removed, even though the removal of longer (costlier) links tends to lead to feasibility more quickly and to require fewer removals in all. An improved version of the algorithm is obtained by selecting a link for removal according to the magnitude of

$$e(i, j) = \text{(increase in average path length when } ij \text{ is removed)}/a_{ij}.$$

Example 5.14 Apply this new greedy algorithm using the data of example 5.13.

Solution Again $v(G)$ is to be optimised and, as before,

$c(G^{(0)}) = 852$ miles of cable,
$v(G^{(0)}) = 2 \times 19 = 38$ hops.

After some calculation, the matrix $(e(i, j))$ is obtained (in which all elements have been multiplied by 10^4 to avoid fractions):

$$(e(i, j)) = \begin{bmatrix} - & 625 & 400 & - & - & 134 \\ & - & 488 & 500 & - & 152 \\ & & - & 400 & 345 & - \\ & & & - & 909 & 152 \\ & & & & - & 137 \\ & & & & & - \end{bmatrix}$$

Link 1-6 has minimal value for $e(i, j)$ and so is removed for a reduction in cost to $852 - 149 = 703$ miles of cable and a new total path length of 42 hops. Next matrix $(e(i, j))$ is updated to obtain

$$(e(i, j)) = \begin{bmatrix} - & 1250 & 400 & - & - & - \\ & - & 488 & 500 & - & 303 \\ & & - & 400 & 345 & - \\ & & & - & 909 & 152 \\ & & & & - & 137 \\ & & & & & - \end{bmatrix}$$

This time link 5-6 is selected and removed giving a reduction in cost of $703 - 146 = 557$ miles of cable. The total path length is 42 hops.   □

This new solution, which just happens to remove the longest two links, has a lower total path length than that found in example 5.13 (42 hops instead of 46 hops) yet requires 32 fewer miles of cable; it is clearly a definitely superior solution.

The algorithm as applied in example 5.14 is fairly typical of *greedy constructive* methods in that an attempt is made to gain as much as possible (in this case reduction in cost) for as small a penalty (in this case increase in total path length) as possible.

The discussion so far has been in terms of the linear problem ONP. The same approach applies, however, if a non-linear objective is used. For example, if the average delay were being minimised when using an (M/M/1) delay function then the method would proceed just as before except that the merit of dropping particular links would be calculated in a different way. Thus, in example 5.14, $e(i, j)$ would be calculated as

$$e(i, j) = \text{(increase in average packet delay when } ij \text{ is removed)}/a_{ij}.$$

Additional constraints can often be incorporated into a heuristic method quite straightforwardly. For example, suppose that the solution to a design problem were required to be 2 node-connected, then all that would be needed would be to reject automatically the dropping of any link leading to 2 node-connectivity being lost. In fact in examples 5.13 and 5.14 above, this would not have altered the solution process. However, if in example 5.13 the cable limit had been 580 miles the greedy method used, ONP-G, would have terminated with the network of figure 5.22 and be unable to proceed as the dropping of any further link would violate the 2 node-connectivity requirement. Since it is apparent that there are 2 node-connected networks constructed from less than 580 miles of cable, this illustrates the following feature of constructive heuristic methods:

in tightly constrained problems a greedy constructive heuristic method may fail to find a feasible solution even though one, or more, exists.

Concave design problems

Unlike ONP, other design problems often require link capacities to be determined. In many physical problems (eg. flow in pipes) there are economies of scale in that cost is a concave function of capacity (cf. figure 5.23). Example 5.2 (section 5.1), however, shows how a concave minimum cost design problem can arise with the objective being concave in terms of flow variables even though link costs are *linear* in terms of capacity.

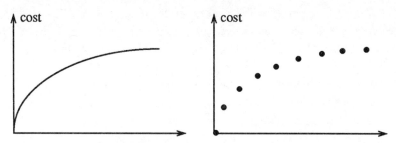

Figure 5.23 An example of concave continuous cost function and a 'concave' discrete cost function.

The difficulty with concave problems is that there are usually many local optima whose values may vary considerably. There is one positive feature though, and that is that there will always be an optimal solution at an extreme point (cf. theorem 3.6, corollary). For a multi-commodity flow problem this means that the condition may be imposed that all flow for any OD pair (r, t) must follow a *single* route from r to t.

The single route restriction is made use of in a method due to Yaged (1971). Given an initial feasible solution $x(0)$ a new solution $x^*(0)$ is generated, as in the Frank-Wolfe method (cf. section 3.3), by solving a set of shortest distance problems with respect to arc lengths $d_{ij} = d\Phi/dx_{ij}$ where Φ is the total cost and x_{ij} is the total flow of all commodities in arc ij. However, knowing that there is an optimal solution at an extreme point, no line search is performed; instead the next approximation $x(1)$ is taken to be $x^*(0)$. Similarly, $x(2) = x^*(1)$ etc. The procedure continues until convergence takes place (ie. $x^*(p+1) = x(p)$ for some p).

Example 5.15 It is required to approximate a minimum cost network using only links from among those shown in figure 5.24.

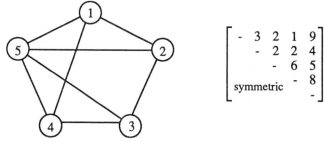

$$\begin{bmatrix} - & 3 & 2 & 1 & 9 \\ & - & 2 & 2 & 4 \\ & & - & 6 & 5 \\ & & & - & 8 \\ \text{symmetric} & & & & - \end{bmatrix}$$

Figure 5.24 The matrix of traffic requirements for example 5.15.

The cost of link ij will be taken to be $0.3x_{ij} + 2\sqrt{x_{ij}}$, this being of the same general form as derived in section 5.1 using cost functions of (5.8) in terms of capacity. Use the Yaged algorithm starting with initial routing

flow between node 1 and node 3 goes via node 2,

flow between node 2 and node 4 goes via node 3,

flow between all other nodes uses the unique single link route,

to obtain an approximation to a minimum cost solution.

Solution The initial link flows are as shown in figure 5.25a (note that flows are symmetric). The length $d_{ij} = d\Phi/dx_{ij} = 0.3 + 1/\sqrt{x_{ij}}$ of each arc ij is indicated in figure 5.25b. Routing with respect to these link lengths leads to flow between nodes 1 and 3 and between nodes 1 and 4 being diverted via node 5; routes for other OD pairs are unchanged and the resulting flow is shown in figure 5.25c. The updated link lengths are shown in figure 5.25d. It is clear that the infinite length of link 1-4 will deter any traffic using that link from now onwards, and accordingly it is dropped from the network. Using the updated link lengths of figure 5.25d it is found that flow between nodes 2 and 4 is diverted via node 5 with other routes being unchanged. The resulting flow pattern and updated link lengths are shown in figure 5.25e, f. The algorithm has now converged with no more route changes taking place.   □

It may be verified that in the above example the total cost is reduced from an initial 49.60 by 0.56 to 49.04. Is the final solution optimal? The answer is no.

Consider the removal of any link, kl say. Then the flow $\delta = x_{kl}$ that previously went along kl must now take an alternative route. The change in costs will be a reduction of $\Phi_{kl}(\delta)$ and an increase of $\Phi_{ij}(x_{ij} + \delta) - \Phi_{ij}(x_{ij})$ in each link ij along which the flow is diverted (recall the single route restriction). The new route may now be determined by selecting a shortest path relative to arc lengths $d_{ij} = \Phi_{ij}(x_{ij} + \delta) - \Phi_{ij}(x_{ij})$. This approach is described more fully in Minoux (1989).

Example 5.16 Continue the solution of the design problem of example 5.15 using the Minoux method.

Solution Figure 5.26a shows the calculation of the net change, Δ_{23}, in the total cost when link 2-3 is removed. It may also be verified that the most favourable change to make is to remove link 2-3 (cf. exercise 5.7).

After this has been done it is found that the most favourable link to drop is 1-2 and the cost change is again -0.76 (cf. figure 5.26b). Finally, the removal of any other link would now cause an increase in cost and so the procedure is terminated. The final cost is 49.04 - 0.76 - 0.76 = 47.52. ☐

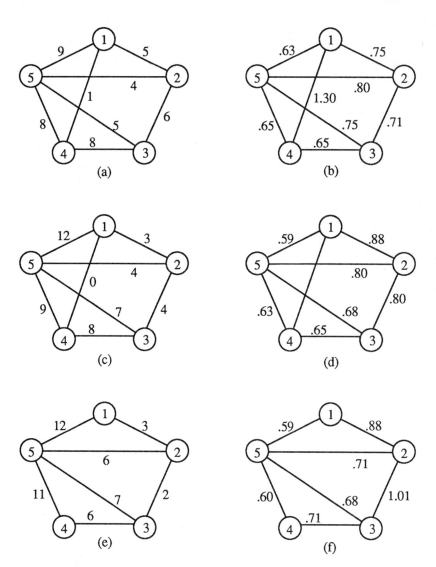

Figure 5.25 Successive stages in the application of the Yaged method.

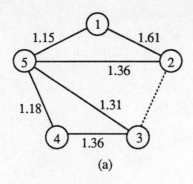

$\Phi_{23}(2) = 3.43.$

The values of d_{ij} for the other links are the increase in costs for those links when flow is increased by 2.

The shortest route between 2 and 3 is via node 5, and has length (cost) of $1.36 + 1.31 = 2.67.$

$\Delta_{23} = 2.67 - 3.43 = -0.76.$

(a)

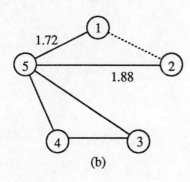

$\Phi_{12}(3) = 4.36.$

$\Delta_{12} = 1.72 + 1.88 - 4.36 = -0.76.$

(b)

Figure 5.26

5.7 LOCAL SEARCH HEURISTICS

An improvement heuristic algorithm

The underlying idea of *improvement heuristics* is to start with a feasible solution and, while maintaining feasibility, make a succession of adjustments each leading to an improvement in solution.

Example 5.17 Devise an improvement heuristic for ONP and, starting with the final solution of example 5.12, apply it to obtain a good solution.

Solution Two types of adjustment will be considered: in the first a link is added to the network (reducing total path length) if this can be achieved without violating the budget constraint. Since the starting solution undershoots the budget by 61 miles there are three links which are candidates for addition, namely 1-2, 2-3 and 3-5. Addition of 1-2 leads to a reduction in total path length of 2 hops for an increase in cost of 32 cable miles. The new network is shown in figure 5.24 together with the updated distance matrix.

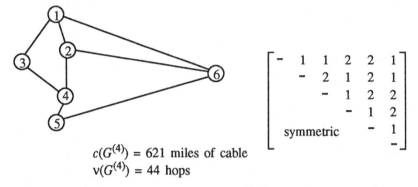

$$c(G^{(4)}) = 621 \text{ miles of cable}$$
$$v(G^{(4)}) = 44 \text{ hops}$$

Figure 5.27 The network of example 5.17 after adding link 1-2.

Now no further link can be added without violating the budget constraint. Consequently, in order to improve the solution, more complex adjustments involving the removal of a link must be considered. Many swaps (adding one link and removing another) lead to no change in $v(G)$. Accordingly a swap which does not change $v(G)$ but leads to a decrease in cost will be accepted as an improvement; this is the second type of adjustment.

Possibilities for swapping in are links 2-3, 3-5 and 4-6. Consider bringing in 2-3 followed by the removal of a link:

if the removed link is 1-2 then $\delta v(G) = 0$ hops, $\delta c(G) = -9$ miles;

1-3 then $\delta v(G) = 0$ hops, $\delta c(G) = 9$ miles;

1-6 then $\delta v(G) = 2$ hops, $\delta c(G) = -117$ miles;

2-4 then $\delta v(G) = 0$ hops, $\delta c(G) = 1$ miles;

2-6 then $\delta v(G) = 0$ hops, $\delta c(G) = -91$ miles;

3-4 then $\delta v(G) = 2$ hops, $\delta c(G) = -18$ miles;

4-5 then $\delta v(G) = 4$ hops, $\delta c(G) = 10$ miles;

5-6 then $\delta v(G) = 4$ hops, $\delta c(G) = -124$ miles.

Consider now bringing in 3-5 followed by the removal of a link:

if the removed link is 1-2 then $\delta v(G) = 0$ hops, $\delta c(G) = 26$ miles;

1-3 then $\delta v(G) = 2$ hops, $\delta c(G) = 8$ miles;

1-6 then $\delta v(G) = 0$ hops, $\delta c(G) = -91$ miles;

2-4 then $\delta v(G) = 2$ hops, $\delta c(G) = 18$ miles;

2-6 then $\delta v(G) = 0$ hops, $\delta c(G) = -74$ miles;

3-4 then $\delta v(G) = 0$ hops, $\delta c(G) = 8$ miles;

4-5 then $\delta v(G) = 0$ hops, $\delta c(G) = 36$ miles;

5-6 then $\delta v(G) = 2$ hops, $\delta c(G) = -88$ miles.

Similarly bringing in 4-6 followed by the removal of a link:

if the removed link is 1-2 then $\delta v(G) = 0$ hops, $\delta c(G) = 100$ miles;

1-3 then $\delta v(G) = 2$ hops, $\delta c(G) = 82$ miles;

1-6 then $\delta v(G) = 2$ hops, $\delta c(G) = -17$ miles;

2-4 then $\delta v(G) = 0$ hops, $\delta c(G) = 92$ miles;

2-6 then $\delta v(G) = 4$ hops, $\delta c(G) = 82$ miles;

3-4 then $\delta v(G) = 0$ hops, $\delta c(G) = 8$ miles;

4-5 then $\delta v(G) = 2$ hops, $\delta c(G) = 110$ miles;

5-6 then $\delta v(G) = 2$ hops, $\delta c(G) = -14$ miles.

There are just four swaps which leave $v(G)$ unchanged but reduce $c(G)$. It is natural to choose one leading to the largest reduction in cost $c(G)$, and so the swap of links 2-3 and 2-6 is accepted leading to

$v(G) = 44$ hops, $c(G) = 530$ miles of cable.

There is now enough slack in the budget constraint to permit the addition of link 3-5 which gives $\delta v(G) = -2$ hops, $\delta c(G) = 50$ miles. The solution is shown in figure 5.28.

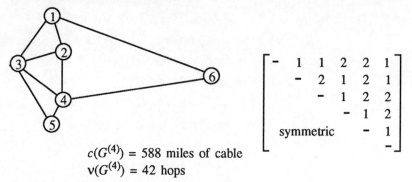

$c(G^{(4)}) = 588$ miles of cable
$v(G^{(4)}) = 42$ hops

Figure 5.28 The network of example 5.17 after adding link 3-5.

If the process were continued then 1-6 would be replaced by 2-6 leading to a slight reduction in cost (17 miles of cable) but no reduction in $v(G)$. □

Local search methods

The improvement method above successively moved from one feasible solution to a 'neighbouring' one. This concept of 'locality' is not absolute but determined by the algorithm designer. Formally, given a combinatorial problem $\min_{x \in F} f(x)$, where F is a discrete set of feasible solutions, a *neighbourhood mapping*, N, is a mapping $N: F \to 2^F$. The set $N(x) \subseteq F$ associated with $x \in F$ is the *neighbourhood* of x and its elements are the *neighbours* of x.

A *local search method* comprises a pair $(N, improve)$ where N is a neighbourhood mapping and *improve* is a subroutine that associates with $x \in F$ a neighbour $improve(x) \in N(x) \cup x$. The word 'subroutine' is appropriate since $improve(x)$ may depend on factors other than the identity of x; for example, $improve(x)$ might be a randomly chosen element of $N(x) \cup x$ or one whose value depends upon the time at which calculation takes place. However, as the name 'improve' suggests, it is the aim that the subroutine should be of such a nature that its application generally 'moves towards better solutions'.

A simple *application* of a local search method consists of choosing an initial feasible solution x_0 then computing

$$x_1 = improve(x_0), \quad x_2 = improve(x_1), \quad x_3 = improve(x_2), \dots .$$

This is continued until a specified termination condition is satisfied. A common choice is to stop when two successive solutions x_i, and x_{i+1}, are the same, that is the sequence has *converged*.

Example 5.18 Devise a local search method for solving

P: $\min 17\xi_1 + 5\xi_2 + 9\xi_3 + 13\xi_4 + 11\xi_5$

subject to

$$8\xi_1 + 2\xi_2 + 6\xi_3 + 5\xi_4 + 6\xi_5 \geq 13$$

$$\xi_1, \dots, \xi_5 \in \{0,1\}.$$

Solution   A solution of P may be represented by the binary number $(\xi_1\xi_2\xi_3\xi_4\xi_5)$ in which each binary digit is 0 or 1.   The simple neighbourhood mapping N defined by taking as $N((\xi_1 \xi_2 \xi_3 \xi_4 \xi_5))$ the set of feasible elements

$$\{(\bar\xi_1 \xi_2 \xi_3 \xi_4 \xi_5), \quad (\xi_1 \bar\xi_2 \xi_3 \xi_4 \xi_5), \quad (\xi_1 \xi_2 \bar\xi_3 \xi_4 \xi_5),$$
$$(\xi_1 \xi_2 \xi_3 \bar\xi_4 \xi_5), \quad (\xi_1 \xi_2 \xi_3 \xi_4 \bar\xi_5)\}$$

where $\bar 0 = 1$ and $\bar 1 = 0$. *improve*$((\xi_1 \xi_2 \xi_3 \xi_4 \xi_5))$ is taken to be the *first* element, $(\xi_1 \ldots \bar\xi_i \ldots \xi_5)$, of $N((\xi_1 \xi_2 \xi_3 \xi_4 \xi_5))$ for which

$$f(\xi_1 \ldots \bar\xi_i \ldots \xi_5) < f(\xi_1 \xi_2 \xi_3 \xi_4 \xi_5)$$

when there is such an element; otherwise $f(\xi_1 \xi_2 \xi_3 \xi_4 \xi_5)$ is taken to be $(\xi_1 \xi_2 \xi_3 \xi_4 \xi_5)$ itself.

By way of illustration let $x_0 = (11111)$ which is a feasible solution, and $f(x_0) = f(11111) = 17 + 5 + 9 + 13 + 11 = 55$.

$N(11111) = \{(01111), (10111), (11011), (11101), (11110)\}$.

Since $f(y) < f(x_0)$ for all $y \in N(x)$ the first element, namely (01111), is selected as x_1. $f(x_1) = f(01111) = 38$.

$N(x_1) = \{(11111), (00111), (01011), (01101), (01110)\}$.

$f(11111) = 55 > f(x_1) = 38$ and (11111) is rejected. However, $f(00111) = 33 < 38$. Set $x_2 = (00111)$. $N(x_2) = \{(10111), (01111)\}$, the other potential elements being infeasible. Neither (10111) nor (01111) leads to a lower value of f, so $x_3 = x_2$ and convergence has taken place. □

At this point some general observations may be made. First, in example 5.16 a *greedy improvement* method is used with, at each stage, a best change $x_i \to x_{i+1}$ being made; on the other hand, in example 5.18 the *first* change $x_i \to x_{i+1}$ found that leads to a *strict* improvement is accepted. The latter approach is frequently adopted since for large neighbourhoods a full search can be very time consuming. The time saved is often better used by taking more starting solutions, thus obtaining several locally optimal solutions, the best of which may be the solution finally adopted. Alternately, the decision maker may choose from among the locally optimal solutions taking into account experience and non-modelled features of the problem.

The neighbourhood mapping used in example 5.18 is not very satisfactory. It would be better to permit also changes in which a 1-bit and a

0-bit are simultaneously complemented (cf. example 5.17).

There is a limit to which the neighbourhoods can be enlarged without incurring an inordinate amount of searching and this means that in general only a *locally* optimal solution will be obtained. How can we avoid getting 'trapped at a local optimum'? We now look at two ways, namely the use of *simulated annealing* and *tabu search*, for doing just this. Another set of techniques, not described here, is that of *genetic algorithms* (Goldberg, 1989).

Simulated Annealing

The feature of improvements methods that inevitably leads to becoming trapped at a local optimum is that a change $x_i \rightarrow x_{i+1}$ is accepted *only* if x_{i+1} is (strictly) better than x_i with regard to the objective concerned. This restriction will now be removed.

Simulated annealing, introduced by Kirkpatrick et al. (1983), has the feature that 'uphill' moves in which x_{i+1} is not as good as x_i may also be accepted; the probability of acceptance is controlled and decreases as the algorithm proceeds.

Algorithm (SA)
{An outline simulated annealing procedure for minimisation problems.
  Input: a neighbourhood mapping N.}

    Select an initial feasible solution x_o.

    Set $i = 0$ and specify values for T_o and m.

    while *not finished* **do**

    begin for m times **do**

      begin

        Generate randomly a solution $\ell \in N(x_i)$ and calculate $p = g(\delta, T)$

        where $\delta = f(\ell) - f(x_i)$, and $0 \leq p \leq 1$.

        with probability p

          set $x_{i+1} \leftarrow \ell$, $i \leftarrow i+1$ (acceptance)

        with probability $1 - p$

          make no changes   (rejection)

      end

      Set $T \leftarrow \gamma T$ where $0 < \gamma < 1$.

    end

{Output: an approximate solution to the problem at hand.}

The function g is selected to have the following properties:

(1) $g(\delta, T) = 1$ if $\delta < 0$ to ensure *automatic* acceptance of changes leading to improvement;

(2) $0 \le g(\delta, T) \le 1$;

(3) g is a monotonic increasing function of T and a monotonic decreasing function of δ.

A function, g, satisfying these requirements is

$$g(\delta, T) = \begin{cases} \exp(-\delta/T) & \text{if } \delta \ge 0. \\ 1 & \text{if } \delta < 0. \end{cases}$$

There are clearly several tuning parameters to be chosen before a specific algorithm results. First, as in other local search methods, an initial solution x_0 and a neighbourhood mapping N are needed. Second, it is important:

(1) to make the initial value of T sufficiently large otherwise the probability of an uphill move is too small;

(2) to make the reductions in T reasonably small otherwise the probabilities for making uphill moves are reduced too quickly;

(3) to make m reasonably large, again to give the algorithm time to find a good solution;

(4) to be able to decide when to terminate.

The triple (T, γ, m) forms what is termed an *annealing* (or *cooling*) *schedule*, from a physical analogy that is explained in Kirkpatrick et al. (1983). A further discussion on choosing an annealing schedule is contained in Johnson et al. (1989).

Simulated annealing tends to make changes that lead to getting structural features right early in its schedule with fine tuning of the solution occurring later (cf. Kirkpatrick et al., 1983).

Tabu search

Simulated annealing is memoryless in the sense that if the current solution is x_i, and the value of T and the number of minor iterations made at that value of T are all known, then the algorithm can proceed. Tabu search, on the other hand, keeps a certain amount of data on the history of the searches already carried out.

The core of tabu search is its *short term memory process* which constitutes a form of aggressive exploration that seeks to make the best move possible subject to requiring that the available choices must satisfy certain constraints (Glover, 1990). The constraints are designed to prevent the reversal or repetition of certain moves (changes) by making selected attributes of these moves forbidden, or *tabu*. A reason for this is to prevent a situation in which at a local optimum, x_p say, a best move $x_p \rightarrow x_{p+1}$ is made only to 'fall back' at the next move $x_{p+1} \rightarrow x_{p+2}$ because $x_{p+2} = x_p$ is the best neighbour of x_{p+1}. Thus a *candidate list* of moves is available which includes all non-tabu moves as determined by a specified neighbourhood mapping.

The move made in tabu search is normally the best available from the current candidate list where 'best' may refer to the objective value only or involve other measure(s) of attractiveness.

It is important to realise that the number of moves that are tabu at any particular time is usually small relative to the number of moves available at that time.

Example 5.19 Suggest a prescription of tabu status for a constrained MST problem such as that of examples 4.3 and 4.4.

Solution For a given number of nodes, n, all spanning trees have the same number of edges (namely n-1). Consequently a suitable neighbourhood mapping is one that removes one edge and adds another. It is reasonable to make tabu any move which involves swapping out the edge just brought into the tree. This is effected by keeping a tabu list of recently added edges. When an edge is brought into the tree it is added to the end of the tabu list. When the list is full, addition of a new edge causes the edge that has been in the list longest to drop out. That is, the tabu list is mainted as a FIFO list (cf. Boffey and Yates, 1989). The tabu list can be surprisingly short; for example the only tabu moves may be the ones which involve swapping out an edge among the last six to be brought into the tree (ie. a tabu list of length 6 is kept). ☐

Tabu search is flexible in that if a really good move becomes available (reaches some prescribed *aspiration* level of improvement) then it will be accepted *even though it is on the tabu list*.

This discussion does not do justice to tabu search which can have other features incorporated, for example, 'longer term memory'. The reader is referred for further information to Glover (1990) wherein will be found references to a variety of successful applications of tabu search.

5.8 EXERCISES

5.1 The Capacity Assignment Problem, CAP, minimises the total cost $\sum_i \sum_j (a_{ij} + p_{ij}c_{ij})$ subject to the delay constraints (5.3). For the corresponding problem of minimising the total delay, $\sum_i \sum_j x_{ij} / (c_{ij} - x_{ij})$ subject to a budget constraint of $\sum_i \sum_j (a_{ij} + p_{ij}c_{ij}) \leq D$ show that the optimal capacities are (with S as in equation (5.10))

$$c_{ij} = x_{ij}\{1 + H/\sqrt{p_{ij}x_{ij}}\} \quad \text{where} \quad SH = D - \sum_i \sum_j (a_{ij} + p_{ij}x_{ij}).$$

Note that this is of precisely the same form as obtained for CAP in section 5.1. Now set D to be the minimal network cost

$$\sum_i \sum_j (a_{ij} + p_{ij}x_{ij}) + \frac{S}{\gamma T}$$

for CAP and show that $H = S/\gamma T$. That is, the same solution is obtained as for CAP when the budget is set accordingly.

5.2 If it is felt that more attention should be given to the more congested links then $\sum_i \sum_j x_{ij}/(c_{ij} - x_{ij})^k$ may be minimised subject to a budget constraint $\sum_i \sum_j (a_{ij} + p_{ij}c_{ij}) \leq D$. Show that the optimal capacities are

$$c_{ij} = x_{ij} + (x_{ij}/p_{ij})^{1/(k+1)}[D - \sum_i \sum_j (a_{ij} + p_{ij}x_{ij})]/\sum_m \sum_n (p_{mn}x_{mn})^{1/(k+1)}$$

and verify that this reduces to the correct form for $k = 1$.

5.3 Consider table 5.4. The lower bound is obtained by taking the starred entries, but this does not correspond to a feasible solution. Branch according as the capacity of link Bu-N is 19.2, 28.8 or higher.

Note, that if the capacity is 19.2 kbps, then in order to restore feasibility (at least) one of the other links must have its capacity increased and so the lower bound may be increased by

$$2 \times \min(2055 - 1278, 2476 - 2065, \ 2526 - 1885, \ ..., \ 1081 - 618).$$

5.4 Sketch a diagram showing the feasible region corresponding to the set of constraints

$$-x + y \leq 1; \quad y \leq 4; \quad x + y \leq 8; \quad x \leq 5; \quad x - y \leq 3; \quad x, y \geq 0.$$

Calculate the values of $Z_1 = -x + 2y$ and $Z_2 = 2x + y$ at each of the vertices. At which vertices are Z_1 and Z_2 maximised? Which, if any, of the vertices corresponds to a solution which is *inferior* (ie. is *dominated by*) some other solution? Identify the *non inferior set*.

Assuming it is justifiable to use the *weighting method* with objective $Z(w) = (1 - w)Z_1 + wZ_2$ to solve the *multiobjective problem*

max (Z_1, Z_2)

subject to the set of constraints (P)

determine optimal solution(s) for all values of w in the range $0 \le w \le 1$.

5.5 Prove that, if $v(a, b)$ denotes the maximum number of pairwise node-disjoint edges between nodes a and b in a graph $G = (V, E)$ then

min $\{ v(a, b) \mid a, b \in V \ \& \ a \neq b \}$

$= $ min $\{ v(a, b) \mid a, b \in V \ \& \ a \neq b \ \& \ \text{there is no edge } ab \}$.

5.6   Find a minimum cost solution for the problem of example 5.9 assuming the extra condition that any connected set of four or more nodes must contain a node of degree at least 3. [Hint: consider the set of nodes {3, 5, 1, 4}.]

5.7   Calculate $\Delta_{12}, \Delta_{15}, \Delta_{23}, \Delta_{25}, \Delta_{34}, \Delta_{35}, \Delta_{45}$, for the problem of example 5.16 (before removal of 2-3).

5.8   Devise simulated annealing and tabu heuristic methods for finding minimal cost 2 edge-connected networks.

Chapter 6

Task and File Allocation

Thus far, only the physical aspects of network design have been treated. However, the communications facility permits a *task* (program or other code sequence) to be spread over the processors of a network. Of course there will, in general, be a need for the constituent parts (called *modules* or *processes*) to exchange information resulting in a communications overhead being incurred. This cost may well be more than offset via:

(1) better turnround resulting from modules being executed concurrently;

(2) better processor utilisation from load balancing;

(3) modules being run on processors best suited to their requirements.

The data dependency between modules will often imply *precedence* requirements. Thus module *a* cannot run before module *b* if module *a* requires data produced by module *b*. Such precedence represent a considerable increase in the complexity of assignment of modules to processors.

Data files also may be spread across a network with, possibly, multiple copies of some files being maintained at separate locations.

Section 6.1 discusses *task allocation*, that is, the assignment of the constituent modules of a task to processors, and shows how this may be tackled by the technique of *dynamic programming*. File allocation is taken up in section 6.2 and in the following section two particular file allocation studies are presented. The powerful computational techniques of variable splitting, surrogate relaxation and BISA are introduced in sections 6.2, 6.3. Section 6.4 looks at the database location problem taking account of updates, and concurrency and consistency control; it concludes by briefly bringing various strands together for the joint optimisation of network and software placing.

6.1 TASK ALLOCATION

There are sometimes advantages in distributing the constituent modules of a task over a computer network rather than executing all of them on a single processor. In *time-critical* situations (as might perhaps arise in military or satellite control applications, or in connection with signal processing) distribution may be advantageous through reduced turnround time obtained by modules executing concurrently on different processors. Distribution may also be adopted to improve system performance through *load sharing* and in this case it is relevant to optimise some measure of the 'evenness' of the work assigned to the different processors.

Stone's model

An early model for process allocation, due to Stone (1977), is based on cost minimisation. Each module i has an associated cost c_{ik} when run on processor k. Let v_{ij} be the volume of communication between module i and module j, and p_{kl} the unit cost of communication between processor k and processor l (in units consistent with those for c_{ik}). Then the objective to be minimised is

$$C = \sum_i \sum_k c_{ik} x_{ik} + \sum_i \sum_j \sum_{\substack{k \\ k<l}} \sum_l v_{ij} p_{kl} x_{ik} x_{jl}.$$

The only constraints to be satisfied are that each module must be allocated to some processor

$$\sum_k x_{ik} = 1,$$

and that the variables x_{ik} be binary, that is

$$x_{ik} \in \{0, 1\}.$$

Here, $x_{ik} = 1$ if module i is assigned to processor k and is zero otherwise. This is a difficult non-linear discrete programming problem. However, it simplifies greatly in the very special case of only two processors and costs given by $p_{12} = p_{21} = p$, $p_{11} = p_{22} = 0$.

For a task subdivided into m modules $M_1, \ldots, M_m$ which are to be assigned to processors S and F, let G denote the network (X, A) where

$$X = \{S, F\} \cup \{1, \dots, m\},$$
$$A = \{ ij \mid i \neq j, \ i, j = 1, \dots, m\} \cup \{ Si \mid i = 1, \dots, m\} \cup \{ jF \mid j = 1, \dots, m\}.$$

The cost of an optimal assignment of modules to processors is then the value of a maximal conserved network flow from S to F when the arc weights (capacities) are given by κ_{ij} where

$$\kappa_{ij} = p v_{ij}, \quad i, j \neq S, F$$
$$\kappa_{Si} = c_{iF}$$
$$\kappa_{jF} = c_{jS}.$$

(For more on network flows see, for example, Boffey, 1982.)

Example 6.1 A task is subdivided into three modules M_1, M_2 and M_3 with traffic demand matrix

$$(v_{ij}) = \begin{bmatrix} - & 2 & 3 \\ & - & 4 \\ & & - \end{bmatrix}$$

Given the task - processor cost matrix

$$(c_{ik}) = \begin{matrix} S & F \\ \begin{bmatrix} 1 & 7 \\ 6 & 2 \\ 3 & 1 \end{bmatrix} \end{matrix}$$

and that $p = 1$, obtain a minimal cost assignment of modules to processors.

Solution First construct G as described above to get the network of figure 6.1b. Now consider the flow of

2 units along S-2-F
2 units along S-1-2-F
3 units along S-1-3-F
1 unit along S-1-F
1 unit along S-3-2-F.

The value of this network flow is $2 + 2 + 3 + 1 + 1 = 9$; that is, 9 units of flow pass from S to F per unit time. Next consider the broken line in figure 6.1 which separates the nodes of the network into two sets

$$\text{LEFT} = \{S, 1\}, \quad \text{RIGHT} = \{2, 3, F\}.$$

The maximum flow per unit time from S to F clearly cannot exceed the maximum flow per unit time across the broken line in the S to F direction; that is

$$\kappa_{S2} + \kappa_{S3} + \kappa_{12} + \kappa_{13} + \kappa_{1F} = 2 + 1 + 2 + 3 + 1 = 9. \qquad (6.1)$$

It follows that

9 ≤ maximum flow from *S* to *F* per unit time ≤ 9

and so the flow considered is maximal.

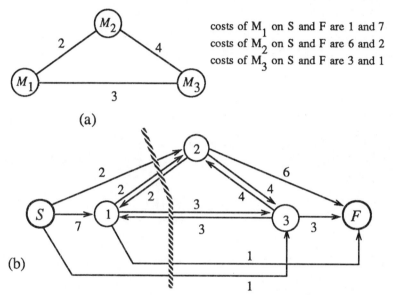

costs of M_1 on S and F are 1 and 7
costs of M_2 on S and F are 6 and 2
costs of M_3 on S and F are 3 and 1

(a)

(b)

Figure 6.1 The network G, corresponding to the 'intermodule communication network' of (a), is shown in (b).

The interpretation of this solution is that module M_1 is assigned to processor S (with cost $c_{1S} = \kappa_{1F}$) and modules M_2 and M_3 are assigned to processor F (cost $c_{2F} + c_{3F} = \kappa_{S2} + \kappa_{S3}$). The resulting intermodule communication cost is $pv_{12} + pv_{13} = \kappa_{12} + \kappa_{13}$ and all terms on the left hand side of (6.1) are accounted for exactly. □

Storage constraints

Next, we look at a model in which storage limitations are also imposed. The problem will be solved via dynamic programming and is first illustrated by means of an example.

Example 6.2 A task has been split into three modules M_1, M_2, M_3 whose storage requirements are m_1, m_2, m_3 respectively, where

i	1	2	3
m_i	9	14	7

The modules are to be run on three interconnected processors whose storage availabilities, A_k, are

k	1	2	3
A_k	10	15	20

The volume v_{ij} of communication between module M_i and module M_j is

$$(v_{ij}) = \begin{bmatrix} - & 1 & 2 \\ & - & 4 \\ & & - \end{bmatrix}$$

and the unit cost p_{kl} of communication between processors k and l is 1 for all $k \neq l$ and 0 if $k=l$. Finally, the costs c_{ik} for executing module M_i on processor k are

$$(c_{ik}) = \begin{bmatrix} 8 & 5 & 3 \\ \infty & 10 & 5 \\ 3 & 2 & 1 \end{bmatrix}$$

Use dynamic programming to obtain a minimal cost allocation of modules to processors.

[Note that the data is in arbitrary units and is chosen merely with a view to illustrating dynamic programming.]

Solution Figure 6.2 shows how allocations may be 'built up'. The allocation has (conceptually) been split into *stages*. Stage 0 corresponds to the initial situation in which no assignments have been made. At stage 1 the assignment of module(s) to processor 1 has been made; at stage 2 modules have been assigned to processor 2, and finally at stage 3 modules have been assigned to processor 3 and the allocation is complete.

The *state* associated with a particular point in the successive assignment of modules to processors is just the set of modules already assigned. (Alternatively, and equivalently the set of modules unassigned could be used to specify the state.) Since the interprocessor unit communication costs are all the same, it follows that the cost of further assignments to processors depends only on this state and not on the particular way the individual modules are assigned.

Now consider figure 6.2 more closely. Initially the only state is $\varnothing$ (no assignments have been made). At stage 1 modules are assigned to processor 1 and, since $A_1 = 10$, the only states that correspond to feasible allocations are $\varnothing$, $\{1\}$ (module 1 only assigned) and $\{3\}$ (module 3 only assigned). The cost 'so far incurred' is zero for the transition $\varnothing \rightarrow \varnothing$, is $c_{11} = 8$ for the transition $\varnothing \rightarrow \{1\}$ and $c_{31} = 3$ for the transition $\varnothing \rightarrow \{3\}$ because at this stage no communication costs have been incurred.

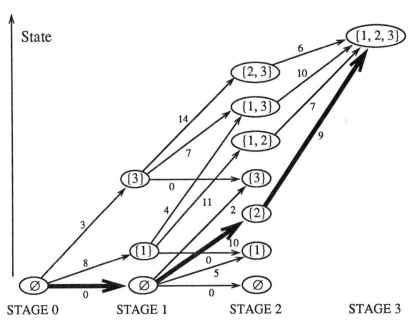

Figure 6.2 Network showing the possible ways in which (modules of) the task in example 6.2 may be allocated to processors, the optimal allocation being indicated by the heavy line. For further details see text.

Storage constraints permit all states to be realised at stage 2 except $\{1, 2, 3\}$. All permissible transitions from a state at stage 1 to a state at stage 2 are shown in figure 6.2. For example, the transition $\{3\} \rightarrow \{1, 3\}$ corresponds to module M_1 being assigned to processor 2 and the resulting cost is $c_{12} = 5$ plus the cost $pv_{13} = (1)(2) = 2$ of communicating between module 3 (on processor 1) and module 1 (on processor 2); the total cost is thus 7.

At stage 3 all modules must have been assigned and so $\{1, 2, 3\}$ is the only feasible state. [Note that the storage constraint for processor 3 forbids transitions from states $\varnothing$, $\{1\}$ and $\{3\}$ at stage 2. In this sense, these states do not correspond to feasible allocations. A clever algorithm with 'lookahead' might detect this situation and not include these states at stage 2.] Again, all permissible transitions are shown in figure 6.2. Consider for example, $\{1,3\} \rightarrow \{1, 2, 3\}$ which corresponds to assigning module M_2 to processor 3 incurring a processing cost $c_{23} = 5$ and communication costs of $pv_{12} + pv_{32} = (1)(1) + (1)(4) = 5$; the cost of transition $\{1,3\} \rightarrow \{1, 2, 3\}$ is thus 10.

Figure 6.3 shows the part of the network of figure 6.2 corresponding to the task allocation

module 3 is assigned to processor 1
module 1 is assigned to processor 2
module 2 is assigned to processor 3.

It is seen that the cost of the path $\varnothing \rightarrow \{3\} \rightarrow \{1,3\} \rightarrow \{1, 2, 3\}$ of figure 6.3 is $3 + 7 + 10 = 20$ and it is readily verified that this is the total cost of the allocation $[20 = (c_{31} + c_{12} + c_{23}) + p(v_{12} + v_{23} + v_{13})]$. An optimal allocation corresponds to a least cost (ie. 'shortest distance') path from state $\varnothing$ at stage 0 to state $\{1, 2, 3\}$ at stage 3 in the network of figure 6.2. This is $\varnothing \rightarrow \varnothing \rightarrow \{2\} \rightarrow \{1, 2, 3\}$ corresponding to the allocation

processor 1 is free

module M_2 is assigned to processor 2

modules M_1 and M_3 are both assigned to processor 3

with total cost 19. This task allocation, while having minimal cost, is poor from the point of view of load sharing as processor 1 has had no work assigned.   □

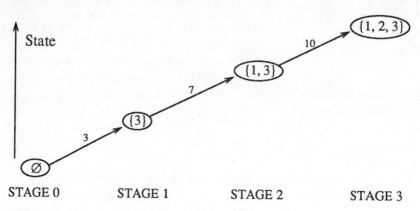

Figure 6.3 A complete allocation of the task of example 6.2.

Dynamic programming

Example 6.2 provides a case in which a problem is solved effectively by means of *dynamic programming* (or DP for short). The DP solution of problems via recurrence equations will now be discussed in somewhat more general terms.

First the problem solving process is split into *stages*. (In the above example this corresponded to assignments of modules to each of processors 1, 2 and 3.) A solution is 'built up' in stages and at any stage other than the last has only been *partially* built up. A *state* $\hat{x}$ is associated with each partial solution x and is such as to specify just that information about a partial solution that is required for the solution process to proceed. Note that, in general, a single state corresponds to more than one partial solution, for example the two partial solutions

$$\begin{bmatrix} \text{module } M_1 \text{ on processor 1} \\ \text{module } M_3 \text{ on processor 2} \end{bmatrix} \qquad \begin{bmatrix} \text{module } M_3 \text{ on processor 1} \\ \text{module } M_1 \text{ on processor 2} \end{bmatrix}$$

both have the same associated state at stage 2, namely $\{1, 3\}$.

In going from a partial solution x at stage s to partial solution y at stage $s+1$ a *decision* is made, and this is mirrored by a *transition* $\hat{x} \rightarrow \hat{y}$ from state $\hat{x}$ to state $\hat{y}$. To each such transition there is associated a *return*, $r(\hat{x}, \hat{y})$, such that the value of the complete solution is the composition of the returns of the individual transitions. In the above example composition was just ordinary addition, but other rules are sometimes applicable.

With the notion of state as described above, the *Principle of Optimality* holds; that is

> any partial solution which can be built upon to
> give an optimal full solution must itself represent
> an optimal way of attaining the partial solution.

This leads to recurrence relations of the form

$$F_{s+1}(\hat{y}) = \min \{F_s(\hat{x}) + r(\hat{x}, \hat{y}) \mid \text{transition } \hat{x} \rightarrow \hat{y} \text{ exists} \},$$
$$F_0(\hat{0}) = 0,$$

(6.2)

where $F_s(\hat{x})$ is the total return associated with state $\hat{x}$ at stage s, and $\hat{0}$ is the initial state. The optimal solution then corresponds to the set of transitions $\hat{x} \rightarrow \hat{y}$ which yield minima in (6.2).

6.2 FILE PLACEMENT

In many situations, a file needs to be accessed from time to time from different nodes of a network. This leads to the question of the best node at which to site the file or, if multiple copies are being considered, what is the best subset of the network nodes at which to site file copies (one at each node of the subset)? The general reference for this type of problem, called the *file placement problem*, is Dowdy and Foster (1982).

Casey's model

An early model, due to Casey in 1972, considers placing a single file and determines the optimal number of copies to be kept and where they should be located. A mathematical formulation of Casey's model (CM) is

CM: minimise $\sum_i \sum_j c_{ij} x_{ij} + \sum_i f_i y_i$

subject to

$$\sum_i x_{ij} = 1 \qquad \text{for all } j \qquad\qquad (6.3)$$

$$x_{ij} \leq y_i \qquad \text{for all } i \text{ and } j \qquad\qquad (6.4)$$

$$x_{ij}, y_i \in \{0, 1\} \quad \text{for all } i \text{ and } j \qquad\qquad (6.5)$$

where

c_{ij} is the cost of satisfying all queries from node j by a copy of the file at i.

f_i is the cost of storing a copy of the file at node i plus the cost of updating this copy from all other nodes.

y_i is 1 if a copy of the file is placed at node i, and 0 otherwise.

x_{ij} is 1 if queries from node j are sent to a copy of the file at i, and 0 otherwise.

[The interpretations of c_{ij} and f_i are considered in more detail in Dowdy and Foster (1982).]

The first set of constraints, (6.3), requires that each node be allocated to a copy of the file regarding queries. Constraints (6.4) state that a query to a copy of the file at i cannot be satisfied unless there is a copy of the file actually placed at node i. Finally, (6.5) are the usual 0-1 conditions.

CM is readily seen to be of exactly the same form as the simple location problem SLP introduced in section 4.4. Consequently, it will not be discussed further here.

A generalisation of CM would be to consider more than one file with multiple copies of each being kept. Specifically, such a model, CM(m), is

CM(m): minimise $\sum_k \sum_i \sum_j c_{kij} x_{kij} + \sum_k \sum_i f_{ki} y_{ki}$
subject to

$$\sum_i x_{kij} = 1 \qquad \text{for all } j \text{ and } k$$

$$x_{kij} \le y_{ki} \qquad \text{for all } i, j \text{ and } k$$

$$\sum_k s_k y_{ki} \le S_i \qquad \text{for all } i \qquad\qquad (6.6)$$

$$x_{kij}, y_{ki} \in \{0, 1\} \qquad \text{for all } i, j \text{ and } k$$

where

S_i is the amount of storage available at node i,

s_k is the amount of storage required by a copy of file k,

and the extra subscript, k, denotes which file is being considered. The 'new' set of constraints (6.6) requires that the storage used by copies of all files at node i should not exceed the total amount of storage available at i. Without these constraints the problem would decompose into separate subproblems of the form of CM, one for each file k.

CM(m) is very similar to the multicommodity location problem studied by Karkazis and Boffey (1981). Indeed, the latter is equivalent to the special case of CM(m) in which (6.6) is replaced by

$$\sum_k y_{ki} \le 1 \text{ all } i.$$

Based on this correspondence one might suspect that a dual ascent method similar to that in Karkazis and Boffey (1981) might also be appropriate for CM(m).

Laning and Leonard's approach

Laning and Leonard (1983) adopted a rather different approach to the storage constrained placement of multiple files. Firstly, they noted that in a large network thousands of files exist of which usually about 20% amount for at least 80% of the storage. Moreover, of this 'interesting' 20% many files may have obvious locations (for security or usage reasons). Consequently, only a relatively few files need to be included in a file placement problem. The overall strategy of Laning and Leonard may be summarised as follows.

Algorithm (LL)
{Laning & Leonard's file allocation algorithm.}

Select a set of m distinct files for analysis.

For each file f specify a maximum number, p_f say, of copies allowed.

For each file f solve a p-median problem for $p = 1, ..., p_f$. From an examination of the results obtain an initial allocation.

Calculate file availabilities (cf. (6.7) below) and compare with the requirements. Resolve any availability infeasibilities.

while a fully feasible solution has not been obtained and further progress might be possible **do**

begin {Delay satisfaction}

Simulate the performance of the network for the current file allocation. Compare observed delays with delay constraints. Attempt to resolve any infeasibilities.

end
{Output: An allocation of files is provided by the current solution}

By the *availability* a_{if} of a file f from node i is meant

a_{if} = probability of a copy of file f being successfully accessed from i

$$= 1 - \prod_{l=1}^{n} (1 - r_{il} y_{lf}) \tag{6.7}$$

where r_{il} is the probability of a successful communication between nodes i and l and y_{lf} is equal to 1 if and only if there is a copy of file f at node l.

The p-median problem referred to in step 3 is just the Simple Location Problem with the extra constraint that there are copies of the file at p nodes and the location cost of every facility is the same. That is

p-MP: minimise $\sum_i \sum_j c_{ij} x_{ij}$

subject to

$$\sum_i x_{ij} = 1 \qquad \text{for all } j$$

$$x_{ij} \leq y_i \qquad \text{for all } i \text{ and } j$$

$$\sum_i y_i = p$$

$$x_{ij}, y_i \in \{0, 1\} \quad \text{for all } i \text{ and } j.$$

Not surprisingly, p-MP can be solved by methods similar to those for solving SLP (cf. Boffey and Karkazis, 1984). For the cost coefficients in p-MP, Laning and Leonard use

$$c_{ij} = \alpha(\text{update cost})_{ij} + (1-\alpha)(\text{query cost})_{ij} + (p/N)\,SC_i$$
SC_i = cost per unit stored at node i
N = total number of nodes in the network.

This is based on the assumption of an even allocation with each median node having approximately the same number, N/p, of allocated nodes. Laning and Leonard applied their approach to the ARPANET configuration of May 1979. For more detail on the resolution of infeasibilities the reader is referred to Laning and Leonard (1983).

A database allocation problem

In some distributed systems, data items are (relatively) seldom used outside a given geographic region. Banks and credit card firms are examples of businesses exhibiting such strong *locality of reference* (Pirkul, 1986). This section describes an allocation problem of relevance to banking which will be used to introduce the technique of 'variable splitting'.

A large bank has many branches dispersed over a wide area with each branch assigned to a particular host computer. Because most transactions involve only a single account belonging to the 'local branch' it seems desirable to assign all accounts belonging to any one branch to the same host; that is, the problem is effectively that of allocating branches to computers.

The aim is to find an allocation of branches to computers so as to minimise overall cost of communication, $\sum_i \sum_j c_{ij} x_{ij}$, where

c_{ij} = cost per unit time when branch i is allocated to computer j.

$$x_{ij} = \begin{cases} 1 & \text{if } i \text{ and } j \text{ are } \textbf{not} \text{ in the same metropolitan area} \\ 0 & \text{otherwise.} \end{cases}$$

Data communication is effected via dedicated point-to-point lines *within* a metropolitan area and via a value added network, such as TYMNET, *between* metropolitan areas. Thus, c_{ij} is composed of two components: c_{ij}^F, the fixed cost of local line rental; and c_{ij}^V, a volume related inter-area network cost. The fixed cost depends on whether bank i at which the transaction originates is in the same area as the computer which holds the relevant database.

$$c_{ij}^F = \begin{bmatrix} \text{local line rental cost from } i \text{ to } j \text{ if } i \text{ and } j \text{ are in the same area} \\ \text{local line rental cost from } i \text{ to nearest node of network plus} \\ \text{the cost of a port into the network, if } i \text{ and } j \text{ are in different} \\ \text{areas.} \end{bmatrix}$$

Now let R_{mi} denote the volume of traffic (in bytes per unit time) arising from transactions generated at branch m which relate to an account at branch i. Also let c_{mj}^N be the *network* cost, per byte, for communication over the network. [If m and j are in the same area then $c_{mj}^N = 0$.] The volume related cost is given by

$$c_{ij}^V = \Sigma_m R_{mi} c_{mj}^N.$$

It may be noted that the case $m = i$, $c_{ij}^N \neq 0$ refers to transactions originating at branch i and relating to an account at that branch, but the database is held remotely. The *Branch Location Problem* (BrLP) may now be stated formally.

BrLP: minimise $\Sigma_i \Sigma_j c_{ij} x_{ij}$ (6.8)

      subject to

$$\Sigma_j x_{ij} = 1 \qquad \text{for all } i \tag{6.9}$$

$$\Sigma_i p_i x_{ij} \leq P_j \qquad \text{for all } j \tag{6.10}$$

$$\Sigma_i v_i x_{ij} \leq V_j \qquad \text{for all } j \tag{6.11}$$

$$\Sigma_i t_i x_{ij} \leq T_j \qquad \text{for all } j \tag{6.12}$$

$$x_{ij} \in \{0, 1\} \qquad \text{for all } i \text{ and } j. \tag{6.13}$$

Constraint (6.9) states merely that each branch must be allocated to some computer. Constraints (6.10), (6.11) and (6.12) relate respectively to limits on available processing capacity of a computer at site j, the available storage of computer at j and communications capacity available for a computer at j. For (6.10), p_i denotes processing requirements (operations per unit time) of transactions directed to the database of branch i, and P_j denotes the maximum processing capacity available to computer j. The interpretations of (6.11) and (6.12) are similar (but note that $t_i = \Sigma_m R_{mi}$). If only one of (6.10) - (6.12) is present the BrLP is just a *Generalised Assignment Problem* (or GAP).

Lagrangean decomposition (or variable splitting)

We will now look at the GAP which results from BLP when (6.11) and (6.12) are omitted from the formulation. Thus:

GAP: minimise $\sum_i \sum_j c_{ij} x_{ij}$ $\qquad$ (6.8*)

subject to

$$\sum_j x_{ij} = 1 \qquad \text{for all } i \qquad (6.9*)$$

$$\sum_i p_i x_{ij} \le P_j \qquad \text{for all } j \qquad (6.10*)$$

$$x_{ij} \in \{0, 1\} \qquad \text{for all } i \text{ and } j. \qquad (6.13*)$$

An obvious strategy to adopt is to apply Lagrangean relaxation; but which set of constraints should be relaxed? An interesting approach is, in a sense, to perform a mixture of the possible relaxations (Jörnsten and Näsberg, 1986). For $0 \le \theta \le 1$, denote by GAP(θ) the problem

GAP(θ): minimise $(1-\theta) \sum_i \sum_j c_{ij} x_{ij} + (\theta) \sum_i \sum_j c_{ij} y_{ij}$ $\qquad$ (6.14)

subject to

$$\sum_j x_{ij} = 1 \qquad \text{for all } i \qquad (6.15)$$

$$\sum_i p_i y_{ij} \le P_j \qquad \text{for all } j \qquad (6.16)$$

$$x_{ij} = y_{ij} \qquad \text{for all } i \text{ and } j \qquad (6.17)$$

$$x_{ij}, y_{ij} \in \{0, 1\} \qquad \text{for all } i \text{ and } j. \qquad (6.18)$$

It is clear, by substituting x_{ij} wherever y_{ij} occurs, that this is equivalent to GAP. Having thus 'split the variables' the next step is to relax, in a Lagrangean way, the constraint set (6.17). The modified objective is

$$\sum_i \sum_j [(1-\theta)c_{ij} + \lambda_{ij}] x_{ij} + \sum_i \sum_j [\theta c_{ij} - \lambda_{ij}] y_{ij}$$

and it is apparent that the relaxed problem decomposes into

P_x: minimise $\sum_i \sum_j [(1-\theta)c_{ij} + \lambda_{ij}] x_{ij}$

subject to

$$\sum_j x_{ij} = 1 \qquad \text{for all } i \qquad (6.15*)$$

$$x_{ij} \in \{0, 1\} \qquad \text{for all } i \text{ and } j \qquad (6.18*)$$

and

P_y: minimise $\Sigma_i \Sigma_j [\theta c_{ij} - \lambda_{ij}] y_{ij}$

subject to

$$\Sigma_i p_i y_{ij} \le P_j \quad \text{for all } j \tag{6.16*}$$

$$y_{ij} \in \{0, 1\} \quad \text{for all } i \text{ and } j \tag{6.18*}$$

and $v(P_x) + v(P_y)$ is a lower bound to $v(\text{GAP})$. P_x solves very easily; all that is needed is, for each i, to find the smallest coefficient $[(1 - \theta)c_{ij} + \lambda_{ij}]$ and set the corresponding x_{ij} to 1. That is,

$$v(P_x) = \Sigma_i [\min_j [(1 - \theta) c_{ij} + \lambda_{ij}].$$

P_y itself decomposes into subproblems, P_y^j, where for each j

P_y^j: minimise $\Sigma_i [\theta c_{ij} - \lambda_{ij}] y_{ij}$

subject to

$$\Sigma_i p_i y_{ij} \le P_j$$

$$y_{ij} \in \{0, 1\} \quad \text{for all } i.$$

Example 6.3 Apply the variable splitting approach to the GAP with

$$(c_{ij}) = \begin{bmatrix} 3 & 6 & 7 \\ 6 & 2 & 8 \\ 7 & 8 & 3 \end{bmatrix} \qquad \begin{matrix} p = (4, 3, 5) \\ P = (3, 4, 5). \end{matrix}$$

Solution For simplicity we take $\theta = 1/2$. Consider the following matrix of Lagrange multipliers

$$(\lambda_{ij}) = \begin{bmatrix} 9 & 7 & 6.5 \\ 3 & 5 & 4 \\ 9 & 9 & 4.5 \end{bmatrix}$$

Then

$$(1/2 c_{ij} + \lambda_{ij}) = \begin{bmatrix} 10.5 & 10 & 10 \\ 6 & 6 & 8 \\ 12.5 & 13 & 6 \end{bmatrix} \quad \begin{matrix} \text{row minima} \\ 10 \\ 6 \\ 6 \\ \overline{22} \end{matrix}$$

and $v(P_x) = 22$. P_y^1 is the knapsack problem

minimise $(1/2c_{11} - \lambda_{11})y_{11} + (1/2c_{21} - \lambda_{21})y_{21} + (1/2c_{31} - \lambda_{31})y_{31}$
subject to

$$p_1 y_{11} + p_2 y_{21} + p_3 y_{31} \le P_1$$
$$y_{11}, y_{21}, y_{31} \in \{0, 1\}$$

or explicitly,

minimise $-7.5y_{11} - 0y_{21} - 5.5y_{31}$
subject to

$$4y_{11} + 3y_{21} + 5y_{31} \le 3$$
$$y_{11}, y_{21}, y_{31} \in \{0, 1\}$$

with optimal solution $y_{11} = 0$, $y_{21} = 0$, $y_{31} = 0$ and $v(P_y^1) = 0$. Similarly it may be verified that $v(P_y^2) = -4$ and $v(P_y^3) = -3$ leading to $v(GAP)$ $\ge 22 - 7 = 15$. However, the feasible solution $x_{12} = x_{21} = x_{33} = 1$ and all other $x_{ij} = 0$ leads to a value of 15 and so must be optimal. $\qquad\square$

Theorem 6.1 The bound $\max_\lambda [v(P_x) + v(P_y)]$ is at least as large as the best bound obtained by Lagrangean relaxation with

    either (a) the semi-assignment constraints (6.15) relaxed,

    or (b) the knapsack constraints (6.16) relaxed.

Proof (cf. Jörnsten and Näsberg (1986).) $\qquad\square$

Example 6.4 Solve the two Lagrangean duals of theorem 6.1 using the data of example 6.3.

Solution Relaxation (a) with multipliers σ_1, σ_2 and σ_3 requires the solution of the following problem:

P_σ: minimise $[(3 - \sigma_1)x_{11} + (6 - \sigma_2)x_{21} + (7 - \sigma_3)x_{31}$
$$+ (6 - \sigma_1)x_{12} + (2 - \sigma_2)x_{22} + (8 - \sigma_3)x_{32}$$
$$+ (7 - \sigma_1)x_{13} + (8 - \sigma_2)x_{23} + (3 - \sigma_3)x_{33}]$$
$$+ \sigma_1 + \sigma_2 + \sigma_3$$

    subject to

$$4x_{11} + 3x_{21} + 5x_{31} \leq 3$$
$$4x_{12} + 3x_{22} + 5x_{32} \leq 4$$
$$4x_{13} + 3x_{23} + 5x_{33} \leq 5$$
$$x_{ij} \in \{0, 1\} \quad \text{for all } i \text{ and } j.$$

Try $\sigma = (10, 6, 7)$; it is then easily seen that the solution of P_σ is

$$(x_{ij}) = \begin{bmatrix} 0 & 1 & 0 \\ 1 & 0 & 0 \\ 0 & 0 & 1 \end{bmatrix}$$

with value $(10 + 6 + 7) - (4 + 4) = 15$. Since there is a zero subgradient this is an optimal solution to the Lagrangean dual.

Relaxation (a) with multipliers τ_1, τ_2 and τ_3 requires the solution of the problem:

P_τ: minimise $[(3 + 4\tau_1)x_{11} + (6 + 4\tau_2)x_{12} + (7 + 4\tau_3)x_{13}$

$\qquad\qquad + (6 + 3\tau_1)x_{21} + (2 + 3\tau_2)x_{22} + (8 + 3\tau_3)x_{23}$

$\qquad\qquad + (7 + 5\tau_1)x_{31} + (8 + 5\tau_2)x_{32} + (3 + 5\tau_3)x_{33}]$

$\qquad\qquad -3\tau_1 - 4\tau_2 - 5\tau_3$

subject to
$$x_{11} + x_{12} + x_{13} = 1$$
$$x_{21} + x_{22} + x_{23} = 1$$
$$x_{31} + x_{32} + x_{33} = 1$$
$$x_{ij} \in \{0, 1\} \quad \text{for all } i \text{ and } j.$$

Try $\tau = (3/4, 0, 0)$; it is then easily seen that a solution of P_τ is

$$(x_{ij}) = \begin{bmatrix} 0 & 1 & 0 \\ 0 & 1 & 0 \\ 0 & 0 & 1 \end{bmatrix}$$

with value $[6 + 2 + 3] - 3(3/4) = 8.75$. The corresponding subgradient is $(0, 1, 0)$ so that subgradient optimisation would give as the next value for τ : $(3/4, \max(0, 0 - \theta), 0) = (3/4, 0, 0)$ where θ is the step length; that is, an optimal solution of the Lagrangean dual has been found.

Notice that $v(P_\tau) = 8.75$, but not $v(P_\sigma)$, is strictly less than the lower bound obtained using variable splitting. $\qquad\qquad\qquad\qquad\square$

For a general strategy based on variable splitting for solving genera-lised Assignment Problems the reader is referred to Jörnsten and Näs-berg (1986).

6.3 SURROGATE DUALITY

In the previous section it was shown how a GAP may be solved by vari-able splitting. However, the Bank Location Problem, BrLP, involves *three* sets of Knapsack constraints so that relaxation of the semi-assign-ment constraints $\sum_j x_{ij} = 1$, for all i, leads to the *multiconstraint* knapsack problem (MKP)

MKP: minimise $\sum_i \sum_j C_{ij} x_{ij}$

   subject to

$$\sum_i p_i x_{ij} \leq P_j \quad \text{for all } j$$
$$\sum_i v_i x_{ij} \leq V_j \quad \text{for all } j$$
$$\sum_i t_i x_{ij} \leq T_j \quad \text{for all } j$$
$$x_{ij} \in \{0, 1\} \quad \text{for all } i \text{ and } j$$

where C_{ij} is written in place $(c_{ij} - \lambda_i)$. MKP is much more difficult to solve than the normal (single constraint) knapsack problem, and in order to solve it Pirkul (1986) used the concept of surrogate relaxation.

Surrogate relaxation

Before applying it to MKP, surrogate relaxation will be described in a more general setting. Consider the problem (cf. section 3.6)

P: minimise φ

   subject to

$$\sum_j a_{ij} x_j \geq b_i, \quad i = 1, ..., m \quad (6.19)$$
$$x = (x_1, ..., x_n) \in \Omega.$$

Now, any solution which satisfies each constraint in the set (6.19) must also satisfy the combined constraint

$$\sum_i \alpha_i (\sum_j a_{ij} x_{ij}) \geq \sum_i \alpha_i b_i,$$

where

$$\alpha_1, \alpha_2, ..., \alpha_n \geq 0.$$

It may also be assumed, without loss of generality, that

$$\alpha_1 + \alpha_2 + ... + \alpha_n = 1.$$

In particular, this statement is true for any optimal solution x^* of P, and hence x^* is a feasible solution of the problem P^α where

P^α: minimise φ
subject to

$$\sum_i \alpha_i (\sum_j a_{ij} x_{ij}) \geq \sum_i \alpha_i b_i,$$

$$x = (x_1, ..., x_n) \in \Omega.$$

Since x^* is not necessarily optimal for problem P^α it follows that

$$v(P^\alpha) \leq v(P).$$

P^α is called the *surrogate relaxation* of P (with respect to constraint set (6.19) and multipliers α_i). There is also the corresponding *surrogate dual problem* (cf. Lagrangean dual problem)

SD: maximise$_{\alpha \geq 0} v(P^\alpha)$

and its optimal value satisfies

$$v(SD) = \max_{\alpha \geq 0} v(P^\alpha) \leq v(P).$$

Two questions arise:

(1) how does surrogate relaxation compare with Lagrangean relaxation with regard to the quality of bounds provided to $v(P)$?

(2) how are 'good' multiplier vectors obtained?

The first question is answered by the following result.

Theorem 6.2 For problem P as defined above

(1) $v(P^\alpha) \geq v(P_\alpha)$ for all $\alpha \geq 0$;

(2) $v(SD) \geq v(LD)$.

Proof It suffices to prove only (1), as (2) then follows immediately. Let Q_α be the problem

Q_α: minimise $\{ \varphi - \Sigma_i \alpha_i (\Sigma_j a_{ij} x_j - b_i) \}$

 subject to

$$\Sigma_i \alpha_i (\Sigma_j a_{ij} x_{ij}) \geq \Sigma_i \alpha_i b_i,$$

$$x \in \Omega$$

then

$v(P^\alpha) \geq v(Q_\alpha)$ since $\varphi - \Sigma_i \alpha_i (\Sigma_j a_{ij} x_j - b_i) \} \leq \varphi$

 $\geq v(P_\alpha)$ since P_α is a relaxation of Q_α. $\square$

As regards the second question, an obvious first try might be to use sub-gradient optimisation. This will, by the above result, lead to at least as good a result as may be obtained by using Lagrangean relaxation, though optimality might not be achieved.

Application to MKP

Applying the above theory to MKP leads to the relaxation

MKP^α: minimise $\Sigma_i \Sigma_j C_{ij} x_{ij}$

 subject to

$$\Sigma_i \Sigma_j (\alpha_1 p_i + \alpha_2 v_i + \alpha_3 t_i) x_{ij} \leq \Sigma_j [\alpha_1 P_j + \alpha_2 V_j + \alpha_3 T_j]$$

$$x_{ij} \in \{0, 1\} \quad \text{for all } i \text{ and } j.$$

This is a normal 0-1 Knapsack problem for which there are effective solution methods. If $C_{ij} \geq 0$ for all i, j the problem solves trivially. However, $C_{ij} = (c_{ij} - \lambda)$ and so some or all the coefficients may be negative. Consequently it is more natural to consider the equivalent problem of maximising $\Sigma_i \Sigma_j (-C_{ij}) x_{ij}$. We shall now illustrate the solution of the surrogate dual for a simpler two constraint problem (such as would arise, for example, if ample space were available to satisfy requirements.

Example 6.5 Use surrogate duality and Lagrangean duality to obtain upper bounds to the optimal value of

MKP: maximise $8x_1 + 4x_2 + 5x_3$

        subject to

$$4x_1 + 5x_2 + 3x_3 \leq 8 \tag{6.20}$$

$$3x_1 + 2x_2 + 4x_3 \leq 6 \tag{6.21}$$

$$x_1, x_2, x_3 \in \{0, 1\}. \tag{6.22}$$

Solution The small size of the problem permits complete enumeration.

x	value
(0, 0, 0)	0
(1, 0, 0)	8
(0, 1, 0)	4
(0, 0, 1)	5
(1, 1, 0)	(6.20) violated
(1, 0, 1)	(6.21) violated
(0, 1, 1)	9
(1, 1, 1)	(6.20) & (6.21) violated

Clearly, (0, 1, 1) is the optimal solution with value 9.

Now incorporate (6.20) and (6.21) into the objective with multipliers λ, $\mu \geq 0$, to get

maximise $(8 - 4\lambda - 3\mu)x_1 + (4 - 5\lambda - 2\mu)x_2 + (5 - 3\lambda - 4\mu)x_3 + 8\lambda + 6\mu$
subject to

$$x_1, x_2, x_3 \in \{0, 1\}.$$

For $(\lambda, \mu) = (6/14, 13/14)$ this becomes

maximise $3.5x_1 + 0x_2 + 0x_3 + 48/14 + 78/14$
subject to

$$x_1, x_2, x_3 \in \{0, 1\}.$$

The solution is clearly $3.5 + 9 = 12.5$. Moreover, this pair of multipliers is optimal as may be verified by finding a zero subgradient. Thus the best upper bound obtainable using Lagrangean relaxation is 12.5.

Now consider the surrogate relaxation with multipliers θ and $1 - \theta$ (no generality being lost by insisting that the multipliers sum to 1). The problem becomes

maximise $8x_1 + 4x_2 + 5x_3$
subject to

$$(3 + \theta)x_1 + (2 + 3\theta)x_2 + (4 - \theta)x_3 \le 6 + 2\theta$$
$$x_1, x_2, x_3 \in \{0, 1\}.$$

$x = (1, 1, 1)$ does not satisfy the constraint for any value of θ and so may be dismissed. The next best potential solution is $x = (1, 0, 1)$ which is feasible provided $\theta \ge 1/2$. If θ is restricted to the range $0 \le \theta \le 1/2$ then the best solution is $x = (1, 1, 0)$ leading to an upper bound of 12. In this case the surrogate dual has provided a strictly better solution than the Lagrangean dual. It is of interest to note that the substitution of the optimal Lagrange multipliers (6/14, 13/14) into the surrogate relaxation leads to a bound of 12 also. □

There are two other Lagrangean dual problems associated with the above knapsack problem; these are obtained by

(1) incorporating only (6.20) into the objective;
(2) incorporating only (6.21) into the objective.

The optimal values in these two cases turn out to be 11.2 and 11.75 respectively (cf. exercise 6.3).

Finding multiplier vectors for surrogate dual problems

For other than trivial problems, complete enumeration is not a viable alternative and another approach is required; that of Gavish and Pirkul (1985) will now be outlined.

Suppose first that there are just two constraints and let $S(\theta)$ denote the problem in which constraints are combined with multipliers θ and $1 - \theta$ as in example 6.5. $S(0)$ corresponds to neglecting the first constraint entirely and $S(1)$ to neglecting the second constraint entirely. It will be assumed that constraint 1 is violated by the solution to $S(0)$ and constraint 2 violated by the solution to $S(1)$, otherwise a solution to the surrogate dual is at hand. The form of $v(S(\theta))$ will be like that of figure 6.4. The number and positions of the straight line sections depend on the size of the problem and the values of the coefficients.

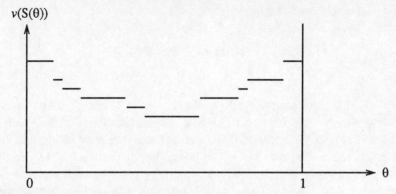

Figure 6.4 The general form taken by the function $v(S(\theta))$.

The following results are established by Gavish and Pirkul (1985).

Theorem 6.3 If x_θ is an optimal solution to $S(\theta)$ then x_θ satisfies at least one of the two constraints.

Theorem 6.4 If the solution x_θ of $S(\theta)$ satisfies the second constraint for $\theta = \theta_H$ say, and $\theta_H \le \theta_1 \le \theta_2 \le 1$, then $v(S(\theta_1)) \le v(S(\theta_2))$.

Theorem 6.5 If the solution x_θ of $S(\theta)$ satisfies the first constraint for $\theta = \theta_L$ say, and $0 \le \theta_3 \le \theta_4 \le \theta_L$, then $v(S(\theta_3)) \ge v(S(\theta_4))$.

Following these results the following algorithm (which is almost identical to that of Gavish and Pirkul) may be proposed.

Algorithm (GP)
{Gavish-Pirkul algorithm for solving $\min_\theta S(\theta)$ approximately.
   Input: problem coefficients and a value for *tolerance*.}
      Set $\theta_L = 0$ and $\theta_H = 1$.
      while $\theta_H - \theta_L > tolerance$ **do**
      begin Set $\theta = (\theta_L + \theta_H)/2$ and solve $S(\theta)$.
            if both constraints are satisfied **then** stop. (An optimal solution has been found.)
            if only the first constraint is satisfied **then** set $\theta_H \leftarrow \theta$.
            if only the second constraint is satisfied **then** set $\theta_L \leftarrow \theta$.
      end
{Output: a value of θ minimising $v(S(\theta))$ accurate to within *tolerance*.}

For more than two constraints Gavish and Pirkul (1985) suggest starting with two of them, finding an optimal combination, finding an optimal combination of this and the third constraint, etc.

A difficulty with the above approach is that a 0-1 knapsack problem is in itself difficult (in the technical sense of being NP-hard, cf. Garey and Johnson, 1979). However, the Linear programming relaxation is very easy to solve and such relaxations can be used to find good multipliers (cf. Gavish and Pirkul, 1985).

Bound improving sequence algorithm (BISA)

Another idea for obtaining a good bound was introduced by Barcia (1985). Suppose an upper bound u_1^* is known for a maximisation problem P, for example, as obtained via Lagrangean or surrogate relaxation. Then the constraint

$$\sum_j c_j x_j \leq u_1^* \tag{6.23}$$

may be added to P since *every* optimal solution to P must satisfy it. Suppose that P is the problem

P: maximise $\sum_j c_j x_j$
   subject to
   $$\sum_j a_{1j} x_j \leq A_1$$
   $$\sum_j a_{2j} x_j \leq A_2$$
   $$x_j \in \{0, 1\} \qquad \text{for all } j.$$

Now a Lagrangean relaxation is formed by taking all constraints other than the 'objective cut' (6.23) into the objective to get the problem PB(1)

PB(1): $v(\text{PB}(1)) = \max \sum_j c_j x_j - \sum_i \lambda_i (A_i - \sum_j a_{ij} x_j)$
   subject to
   $$\sum_j c_j x_j \leq u_1^*$$
   $$x_j \in \{0, 1\} \quad \text{for all } j.$$

Solving this will give a new set of multipliers and a value $v(\text{PB}(1)) \leq u_1^*$ which is also an upper bound to $v(\text{P})$. Next let $u_2^* = v(\text{PB}(1))$ and solve PB(2), the problem P with u_2^* replacing u_1^*. This in turn yields a new upper bound u_3^*, and so on. The sequence of bounds $\{u_i^*\}$ satisfies

$$u_1^* \geq u_2^* \geq u_3^* \geq u_4^* \geq \ldots \geq v(P).$$

Since monotonic decreasing and bounded below, this sequence must converge to a limit, v^* say, which satisfies $v^* \geq v(P)$. Barcia established that, in fact, equality holds:

Theorem 6.6 (Barcia) If the problem P is non-degenerate then $v^* = v(P)$.
Proof (cf. Barcia, 1985.)   □

Example 6.6 Apply BISA to the problem of example 6.5.
Solution When both constraints are relaxed to form Lagrangean relaxations the best upper bound obtainable is 12.5 (cf. example 6.5). Accordingly, we set $u_1^* = 12.5$ and solve

$P_{\lambda,\mu}$: maximise $(8 - 4\lambda - 3\mu)x_1 + (4 - 5\lambda - 2\mu)x_2 + (5 - 3\lambda - 4\mu)x_3 + 8\lambda + 6\mu$
         subject to
$$8x_1 + 4x_2 + 5x_3 \leq 12.5$$
$$x_1, x_2, x_3 \in \{0, 1\}.$$

It may be verified that an optimal set of multipliers (ie. a set minimising $v(P_{\lambda,\mu})$) is $(\lambda, \mu) = (0.8, 0)$ and that there are two corresponding solutions $x = (1, 0, 0)$ and $(1, 1, 0)$ both with value 11.2. u_2^* is now set to 11.2 (11 could be used if the integrality of $v(P)$ were invoked). The new problem, P(2) is

     maximise $(8 - 4\lambda - 3\mu)x_1 + (4 - 5\lambda - 2\mu)x_2 + (5 - 3\lambda - 4\mu)x_3 + 8\lambda + 6\mu$
         subject to
$$8x_1 + 4x_2 + 5x_3 \leq 11.2$$
$$x_1, x_2, x_3 \in \{0, 1\}.$$

$(\lambda, \mu) = (0, 0)$ leads to $v(P(2)) = 9$. Moreover the solution $x = (0, 1, 1)$ has value 9 and so must be optimal.   □

It is also possible to combine the techniques of surrogate relaxation and BISA.

6.4 FURTHER TOPICS

A major advance in modelling was due to Morgan and Levin (1977). Their innovation was to take account of dependencies between files (or fragments of databases) and programs that are present in database systems. A request originating at node i of the network requires the execution of a program p, a copy of which is at node j, which in turn uses data from a file f, a copy of which is stored at node k (cf. figure 6.5).

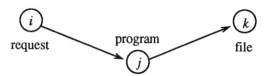

Figure 6.5 Dependency between files and programs.

Associated with such a system is a cost which is the sum of

    Cc = communication costs
    PSc = program storage costs
    FSc = file storage costs
    Qc = query costs
    Uc = update costs.

These will be considered in turn. First, $Cc = \sum_{i,p,j,f} c_{ipjf}\, x_{ipjf}$ where

$$x_{ipjf} = \begin{cases} 1 & \text{if request, originating at } i, \text{ uses } p \text{ at } j, \text{ which in turn} \\ & \text{uses file } f \\ 0 & \text{otherwise.} \end{cases}$$

c_{ipjf} = cost of communication from i to j resulting from a request to p at j using file f.

Program storage costs are $PSc = \sum_{p,j} g_{pj}\, y_{pj}$ where

$$y_{pj} = \begin{cases} 1 & \text{if a copy of program } p \text{ is located at } j \\ 0 & \text{otherwise.} \end{cases}$$

g_{pj} = cost of storing program p at node j.

File storage costs are $FSc = \sum_{k,f} h_{kf}\, z_{kf}$ where

$$z_{kf} = \begin{cases} 1 & \text{if a copy of file } f \text{ is located at } k \\ 0 & \text{otherwise} \end{cases}$$

h_{kf} = cost of storing a copy of file f at node k.

Query and update costs are interesting because of the lack of symmetry: when a program needs data from file f it may get it from *any* copy of f, whereas if a program is updating f then *all* copies must be updated (to maintain integrity).

$$Qc = \Sigma_{i,p,j,k,f} \, d_{ipjkf} \, w_{jkf} \, x_{ipjf}$$

$$Uc = \Sigma_{i,p,j,k,f} \, e_{ipjkf} \, z_{kf} \, x_{ipjf}$$

where

$$w_{jkf} = \begin{cases} 1 & \text{if a request using file } f \text{ at } k \text{ is located at } j \\ 0 & \text{otherwise.} \end{cases}$$

and d_{ipjkf} and e_{ipjkf} are appropriate constants.

The model of Morgan and Levin (1977) becomes

MLM: minimise Cc + PSc + FSc + Qc + Uc
        subject to

$$\Sigma_j \, x_{ipjf} = 1 \quad \text{for all } i, p \text{ and } f \tag{6.24}$$

$$\Sigma_k \, w_{jkf} = 1 \quad \text{for all } j \text{ and } f \tag{6.25}$$

$$x_{ipjf} \leq y_{pj} \quad \text{for all } i, p, j \text{ and } f \tag{6.26}$$

$$w_{jkf} \leq z_{kf} \quad \text{for all } j, k, f \tag{6.27}$$

$$x_{ipjf}, y_{pj}, w_{jkf}, z_{kf} \in \{0, 1\} \quad \text{for all } i, p, j, k \text{ and } f. \tag{6.28}$$

Constraint (6.24) states that each request from i for program p using file f must be satisfied; (6.25) states that each request for file f from j must be serviced; (6.26) requires that the services of program p cannot be rendered from a particular site unless p is located there; the interpretation of (6.27) is similar.

This is a difficult discrete *non-linear* problem. Morgan and Levin observed that programs usually require relatively small amounts of storage and it is not unreasonable to omit the cost PSc (ie. set $g_{pj} = 0$ for all p and j). This results in MLM decomposing into problems MLM_f, one for each file f.

Morgan and Levin (1977) suggested a heuristic solution method for solving MLM. Fisher and Hochbaum (1980), with essentially the same model, used a dual ascent approach. They reported that the effectiveness of dual ascent, while quite good, was not as good as for the Simple Location Problem SLP (cf. section 4.4). Again, Carraresi and Gallo (1982) using essentially the Morgan-Levin model, transformed it and applied Benders decomposition; in their method the extra constraints that $g_{pj} = 0$ need not be imposed. They were able to solve '10 processor - 10 file - 5 program' problems in a modest amount of computing time.

Jagannathan and Mirchandani have considered a distributed database in which there is a copy of the database management system (DBMS) at each node. Since the DBMS provides the programs for processing queries and updates, this means, in the terminology used above, that

$x_{ipjf} = \delta_{ij}$ (ie. 1 if $i = j$, 0 otherwise)

$y_{pj} = 1$ for all p and j

$c_{ipjf} = 0$ for all i, p, j and f

$g_{pj} = 0$ for all p and j.

As observed earlier, $g_{pj} = 0$ implies that the problem decomposes into a set of subproblems, one for each file:

JMM(f):   minimise $\sum_k h_{kf} z_{kf} + \sum_{p,j,k} d_{jpjkf} w_{jkf} + \sum_{p,j,k} e_{jpjkf} z_{kf}$

         subject to

$$\sum_k w_{jkf} = 1 \qquad \text{for all } j$$

$$w_{jkf} \leq z_{kf} \qquad \text{for all } j \text{ and } k$$

$$w_{jkf}, z_{kf} \in \{0, 1\} \qquad \text{for all } j \text{ and } k$$

which is just SLP if 'kf' is replaced by a single index. This is the general framework, but Jagannathan and Mirchandani add further features. In particular an extra term, CCc, is added to the objective to account for the cost of providing concurrency and consistency control. *Concurrency* control involves the proper sequencing of concurrent transactions accessing the same portion of a data file so that data integrity is maintained. On the other hand, it is clearly important that a user accessing a data item from a file should be able to obtain the *same* value from *any* copy of the file, and *consistency* control maintains this by ensuring that *all* copies of a data file are updated 'simultaneously'.

There is a delay and overhead associated with simultaneous updates, the cost being an increasing function F of the number $\sum_k z_{kf}$ of copies of the file. The decomposition by file, as in JMM(f), is still valid if F is a linear function, and then JMM(f) is still an SLP. However, Jagannathan and Mirchandani suggest that F is more likely to be a convex increasing function, and they extend the methodology of Erlenkotter (1978) by proposing an iterative solution with each iteration solving an SLP using the DUALOC procedure (of which algorithm (BKE) forms part, cf. section 4.4).

Comprehensive models

So far we have treated separately the physical design of a network and the location of software on a network. We shall conclude this book by briefly mentioning the work of D. Stiles and colleagues at Utah State University.

It is assumed that the following information is given:

- the number and locations of the computers (nodes);
- the number of databases and their characteristics;
- the choices of computers available;
- the choices of links available.

The aim is then to minimise the total cost which includes

- the costs of computers;
- the costs of links;
- query communication costs;
- update communication costs.

The minimisation is carried out subject to the following constraints:

- there must be a computer at every node;
- a copy of each database must be stored somewhere;
- storage capacity available must not be exceeded;
- processing capacity available must not be exceeded;
- a query to a database can only be serviced at a node if a copy of the database is stored there;
- if node i sends a query to node j then a path containing no more than two links must exist between node i and node j.

While most of the features above have appeared earlier in this text the significance of the work of Stiles et al. is that they minimise cost while taking account of topology, link capacities, database location and routing of messages. The 'two hop' restriction is not an essential requirement but is imposed in order to limit the complexity of the problem. Indeed the problem as described is already immensely complex and it is necessary to resort to the use of heuristics for problems involving more than a very few nodes (about 5 or 6 only!). However, simulated annealing has successfully been applied to very much larger problems (up to 100 nodes).

While the use of heuristics is likely to lead to somewhat suboptimal solutions (to the *model* problem), the alternative of decomposing into subproblems can also lead to suboptimality, even when the subproblems are solved exactly. It may be that the better approach from a practical point of view is the approximate treatment of the comprehensive model.

6.5 EXERCISES

6.1 Messages are to be sent through a fixed network from node r to node t. The probability that a link i-j will be working is p_{ij}; $\{ p_{ij} \}$ is assumed to form an independent set. Let $\hat{x}$ be the state of the system in which the message has reached node x (that is, without encountering a failed link). Denote by $F_s(\hat{x})$ the probability that state $\hat{x}$ can be attained after s links have been traversed. Verify that

$$F_{s+1}(\hat{y}) = \max \{ F_s(\hat{x}) \times p_{xy} \mid \text{there is a link } xy \}$$
$$F_o(\hat{r}) = 1.$$

Discuss the similarity of this to the development of DP at the end of section 6.1. [Note that $p_{ra}p_{ab}\cdots p_{ex}$ is maximised when $-\log(p_{ra}p_{ab}\cdots p_{ex})$ is minimised.]

6.2 Suppose that the cost matrix (c_{ij}) for Casey's model CM is given by

$$\begin{bmatrix} 5 & 8 & 12 & 9 \\ 7 & 6 & 13 & 5 \\ 6 & 12 & 4 & 7 \end{bmatrix}$$

Separately find optimal locations for three files A, B and C for which the vectors of fixed costs $f = (f_i)$ are given by $(2, 3, 2)$, $(4, 6, 4)$ and

(6, 9, 6) respectively. [Note that these problems are small enough to solve by complete enumeration.] Also find values of the dual variables λ_j by using algorithm (BKE).

Now suppose that all three files are considered together. The separate treatment above would indicate a copy of all three files at node 3 and copies of A and B at node 2. However, associated with node 3 there is (using an obvious notation) a storage constraint of

$$2y_{C1} + 4y_{C2} + 6y_{C3} \leq 6$$

which is violated. Add this constraint to the formulation of the problem to obtain an instance of CM(3) in which only one storage constraint is included. Now relax the storage constraint with Lagrange multiplier σ. Solve the problem when $\sigma = 2$ to obtain an improved lower bound for this instance of CM(3).

6.3 For the problem of example 6.5, show that relaxing constraint set (6.20) only gives at best an upper bound of 11.2 and that relaxing set (6.21) only gives at best an upper bound of 11.75.

6.4 Apply the variable splitting approach with $\theta = 1/2$ to the problem of example 6.5. Can you obtain in this way a better bound than

$$\min(11.2, 11.75) = 11.2$$

obtained in question 6.3?

6.5 Consider the problem

min $3x_1 + 2x_2$

subject to

$$
\begin{aligned}
x_1 + y_1 &\geq 1 & \dots (\mu_1) \\
x_2 + y_2 &\geq 1 & \dots (\mu_2) \\
y_1 + y_2 &= 1 \\
x_1, x_2, y_1, y_2 &\in \{0,1\}.
\end{aligned}
$$

Find $v(p^\mu)$ and $v(p_\mu)$ as a function of $\mu = (\mu_1, \mu_2)$ for $0 \leq \mu_1 \leq 3$ and $0 \leq \mu_2 \leq 2$, where p_μ and p^μ are respectively the Lagrangean and surrogate relaxations when multipliers μ_1 and μ_2 are associated with the first two constraints.

6.6   Discuss whether it is necessary for all constraints other than the 'objective constraint', $\sum_j c_j x_j \leq u_1^*$, and the 0-1 constraints, $x_j \in \{0, 1\}$, to be relaxed and taken into the objective in the BISA approach (cf. problem PB(1) in section 6.3).

6.7 Consider and discuss the last sentence of section 6.4.

Appendix A

Poisson Processes

A *Poisson process* in time is a process for which the following three conditions hold.

Condition 1: The numbers of *events* occurring in non-overlapping intervals are independent.

Condition 2: The probability of exactly one *event* occurring during a very small time interval h is approximately λh; more precisely $\lambda h + O(h^2)$.

Condition 3: At most one event can occur during a very small time interval h; more precisely, the probability of more than one event in the interval is $O(h^2)$.

If $p_n(t)$ = probability of n events occurring during time t, then, to first order in h,

$$p_0(h) = 1 - \lambda h, \quad p_1(h) = \lambda h, \quad p_n(h) = 0 \text{ if } n > 1 \qquad (A.1)$$

for some constant λ. By condition 1,

$$p_n(t+h) = p_n(t)p_0(h) + p_{n-1}(t)p_1(h), \quad n \geq 0. \qquad (A.2)$$

(cf. figure A.1) where $p_{-1}(t)$ is taken to be zero to make the formula correct when $n = 0$.

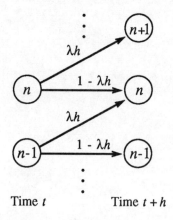

Time t Time $t + h$

Figure A.1 The possible transitions to state n during a very small time interval h.

Substitution of (A.1) into (A.2) gives

$$p_n(t+h) = p_n(t)(1-\lambda h) + p_{n-1}(t)\lambda h, \quad n \geq 0.$$

From which,

$$dp_n(t)/dr = \text{Limit}_{h \to 0}[p_n(t+h) - p_n(t)]/h = -\lambda p_n(t) + \lambda p_{n-1}(t). \tag{A.3}$$

It is readily verified by substitution that a solution of (A.3) is

$$p_n(t) = \frac{(\lambda t)^n \exp(-\lambda t)}{n!}. \tag{A.4}$$

This is the well-known Poisson distribution whose mean (and variance!) is λt. The parameter λ is thus seen to be the mean number of events per unit time, that is, the mean event rate. Now let

$f(t) = $ *probability density function* of the time between successive
events being $t > 0$.

The corresponding *cumulative density function*, F, is defined by

$$F(t) = \int_0^t f(t)\,dt$$

and clearly satisfies

$$1 - F(T) = \text{Prob}\{ \text{ inter-event time is at least } T \}$$
$$= \text{Prob}\{ \text{ no event occurs during time } T)$$
$$= p_0(T)$$
$$= \exp(-\lambda T) \quad \text{from (A.4).}$$

Differentiating both sides with respect to T gives

$$f(t) = \lambda \exp(-\lambda T).$$

This is the (*negative*) *exponential* distribution whose mean is $1/\lambda$. Note that this is as might be expected since λ is the mean event rate.

From condition 1, a Poisson process may be said to be memoryless in that what happens within a particular interval does not depend in any way on what happened prior to the start of the interval. This is reflected by the exponential distribution as

$$\text{Prob}\{ t > T + S \mid t > S \} = \text{Prob}\{ t > T + S, \ t > S \} / \text{Prob}\{ t > S \}$$
$$= \text{Prob}\{ t > T + S \} / \text{Prob}\{ t > S \}$$
$$= \exp(-\lambda(T+S)) / \exp(-\lambda S))$$
$$= \exp(-\lambda T).$$
$$= \text{Prob}\{ t > T \}.$$

Finally, if the process concerned is the arrival of items to a queue then λ is the mean arrival rate, and if the process is a server process then λ (usually denoted by μ in this case) is just the mean service rate.

Appendix B

Linear Programming Duality Theorem

The reader is assumed to have an elementary knowledge of linear programming including the modelling of simple problems as linear programs (LPs), geometric representation of an LP in two decision variables and its solution by geometric means. An acquaintance with the (standard primal) simplex algorithm is desirable. The requisite material is available in many introductory texts (eg. Taha, 1987).

A standard form for a linear program is

P: maximise $x_0 = c_1 x_1 + \ldots + c_n x_n$
   subject to

$$a_{11} x_1 + \ldots + a_{1n} x_n \leq b_1 \qquad (y_1)$$

$$\vdots \qquad \vdots \quad \vdots \qquad \vdots$$

$$a_{m1} x_1 + \ldots + a_{mn} x_n \leq b_m \qquad (y_m)$$

$$x_1, \ldots, x_n \geq 0.$$

If an LP is not already in this form then it may be transformed so that it is; for example an equality constraint $\sum_j a_{ij} x_{ij} = b_j$ may be replaced by the equivalent pair of inequality constraints

$$\sum_j a_{ij} x_{ij} \leq b_j \qquad \sum_j (-a_{ij}) x_{ij} \leq (-b_j).$$

Associated with the problem P (which will be called the *primal* problem) there is an associated problem, D, called the *dual* problem. Its form is:

D: minimise $y_0 = b_1 y_1 + \ldots + b_m y_m$
   subject to

$$a_{11} y_1 + \ldots + a_{m1} y_m \geq c_1 \qquad (x_1)$$

$$\vdots \qquad \vdots \quad \vdots \qquad \vdots$$

$$a_{1n} y_1 + \ldots + a_{mn} y_m \geq c_n \qquad (x_n)$$

$$y_1, \ldots, y_m \geq 0.$$

Note the ordering of the subscripts of the coefficients a_{ij}. Also D has '$\geq$' constraints where P has '$\leq$' constraints. Finally, the objective coefficients of P become the right hand side constants for D, and the right hand side constants of P become the objective coefficients for D.

It will be seen that there is a certain kind of symmetry between the two problems and it is readily proved that if D is regarded as the primal problem then its dual would be P. Thus it is better to speak of a *primal - dual pair* of LPs. Which is regarded as the primal and which the dual is a matter of choice.

Now let $x_1^*, ..., x_n^*$ be an optimal solution of P with x_o^* its associated value, and let $y_1^*, ..., y_m^*$ be an optimal solution of D with y_o^* its associated value. Then

Theorem (Duality)

(1) $x_o^* = y_o^*$

(2) $x_j^* \left(\sum_i a_{ij} y_i^* - c_j \right) = 0$ for $j = 1, ..., n$

(3) $\left(b_i - \sum_j a_{ij} x_j^* \right) y_i^* = 0$ for $i = 1, ..., m$.

[Relations (2) and (3) are known as *Complementary Slackness* relations.]

References

Baratz, A. A. and Jaffe, J. M. (1986) Establishing virtual circuits in large computer networks. *Computer Networks and ISDN Systems*, **12**, 27-37.

Barcia, P. (1985) The bound improving sequence algorithm. *Oper. Res. Lett.*, **4**, 27-30.

Barnett, R. and Maynard-Smith, S. (1988) *Packet Switched Networks: Theory and Practice*. Sigma, Wilmslow, UK.

Bertsekas, D. P. and Gafni, E. M. (1982) Projection methods for variational inequalities with application to the traffic assignment problem. *Math. Prog. Study*, **17**, 139-159.

Bertsekas, D. P. and Gallager, R. (1987) *Data Networks*. Prentice-Hall, Englewood Cliffs, NJ.

Bilde, O. and Krarup, J. (1977) Sharp lower bounds and efficient algorithms for the simple plant location problem. *Ann. Disc. Math.*, **1**, 79-97.

Blake, I. F. and Poor, H. V. (1986) *Communications and Networks: A Survey of Recent Advances*. Springer-Verlag, New York.

Boffey, T. B. (1982) *Graph Theory in Operations Research*. Macmillan, London.

Boffey, T. B. (1989) Location problems arising in computer networks. *J. Opl Res. Soc.*, **40**, 347-354.

Boffey, T. B. and Karkazis, J. (1984) *p*-Medians and multimedians. *J. Opl Res. Soc.*, **35**, 57-64.

Boffey, T. B. and Yates, D. F. (1989) *Introduction to Computer Data Structures*. Chartwell-Bratt, London.

Boorstyn, R. R. and Frank, H. (1977) Large-scale network topological optimization. *IEEE Trans. Commun*, **COM-25**, 29-47.

Camerini, P. M., Fratta, L. and Maffioli, F. (1975) On improving relaxation methods by modified gradient techniques. *Math. Prog. Study*, **3**, 26-34.

Carrarresi, P. and Gallo, G. (1982) Optimum location of files and programs in computer networks. *Math. Prog. Study*, **20**, 39-53.

Chandy, K. M. and Russell, R. A. (1972) The design of multipoint linkages in a teleprocessing tree network. *IEEE Trans. Comput.*, **C-21**, 1062-1066.

Chou, W. (1985) *Computer Communications : volume II Systems and Applications*. Prentice-Hall, Englewood Cliffs, NJ.

Christofides, N. (1975) *Graph Theory: an Algorithmic Approach*. Academic Press, New York.

Clarke, G. and Wright, J. (1963) Scheduling of vehicles from a central depot to a number of delivery points. *Oper. Res.*, **11**, 568-581.

Cohon, J. L. (1978) *Multiobjective Programming and Planning*. Academic Press, New York.

Courant, R. (1934) *Differential and Integral Calculus, Vol I*. Blackie, London.

Courant, R. (1936) *Differential and Integral Calculus, Vol II*. Blackie, London.

Curtois, P.-J. and Semal, P. (1981) An algorithm for the optimization of nonbifurcated flows in computer communication networks. *Performance Evaluation*, **1**, 139-152.

Dowdy, L. W. and Foster, D. V. (1982) Comparative models of the file assignment problem. *Computing Surveys*, **14**, 187-313.

Erlenkotter, D. (1978) A dual-based procedure for uncapacitated facility location. *Oper. Res.*, **26**, 992-1009.

Esau, L. R. and Williams, K. C. (1966) On teleprocessing system design. *IBM Syst. J.*, **5**, 142-147.

Even, S. (1975) An algorithm for determining whether the connectivity of a graph is at least *k*. *SIAM J. Comput.*, **4**, 393-396.

Fisher, M. L. and Hochbaum, D. S. (1980) Database location in computer networks. *JACM*, **27**, 718-735.

Florian, M., Guélat, J. and Spiess, H. (1987) An efficient implementation of the "Partan" variant of the linear approximation method for the network equilibrium problem. *Networks*, **17**, 319-339.

Florian, M., Nguyen, S. and Pallottino, S. (1981) A dual simplex algorithm for finding all shortest paths. *Networks*, **11**, 367.

Floyd, F. W. (1962) Algorithm 97: shortest path. *Commun. ACM*, **5**, 345.

Ford, L. R. jr and Fulkerson, D. R. (1962) *Flows in Networks*. Princeton University Press.

Frank, M. and Wolfe, P. (1956) An algorithm for quadratic programming. *Naval Res. Logist. Quart.*, **3**, 149-154.

Fratta, L., Gerla, M. and Kleinrock, L. (1986) The flow deviation method - an approach to store-and-forward communication networks. *Networks*, **3**, 97-133.

Gallager, R. G. (1977) A minimum delay routing algorithm using distributed computation. *IEEE Trans. Commun.*, **COM-25**, 73-85.

Gallo, G. and Pallottino, S. (1982) A new algorithm to find the shortest paths between all pairs of nodes. *Disc. Appl. Math.*, **4**, 23-35.

Gallo, G. and Pallottino, S. (1986) Shortest path methods: a unifying approach. *Math. Prog. Study*, **26**, 38-64.

Garey, M. R. and Johnson, D. S. (1979) *Computers and Intractability: a guide to the theory of NP-completeness.* Freeman, San Francisco.

Gavish, B. (1982) Topological design of centralized computer networks - formulations and algorithms. *Networks*, **12**, 355-377.

Gavish, B. (1983) Formulations and algorithms for the capacitated minimal directed tree problem. *JACM*, **30**, 118-132.

Gavish, B. (1985) Augmented Lagrangean based algorithms for centralized network design. *IEEE Trans. Commun.*, **COM-33**, 1247-1257.

Gavish, B. and Hantler, S. L. (1983) An algorithm for optimal route selection in SNA networks. *IEEE Trans. Commun.*, **COM-31**, 1154-1161.

Gavish, B. and Neumann, I. (1989) A system for routing and capacity in computer communication networks. *IEEE Trans. Commun.*, **37**, 360-366.

Gavish, B. and Pirkul, H. (1985) Efficient algorithms for solving multi-constraint zero-one knapsack problems to optimality. *Math. Prog.*, **31**, 78-105.

Gavish, B. and Pirkul, H. (1986) Computer and database location in distributed computer systems. *IEEE Trans. Comput.*, **C-35**, 583-590.

Geoffrion, A. M. (1974) Lagrangean relaxation for integer programming. *Math. Prog. Study*, **2**, 82-114.

Gerla, M. (1985) In *Computer Communications : volume II Systems and Applications* (ed. Chou, W). Prentice-Hall, Englewood Cliffs, NJ.

Gerla, M. and Kleinrock, L. (1977) On the topological design of distributed computer networks. *IEEE Trans. Commun.*, **COM-25**, 48-60.

Gerla, M. and Kleinrock, L. (1980) Flow control: a comparative survey. *IEEE Trans. Commun.*, **COM-28**, 553-574.

Glover, F., Klingman, D., Phillips, N. V. and Schneider, R. F. (1985a) New polynomial shortest path algorithms and their computational attributes. *Mgmt. Sci.,* **31**, 1106-1128.

Glover, F., Klingman, D. and Phillips, N. V. (1985b) A new polynomial shortest path algorithm. *Oper. Res.*, **33**, 65-73.

Glover, F. (1990) TABU search: a tutorial. *Interfaces*, **20**, 74-94.

Goldberg, D. E. (1989) *Genetic Algorithms in Search, Optimization and Machine Learning*. Addison-Wesley, Reading, USA.

Hansen, J. V. and Giauque, W. C. (1986) Task allocation in distributed processing systems. *Oper. Res. Lett.*, **5**, 137-143.

Hansler, E. (1972) A fast recursive algorithm to calculate the reliability of a communication network. *IEEE Trans. Commun.*, **COM-20**, 637-640.

Hart, P., Nilsson, N. and Raphael, B. (1968) A formal basis for the heuristic determination of minimum cost paths. *IEEE Trans. Syst. Man Cybernet.*, **4**, 100-107.

Jennings, F. (1986) *Practical Data Communications: modems, networks and protocols*. Blackwell Scientific Publications, Oxford..

Johnson, E. L. and Padberg, M. W. (1981) A note on the knapsack problem with special ordered sets. *Oper. Res. Lett.*, **1**, 18-22.

Johnson, D. S., Aragon, C. R., McGeoch, L. A. and Schevon, C (1989) Optimization by simulated annealing: an experimental evaluation; part 1, graph partitioning. *Oper. Res.*, **37**, 865-892.

Jörnsten and Näsberg (1986) A new Lagrangian relaxation approach to the generalised assignment problem. *Eur. J. Oper. Res.*, **27**, 313-323.

Karkazis, J. and Boffey, T. B. (1981) The multi-commodity facilities location problem. *J. Opl Res. Soc.*, **32**, 803-814.

Karwan, M. H. and Rardin, R. L. (1979) Some relationships between Lagrangian and surrogate duality in integer programming. *Math. Prog.*, **17**, 320-334.

Kennington, J. L. and Helgason, R. V. (1980) *Algorithms for Network Programming*. Wiley, New York.

Kershenbaum, A. (1987) Capacitated facility location. In Yemini (1987).

Kershenbaum, A. and Boorstyn, R. R. (1983) Centralised teleprocessing network design. *Networks*, **13**, 279-293.

Kershenbaum, A., Boorstyn, R. R. and Oppenheim, R. (1980) Second-order greedy algorithms for centralized teleprocessing network design. *IEEE Trans. Commun.*, **COM-28**, 1835-1838.

Kirkpatrick, S., Gellatt, C. D. jr and Vecchi, M. P. (1983) Optimization by simulated annealing. *Science*, **220**, 671-680.

Kleinrock, L. (1964) *Communication Nets: Stochastic Message Flow and Delay.* McGraw-Hill, New York.

Kleinrock, L. and Kamoun, F. (1977) Hierarchical routing for large networks: performance, evaluation and optimization. *Computer Networks*, **1**, 155-174.

Kleitman, D. (1969) Methods for investigating the connectivity of large graphs. *IEEE Trans. Circuit Theory*, **CT-16**, 232-233.

Klincewicz, J. G. and Luss, H. (1986) A Lagrangian relaxation heuristic for capacitated facility location problems with single-source constraints. *J. Oper. Res. Soc.*, **37**, 495-500.

Körkel, M. (1989) On the exact solution of large-scale simple plant location problems. *Europ. J. Oper Res.*, **39**, 157-173.

Kruskal, J. B. (1956) On the shortest spanning subtree of a graph and the traveling salesman problem. *Proc. Amer. Math. Soc.*, **7**, 48-50.

Lane, J. E. (1987) *Packet SwitchStream (PSS) - A user's guide.* NCC Publications, Manchester, England.

Laning, L. J. and Leonard, M. S. (1983) File allocation in a distributed computer communication network. *IEEE Trans. Comput.*, **C-32**, 232-244.

Lawler, E. L. (1976) *Combinatorial Optimization: Networks and Matroids.* Holt, Rinehart Winston, New York.

LeBlanc, L. J. and Simmons, R. V. (1989) Continuous models for capacity design of large packet-switched telecommunication networks. *ORSA J. Comput.*, **1**, 271-286.

Lupi, M. (1986) Convergence of the Frank-Wolfe algorithm in transportation networks. *Civil Eng. Syst.*, **3**, 7-15.

McGregor, P. and Shen, D. (1977) Locating concentration points in communication networks. *IEEE Trans. Commun.*, **COM-25**,

McKeown, G. P., Rayward-Smith, V. J. and Turpin, H. J. (1991) Branch-and-Bound as a higher order function. *Annals of O. R.*, in press.

McQuillan, J. Richer, I. and Rosen, E. (1980) The new routing for ARPANET. *IEEE Trans. Commun.*, **28**, 711-719.

Magnanti, T. L, Mireault, P. and Wong, R. T. (1986) Tailoring Benders decomposition for uncapacited network design. *Math. Prog. Study*, **26**, 112-154.

Minoux, M. (1989) Network synthesis and optimum network design problems: models, solution methods and applications. *Network*, **19**, 313-360.

Monma, C. L. and Shallcross, D. F. (1989) Methods for designing communications networks with two-connected survivability constraints. *Oper. Res.*, **37**, 531-541.

Morgan, H. L. and Levin, K. D. (1977) Optimal program and data locations in computer networks. *Commun. ACM*, **20**, 315-322.

Narasimhan, S. (1990) The concentrator location problem with variable coverage. *Computer Networks & ISDN Systems*, **19**, 1-10.

Nemhauser, G. L. (1972) A generalized permanent label setting algorithm for the shortest path between all nodes. *J. Math. Analysis & Applic.*, **38**, 328-334.

Perko, A. (1983) A representation of disjoint sets with fast initialization, *Information Processing Lett.*, **16**, 21.

Perko, A. (1986) Implementation of algorithms for *K* shortest loopless paths, *Networks*, **16**, 149-160.

Pirkul, H. (1986) An integer programming model for the allocation of databases in a distributed computer system. *Eur. J. Opl Res.*, **26**, 401-411.

Pirkul, H. (1987) Efficient algorithms for the capacitated concentrator location problem. *Computers Opns Res.*, **14**, 197-208.

Pirkul, H., Narasimhan, S. and De, P. (1988) Locating concentrators for primary and secondary coverage in a computer communications network. *IEEE Trans. Commun.*, **COM-36**, 450-458.

Prim, R. C. (1956) Shortest connection networks, and some generalizations. *Bell Syst. Tech. J.*, **36**, 1389-1401.

Quartermain, J. S. and Hoskins, J. C. (1986) Notable computer networks. *CACM*, **29**, 932-971.

Rudin, H. (1976) On routing and Delta routing: a taxonomy and performance comparison of techniques for packet-switched networks. *IEEE Trans. Commun.*, **COM-24**, 43-59.

Sandi, C. (1979) 'Subgradient optimization', in Christofides, Mingozzi and Toth (eds), *Combinatorial Optimization*, Wiley, Chichester, 73-91.

Schwartz, M (1987) *Telecommunication Networks : Protocols, Modeling and Analysis.* Addison-Wesley, Reading, MA.

Schwartz, M. and Stern, T.E. (1980) Routing techniques used in computer communications networks. *IEEE Trans. Commun.*, **COM-28**, 539-552.

Sinha, P. and Zoltners, A. A. (1979) The multiple-choice knapsack problem. *Oper. Res.*, **27**, 503-515.

Sofianopoulou, S. (1990) Optimum allocation of processes in a distributed environment: a process to process approach. *J. Opl Res. Soc.*, **41**, 329-337.

Spira, P. M. (1973) A new algorithm for finding shortest paths in a graph of positive arcs in $O(n^2 \log\log n)$. *SIAM J. Comput.*, **2**, 28-32.

Stallings, W. (1988) *Data and Computer Communications.* Macmillan,

Stone, H. S. (1977) Multiprocessor scheduling with the aid of network flow algorithms. *IEEE Trans. Soft. Eng.*, **SE-3**, 85-93.

Taha, H. A. (1987) *Operations Research, an Introduction*, fourth edition. Macmillan, New York.

Tanenbaum, A. S. (1989) *Computer Networks.* 2nd ed. Prentice-Hall, Englewood Cliffs.

Tang, D. T. Woo, L. S. and Bahl, L. R. (1978) Optimization of teleprocessing networks with concentrators and multiconnected terminals. *IEEE Trans. Comput.*, **C27**, 594-604.

Topkis, D. M. (1988) A k shortest path algorithm for adaptive routing in communication networks. *IEEE Trans. Commun.*, **COM-36**, 855-859.

Tymes, L. (1981) Routing and flow control in TYMNET. *IEEE Trans. Commun.*, **29**, 392-398.

Vernekar, A., Anandalingam, G. and Dorny, C. N. (1990) Optimization of resource location in hierarchical computer networks. *Computers Opns Res.*, **17**, 375-388.

Walsh, G. R. (1975) *Methods of Optimization*, Wiley.

Wecker, S. (1980) DNA: the Digital Network Architecture. *IEEE Trans. Commun.*, **COM-26**, 510-526.

Yaged, B. (1971) Minimum cost routing for static network models. *Networks*, **1**, 139-172.

Yemini, Y. ed. (1987) *Current Advances in Distributed Computing and Communications.* Computer Science Press, Rockville, Ma.

Index